War of Cosmologies

When Belief Systems Collide

Gray Matter Publications

By, S. A. Cooper

War of Cosmogonies: Genesis, Science, and the Battle for Reality

Copyright © 2025 by **S. A. Cooper**

All rights reserved. No part of this publication may be reproduced, distributed, or transmitted in any form or by any means, including photocopying, recording, or other electronic or mechanical methods, without the prior written permission of the publisher, except in the case of brief quotations embodied in critical reviews and certain other noncommercial uses permitted by copyright law.

For inquiries:

writer.sacooper@gmail.com

ISBN: 979-8-9921788-5-2

The United States of America

Table of Contents

INTRODUCTION

Moses' Account 7

CHAPTER 1

WHO, WHEN, WHAT, WHERE, WHY, HOW 19

CHAPTER 2

Stardust, Soup to Sapiens 31

CHAPTER 3

Geologism 41

CHAPTER 4

Values 61

CHAPTER 5

Behind the Throne 69

CHAPTER 6

Accuracy, Honest, and Confidence 85

CHAPTER 7

Thoughtcrimes 103

CHAPTER 8

Kitzmiller v. Dover 119

TABLE OF CONTENTS

CHAPTER 9

Master Strategist 151

CHAPTER 10

The in-Crowd 167

CHAPTER 11

Dystopian Tale..209

CHAPTER 12

Radical Metaphysics 215

CHAPTER 13

Sensational Science 219

CHAPTER 14

The Chocking Truth..243

CHAPTER 15

Celebrity Scientist..251

In the beginning God created the heaven and the earth. And the earth was without form, and void; and darkness was upon the face of the deep. And the Spirit of God moved upon the face of the waters. And God said, Let there be light: and there was light. And God saw the light, that it was good; and God divided the light from the darkness. ... And God said, Let us make man in our image, after our likeness... So God created man in his own image, in the image of God created he him; male and female created he them. ... And the LORD God formed man of the dust of the ground, and breathed into his nostrils the breath of life; and man became a living soul. — Genesis 1–2 (selected, KJV)

Introduction

Moses' Account

Only take heed to thyself... lest thou forget the things which thine eyes have seen... but teach them thy sons, and thy sons' sons... the day that thou stoodest before the Lord thy God in Horeb...[1] —Moses

There's a question nearly everyone has considered, even if only in passing. Few, however, have stopped to examine it seriously. More often than not, we accept an answer by assumption or inheritance—filtered through presuppositions we rarely confront. We seldom engage with the reasoning behind opposing views. The question is simple, but everything leads to it:

Are we the result of coincidence, or the product of purpose?

Think back to your earliest memories—sitting in a classroom, playing in the woods or at the park, hearing a family member's voice, or blowing out candles at a birthday party, then the thrill of opening gifts. Remember something you hoped for, something you feared, your first crush, and how you imagined the future. This is the reality you carry with you—experiences that live alongside the present. Those memories are essential to who you are and confirm that you exist.

Ask yourself: can all that I know and have experienced be explained as the product of random processes arising from nothing? Or could there be meaning behind it all—perhaps—something ordered by a mind?

These questions aren't new. They've echoed through every age and civilization. And no figure has stood more clearly at the center of the conflict between questions of coincidence and purpose than Moses. His creation account in Genesis has shaped how billions understand the origin of the world. From the ancient world to the modern world, his vision of the beginning has been challenged, dismissed, and reinterpreted—only to be later embraced again through a different model, after centuries of insisting there was no beginning at all.

The greatest offensive against Moses' account of origins came at the tail end of the Enlightenment. Figures like the geologist Charles Lyell challenged the idea of a young Earth and a recent creation, proposing instead that the world was shaped by slow, gradual, and cyclic processes over immense spans of time. Where Genesis presented a world measured in generations, Lyell's model demanded eons. The intellectual shift was monumental: time itself was redefined in a way that made divine intervention or recent creation appear unscientific by default.

Building on Lyell's ideas, Charles Darwin applied the same principle to biology, arguing that natural selection—not special creation by God—better explained the diversity of life. Darwin's ideas gained institutional strength through a lesser-known but influential group called the X Club, which worked earnestly to define science in materialist terms and push theological interpretations to the margins. The divide the X Club perfected has defined the standoff between methodological naturalism and Moses to this day; their influence still determines the terms on which origins are debated. Too often, debates about the origin of the universe, life, or consciousness operate within the materialist-only framework of methodological naturalism—one that turns a blind eye to a more fundamental question: the origin of reality itself. Our reality is something Moses speaks to directly.

Yet in the centuries leading to Darwin, the Enlightenment elevated human reason, empirical observation, and skepticism toward tradition—preparing the way for the dominance of Darwin's ideas and their ultimate arbiter, the X Club. The Bible, as the central text of the Christian tradition and often tied to state and church power, became a primary target for reassessment.[2] While many Enlightenment thinkers were themselves Christians and made lasting contributions to theology, ethics, and science, the broader movement gave rise to more radical critiques of biblical authority.

In time, this evolved into a framework where supernatural claims were increasingly excluded—not necessarily because of contrary evidence, but because they no longer fit within the assumptions of empirical rationalism. The Enlightenment thinkers who helped define modern intellectual thought did not begin from a neutral stance. From then to now, many of these thinkers have been especially troubled by the persistence of belief in the Mosaic text that describes divine judgment and intervention—views they see as philosophically unacceptable.

Among any metaphysical interpretations of reality, the biblical account has proven far more disruptive to Western secular assumptions—far more so than ancient myths few take seriously. The concept of a God who acts in history challenged the idea of a closed, self-governing universe and was a problem because it introduced moral accountability and divine judgment. As a result, Enlightenment scholars dismissed biblical accounts of creation, the flood, or the Exodus as little more than fables.[3]

Materialists believe that matter is the fundamental basis of all reality, and that everything, including thought and consciousness, arises from matter. Though materialists often claim that science simply ignores religion as irrelevant, it's rare to find one who does not take up the sword against Moses when the topic turns to origins—whether biological or cosmological. Because of this dominate belief system, rather than remaining neutral, the discussion is often dominated by efforts to discredit the biblical account. Secularists have relentlessly warred against Moses' writings, as if erasing their influence were necessary to preserve the materialist worldview.

For much of the 19th and 20th centuries, academic consensus continued to dismiss the biblical Moses as a literary invention. To them, they claimed, if he existed at all, he was an amalgamation of myth, legend, and later theological reflection. This opinion was not solidified by a lack of evidence, but by the lack of evidence scholars were willing to consider admissible. Even sections of the Bible that contained names, dates, and political references were treated with suspicion. The assumption was that such details were added later to give authority to religious ideas or national identity, not because they reflected real events.

In time, this dictated how universities, historians, and archaeologists handled ancient texts. This assumption became the foundation of Biblical criticism within academia. Biblical texts were placed in a separate category from other ancient writings. Rather than being studied alongside Egyptian, Sumerian, or Hittite records with the same criteria, the Bible was treated as a theological artifact, not a historical one.[4] Its contents had to be independently confirmed before being considered trustworthy, while other ancient texts were presumed to have historical value unless disproven.

Moses, they said, had no place in Egyptian records. There were no ancient inscriptions naming him, no monuments commemorating his deeds, no Egyptian texts acknowledging his confrontation with Pharaoh. They insisted what existed was a heavily redacted religious text, compiled centuries after the supposed events, and written with a clear theological *motive*. That was enough, for many, to reject Moses outright.

Yet in more recent times, a quiet reversal has taken place, not through any grand discovery, but through a series of smaller, cumulative realizations that gradually undercut the older position. These shifts have occurred across multiple disciplines: archaeology, Egyptology, epigraphy, and historiography. In each case, scholars denied a particular element of the Exodus narrative or the Mosaic tradition—only to revise or retract their position in light of new findings, new technologies, or a broader methodological rethink. The results do not "prove" Moses in the way one might verify the reign of an Egyptian pharaoh, but they have made the blanket denial of his plausibility increasingly difficult to defend.

One of the earliest cracks in the scholarly wall came from an Egyptian victory inscription. In 1896, British archaeologist Flinders Petrie uncovered a granite stele commissioned by Pharaoh Merneptah. Dated to roughly 1208 BC, it records a military campaign in Canaan and famously declares:

Israel is laid waste, his seed is no more.[5]

This inscription forced scholars to admit that a people called "Israel" were already present in the land much earlier than was thought. That one line contradicted the prevailing assumption that Israel emerged only in the 12th or even 11th century as a settled agricultural society.

Much of the standard timeline relies on equating Pharaoh Shoshenq I with the biblical Shishak who attacked Jerusalem during the reign of Rehoboam. Egyptologist David Rohl and others have challenged this synchronism, arguing that Shoshenq's campaign doesn't align with the biblical description or geography.[6] If Shishak is instead identified with a 19th Dynasty pharaoh—such as Ramesses II or III—the Exodus would fall earlier in Egyptian history—possibly in the Middle Bronze Age—aligning more closely with the Semitic presence at Avaris and with an earlier date for Israel's emergence in Canaan.

This timeline adjustment entails compressing Egypt's Third Intermediate Period, a phase marked by fragmented rule and overlapping dynasties. Scholars like Rohl argue that this period has been artificially extended, stretching the chronology and pushing New Kingdom events too far back. By reducing its duration, earlier events such as the Exodus shift forward in time, narrowing the gap between biblical accounts and archaeological layers.

Another major point of contention had long been Hebrew literacy. Many 20th-century scholars rejected the idea that Moses could have written anything, including the law or historical narratives. Writing was assumed to be the work of elite scribes, not nomadic Hebrews. The Torah was, according to this view, a late creation attributed retroactively to Moses by editors of the exile period. This position began to unravel with the discovery of Proto-Sinaitic inscriptions at Serabit el-Khadim in the Sinai Peninsula.[7]

Dated to the late 19th to 15th centuries BC, these inscriptions are thought to have been created by Semitic-speaking workers employed at Egyptian turquoise mines.[8] Initially dismissed as indecipherable or irrelevant, they have since attracted renewed interest. One inscription—located west of the main mining complex and interpreted by William H. Shea—stands out for its distinct content and context.[9] In his findings, Shea argued it does not reflect routine labor activity but instead refers to "the congregation," "Hobab," and "the Mighty One of the cherubim"—elements directly tied to the Exodus narrative and Israelite worship.[10]

Some researchers, such as Douglas Petrovich, go further by proposing that certain inscriptions mention figures like "Moses" or the term "Hebrews." While some critics often dismiss his interpretations due to perceived religious bias, their focus on motive rather than evidence raises deeper questions about the assumptions of those who view reality as consisting solely of matter. Though interpretations such as Petrovich's remain debated, the broader conclusion is gaining ground: Semitic-speaking peoples in the right time and place were writing, and some inscriptions may preserve aspects of the same cultural and theological worldview attributed to Moses and early Israelite tradition.

These peoples used an early script considered a precursor to the alphabet, showing clear linguistic connections to Northwest Semitic languages, including early Hebrew. The existence of Semitic laborers, literate in a rudimentary alphabet, at Sinai, during the same era that biblical chronology places Moses there, made the claim of Israelite illiteracy much harder to sustain. Notably, this early use of alphabetic writing by Semitic laborers at Sinai suggests a theological shift.

Unlike the gods of surrounding cultures, who were approached through ritual specialists and obscure scripts, the God of Moses is portrayed as communicating directly, through written words, in a script accessible to common people. This points to a distinct conception of divinity: not a distant force mediated by elites, but a personal God who reveals Himself in clear, lasting, and widely understandable terms. Such a model stands apart from the temple-based systems of the ancient world and may explain why early Hebrew tradition placed such emphasis on law, literacy, and covenant memory.

Critics often compare the Bible to other religious traditions—such as Hindu, Indigenous Australian, or Native American cosmogonies—arguing that all contain symbolic stories and mythic elements. As noted, however, the Mosaic tradition makes a fundamentally different claim: that God revealed Himself directly to a nation in historical time, using a common script, with laws recorded and preserved in writing. This emphasis on public, accessible communication—not just private visions or mythic imagery—sets it apart from most religious systems, which often rely on symbolic narratives, esoteric knowledge, or ritual intermediaries. It's this historical and textual specificity that makes the Bible harder to dismiss using the same framework applied to other religions.

Another key difference is that the Mosaic texts are filled with specific names, dates, and geographical references. Unlike many mythological traditions, which are often symbolic or timeless, the Bible anchors its narratives in identifiable historical settings—genealogies, real places, known kingdoms, named rulers, and datable events. In other ancient texts, named figures do appear, but usually as isolated mythic characters without clear historical grounding. These figures are rarely connected to a broader framework of traceable locations, timelines, or political developments. In comparison, the biblical narrative presents a sustained historical structure, making other accounts seem more like mythic spin-offs or symbolic echoes than full historical traditions. This level of historical integration is rare, and it's what allows the biblical narrative to be tested against archaeology in ways most other religious texts cannot.

If Semitic-speaking people were writing in Sinai using alphabetic characters centuries before the Babylonian exile, then the idea of a literate Moses ceased to be anachronistic. Nevertheless, even the idea that Moses couldn't have written anything because nomadic Hebrews weren't literate is a minimalist argument. It's widely accepted among critical scholars, yet rests on assumptions that dismiss key contextual evidence from the outset—including Moses' Egyptian royal upbringing, which, according to Genesis, would have placed him within the elite and given him access to high-level scribal education. When this broader context is excluded from consideration, it raises a question: can such a view be considered a fair historical assessment, or is it a predetermined verdict?

The argument against the historicity of the Mosaic text is also challenged by Egyptian inscriptions from the reign of Amenhotep III (~1400 BC), which refer to "the land of the Shasu of Yhw."[11] This toponym likely references a deity named Yhw—widely understood to be an early form of Yahweh—associated with a nomadic group called the *Shasu*, located in the southern Transjordan or northern Arabian region.[12] These references place the name Yahweh, and possibly those who worshipped him, in both geographic proximity to early Israelite movements and chronological alignment with the biblical period of Moses. Rather than reconsidering Moses' role in introducing Yahweh, some scholars simply shifted the claim: Yahweh may have existed earlier, they now argue, but as the god of a non-Israelite tribal group—later adopted into Israelite religion.

Such a position, however, raises intriguing questions. If Yahweh was merely a borrowed deity from surrounding peoples like the Shasu, why is it only the Israelites who preserved His name, laws, and character in writing? Why don't we find Shasu hymns, prayers, or narratives about Yahweh—only Egyptian references and an extensive Hebrew tradition? The silence from the supposed source culture, and the depth of articulation from the supposed borrower, casts doubt on the idea that Yahweh worship originated with a different people. In fact, the conclusion that Yahweh was borrowed is rooted in a materialist framework—one in which every belief must evolve from something prior. The interpretation is not drawn from the evidence; it's an expression of the framework itself. In this view, the interpretation becomes the evidence.

At the same time, scholars long dismissed the Exodus account because Egypt had no "Exodus story" of its own. Yet fragments began to surface. The 3rd-century BC Egyptian priest Manetho, whose writings survive only through quotations in the 1st-century AD Jewish historian Josephus, describes a group of foreigners expelled from Egypt after defiling temples and defying Pharaoh.[13] He names their leader Osarsiph, an Egyptian priest who turned against native religion and led his people out—whom Manetho identified as Moses.[14] This account, though filtered through hostile Egyptian sources, suggests that the memory of an expulsion involving a Moses-like figure was known in Egyptian tradition. It was once viewed as a fabrication designed to mock Jewish identity. Now it is being reconsidered as a distorted but real memory of upheaval during Egypt's 18th or 19th Dynasty.

The biblical account following *Joseph* says that the Israelites settled in Goshen, a fertile area suited to pastoral life, and that they helped build the store cities of Pithom and Raamses. For decades, scholars claimed no such settlement was known, no such cities existed, and no evidence tied Semites to Egypt in this period. Then evidence began turning up in the ground. Archaeologists were excavating the exact region the Bible associates with Israelite enslavement: the land of Goshen, in the eastern Nile Delta.[15] At Tell el-Dab'a—identified as ancient Avaris—excavations led by Manfred Bietak revealed a major Semitic population living there during the Second Intermediate Period and into the early New Kingdom.[16]

Avaris, later rebuilt as Pi-Rameses, was occupied by Asiatic peoples who bore names, burial customs, and material culture tied to Canaan.[17] The parallels were unsettling. Archaeologists uncovered large Semitic-style houses, graves showing Asiatic morphology, and scarabs inscribed with names like "Yaqub" (Jacob)—once dismissed as biblical fiction, now etched into artifacts from the Delta.[18] And Pi-Rameses matched both the name and location given in the Exodus as the Israelites' departure point.[19]

The argument that Israelites were never in Egypt continued to shift. The new claim became: these weren't "Israelites," just generic Canaanite migrants. Perhaps. But *the text of Exodus never claimed otherwise*. It describes a Semitic people who came from Canaan, settled in Egypt, were enslaved, and eventually left.

Scholars typically associate the Second Intermediate Period with the rise of the Hyksos—a group of Semitic rulers who gained power in Egypt during a time of internal decline. Though the Hebrews and Hyksos were both Semitic and may have occupied similar regions in the Delta, the biblical account presents the Hebrews as arriving peacefully under Joseph and later falling into slavery. In the revised chronology advanced by Rohl, the Hebrews departed Egypt during the Exodus, and it was only after this collapse that the Hyksos entered and took control.[20] Their ascent, according to his view, reflects Egypt's weakened state—aligning with Moses' narrative of judgment following the plagues and Israelite departure.

As for the plagues of Egypt: frogs, hail, locusts, and bloody rivers made for strong literary effect but little historical credibility, it was argued. Environmental studies, however, especially those focused on the ecology of the Nile, began to change that. Scholars noted that the sequence of plagues described in Exodus follows a chain of environmental collapse that can occur when Nile flooding patterns are disrupted. Reddish algae blooms (which turn water blood-colored and kill fish), frog migrations, insect swarms, and livestock disease all occur in interdependent order in such collapses.

One rarely mentioned Egyptian text (the Ipuwer Papyrus) complicates the standard dismissal of the biblical Exodus. It describes national collapse: blood in the Nile, the rise of servants over masters, and widespread disorder. Though poetic in form, it contains no gods, no creation myth, no sacred drama. Its tone is observational, not mythic. Most scholars treat it as a reflection of real crisis, preserved in civil script and context—likely cultural memory shaped by trauma. [21]

The biblical account records similar conditions: ecological disaster, social inversion, and a Semitic population leaving Egypt. Yet it is not granted the same consideration. Where Ipuwer is accepted as plausible history filtered through lament, Exodus is treated as theological invention. Ipuwer describes collapse, and his account is preserved—if for nothing else, then for its context. But Moses, who witnesses something similar and interprets it as meaningful, is dismissed for doing so.

Here, the standard changes, not because of a lack of parallel, but from discomfort with the implications. The overlaps are substantive, structured correlations, even occurring in similar sequence. The argument, however, is not that Ipuwer proves Exodus, but that it represents a non-Israelite memory of the same or similar event—making it a piece of cultural evidence that deserves to be considered, not redefined to avoid the conclusion it suggests.

Add in a volcanic eruption such as the Thera explosion—now dated by many scholars to the mid-second millennium BC, close to the conventional window for the Exodus—and combine that with atmospheric anomalies, and even for those incredulous to miracles, phenomena like darkness, fiery hail, and ashfall begin to resemble remembered catastrophe more than religious fantasy.[22] What ancient texts describe as divine judgment may, in this light, represent culturally preserved accounts of real natural disasters.

The earlier posture of categorical denial—Moses never existed, the Exodus never happened, Israel invented its past—is no longer sustainable in light of the accumulating data. Instead, a more cautious, layered approach has emerged. More scholars are now more willing to contemplate the possibility of a historical Moses, an exodus of Semitic peoples from Egypt, and a wilderness tradition rooted in real geography and cultural memory. Moses is now, at the very least, a memory rooted in a real cultural crisis, passed down through generations who had every reason to preserve it.

Furthermore, the academic dismissal of special creation once appeared settled. But advances in modern biology—particularly in cellular complexity—have led to renewed debate over how decisively evolutionary materialism can account for life's origins. In the early 20th century, Darwinian evolution by natural selection had become the *central organizing principle of biology*. Any suggestion of design, intent, or non-randomness in origins was dismissed as pseudoscience, and frequently made the butt of academic ridicule.[23] But the 21st century has not maintained that posture as confidently as the 20th. The steadily emerging evidence of irreducible complexity has muted much of the earlier dismissal of special creation, as Darwin and later disciples of his were unaware of the intricate, magnitudes-far-from-simple systems within the cell—many of which systems we still cannot fully grasp.

The original Darwinian model relied on a relatively simple vision of life's building blocks—cells as protoplasmic blobs, mutations as noise, and deep time as the great innovative sculptor. But molecular biology has replaced that simplicity with layers of encoded complexity. The structure of DNA, the role of epigenetics, and the existence of fine-tuned regulatory systems have raised questions that random variation and natural selection struggle to answer.

The genetic code is not like a language—it is a language, but it arose through random mutations. DNA is the blueprint, though not in any intentional sense. Regulatory networks govern cellular behavior algorithmically, but that's just how chemistry unfolds. It's not designed—it only behaves as if it were. It's all physical, yet somehow informational. There's no message, but it's encoded. There's no purpose—only feedback systems that adjust and respond. It looks engineered, but that's the illusion natural selection creates.

Many researchers now, however, openly concede that the emergence of these integrated systems poses a profound challenge. No longer a problem on the verge of resolution, it has become even more perplexing for their worldview as discoveries increase.[24] Random mutation no longer appears sufficient as the engine.

The "Cambrian Explosion" presents another major challenge to Darwin's theory. As Darwinian evolution gained institutional acceptance, it struggled to account for such more direct anomalies: the sudden appearance of complex body plans, interdependent biological systems, and detailed genetic instructions in the fossil record—without evolutionary precursors. Ironically, the sudden emergence of new lifeforms in the fossil record aligns more closely with Moses' account—yet it's often dismissed by treating the absence of evidence as if it were evidence itself.

The final frontier of reversal lies in the cosmos. For centuries, the dominant cosmological assumption was that the universe was eternal and uncreated. An eternal universe required no origin and no cause—no need for a beginning, and therefore no space for a beginner. What critics once dismissed as legend has returned with force. *In the beginning*, they now say, was a "Big Bang."

Instead of fading, Moses' account is proving more formidable than ever—quite literally standing the test of time.

Chapter 1

WHO, WHEN, WHAT, WHERE, WHY, HOW

> *"The problem of cosmogony is to explain the origin of the universe and its present structure."* —James Jeans, Astronomy and Cosmogony (1928)[25]

Barbara Ryden's *Introduction to Cosmology* opens by citing Paul Gauguin: "Where do we come from? What are we? Where are we going?"[26] She follows by narrowing these questions into measurable terms: what the universe is made of, whether it is finite or infinite, whether it had a beginning, and whether it will have an end. In doing so, she shifts the focus from the broader question of origin to narrower, measurable concerns: composition, geometry, and timescale.

The original existential questions are not openly dismissed, but they are redefined within a materialist framework that makes certain answers impossible and others automatic. It's like someone asking, 'Where did the egg come from?' and being answered with a breakdown of its mass, shape, chemical composition, and shell curvature—all of which are accurate but don't address the origin in the sense the question intends.

This narrowing of focus is not unique to Ryden—it reflects a broader pattern. While the modern term *cosmology* has grown to dominate discussions of the universe, it has increasingly displaced the older term *cosmogony*, which once named the question more directly. Where cosmology describes the structure and behavior of the universe, cosmogony directly asks how it came to be in the first place. Yet today, even when origin is discussed, it is almost always framed in cosmological terms—as if a question with obvious metaphysical weight could be fully addressed by physics alone. It is retold as a problem of expansion rates and field dynamics. it's a narrowing of both language and thought. It appears in academic literature and in public-facing reference works, where cosmogony is now treated as a subfield rather than a central problem.

Wikipedia participates in this trend. Its entry on cosmogony begins with a simple sentence: "Cosmogony is any model concerning the origin of either the cosmos or universe."[27] It then defines cosmogony as "the study of the origin of particular astrophysical *objects* or systems," including the universe.[28] Yet it immediately declares that "the prevalent cosmological model of the early development of the universe is the Big Bang theory."[29] In doing so, it presents a cosmological model as if it were a cosmogonic explanation, without acknowledging the distinction, despite maintaining separate entries for cosmology and cosmogony. This normalizes the modern habit of treating cosmological models as sufficient cosmogonic explanations, while avoiding the metaphysical weight the term cosmogony traditionally carried.

The *Stanford Encyclopedia of Philosophy* reinforces this narrowing of scope. It has no dedicated entry for "cosmogony" at all. Where the term appears—in entries on pre-Socratic philosophers, religious metaphysics, or ancient cosmologies—it is generally treated as a relic of pre-scientific thinking, confined to myth or theology. Meanwhile, its entry on cosmology begins with Einstein and modern physics, avoiding cosmogonic roots and longstanding metaphysical context.[30] Like Wikipedia, it reflects the prevailing assumption that cosmology is a strictly materialistic enterprise—yet it does so by ignoring the most basic reality: that something cannot come from nothing without explanation. It stashes the primary questions of what exists and their necessary preconditions. It substitutes theoretical constructs for observed reality, and proceeds to treat those constructs as if they were evidence. This standard discourse redefines *scientific* as whatever sustains the model—regardless of coherence, causality, or origin—an ultimate case of pretending the emperor has clothes on.

CHAPTER 1   WHO, WHEN, WHAT, WHERE, WHY, HOW

> COSMOG'ONIST, *n.* [See *Cosmogony.*]
> One who treats of the origin or formation of the universe. *Enfield.*
> COSMOG'ONY, *n. s* as *z.* [Gr. κοσμογονια; κοσμος, world, and γονη, generation.]
> The generation, origin or creation of the world or universe. In *physics,* the science of the origin or formation of the universe. *Enfield. Encyc.*
> COSMOG'RAPHER, *n.* [See *Cosmography.*] One who describes the world or universe, including the heavens and the earth.
> COSMOGRAPH'IC, } *a.* Relating to
> COSMOGRAPH'ICAL, } the general description of the universe.
> COSMOGRAPH'ICALLY, *adv.* In a manner relating to the science of describing the universe, or corresponding to cosmography.

Figure 1.1: From *An American Dictionary of the English Language* by Noah Webster (1828). This definition clearly show that creation, origin, and structure were once integrated—with science being part of, not isolated from, these foundational questions. Image source: harchive.org

The word cosmogony once marked one of the most seriously investigated questions: where did the world come from? In Noah Webster's 1828 dictionary, the term was defined as "the generation, origin or creation of the world or universe. In physics, the science of the origin or formation of the universe."[31] That definition made no attempt to separate origin science from philosophical or theological meaning.

The question of beginnings was once open to all apparent lines of inquiry: metaphysics, creation, and methodological naturalism all had a seat at the table. Science, as a method, was not claimed by any single philosophy, and certainly not by one that must suppress the implications of its own findings.

In modern dictionaries, cosmogony is still defined as "the creation or origin of the world or universe."[32] However, earlier definitions that explicitly described cosmogony as a scientific discipline have largely been removed or reframed, reflecting an ideological shift away from treating it as a formal branch of science.[33] Though the defining lens of materialism (methodological naturalism) has moved further from being able to coherently address the questions of where the universe, life, and consciousness came from, openness to alternatives outside materialist assumptions remains actively closed off. The true question of origin is now framed as one science cannot answer. However, it increasingly appears to be an inquiry that is deliberately guarded.

A century ago, a leading physicist could speak as James Jeans did, framing the origin of the universe and its structure as a legitimate "problem of cosmogony."[34] In the early decades of the 20th century, figures like Jeans, George Darwin, and Georges Lemaître all addressed the question of beginnings with language that acknowledged what they were doing. Lemaître even titled a major 1950 essay *The Primeval Atom: An Essay on Cosmogony*.[35] The problem was not hidden. These were scientific efforts to explain the origin of the cosmos, and they were willing to call it that.

Two decades later, the great physicist John Archibald Wheeler was still speaking the same language of cosmogony. In a 1968 lecture—and again in his seminal 1977 paper, "Is Physics Legislated by Cosmogony?"—he argued that the laws of physics may have been "laid down" in the act of cosmic birth.[36] For Wheeler, cosmogony (how the universe comes to be) and fundamental physics (the rules it obeys) are "aspects of one and the same problem."[37]

He argued that treating spacetime as pure geometry is an incomplete reduction—no deeper, he said, than treating a solid as pure elasticity.[38] Just as solids reduce to atoms and electrons, geometry must reduce to something more fundamental, which he called pregeometry—a deeper layer of structure that may not involve space or time at all.[39]

What stands out is not that these thinkers used theological language—they didn't—but that they made no effort to conceal the metaphysical structure of the question. They knew they were telling a story about origin, and they spoke in terms that carried that weight. As Jeans wrote in *The Mysterious Universe* (1930):

> The stream of knowledge is heading toward a non-mechanical reality; the universe begins to look more like a great thought than like a great machine. Mind no longer appears as an accidental intruder into the realm of matter; we are beginning to suspect that we ought rather to hail it as the creator and governor of the realm of matter—not, of course, our individual minds, but the mind in

which the atoms out of which our individual minds have grown exist as thoughts.[40]

For Jeans, this wasn't theological language. He simply acknowledged that physics radiated into metaphysics. He understood the cosmogonic question was not just as a physical one, but he saw it as one that ultimately pointed toward intelligence embedded in the structure of reality.

Wheeler, too, reached a similar conclusion, though from a different angle. He proposed what he called the Participatory Anthropic Principle, writing:

> We are not only observers. We are participators. In some strange sense, this is a participatory universe.[41]

For Wheeler, observation played a constitutive role in reality itself. "The universe," he suggested, "does not exist 'out there' independent of all acts of observation."[42] It takes form only through conscious engagement. He saw this as a serious conclusion drawn from quantum mechanics and cosmological reasoning.

By the late 20th century, the word cosmogony had largely disappeared from scientific discourse. It was too direct. In its place, cosmology became the preferred label: measured, mathematical, and allegedly neutral. It offered an epistemological break from cause, from intention, and from meaning. This was no longer about how reality could come to be, but about how mathematical constructs—untethered from observed conditions—could be used to explain structure.

A comparison between two versions of Wikipedia's *cosmogony* entry (one from 2004 and one from May 2025) shows a clear shift in how the subject is framed.[43] The 2004 archived version recognizes that cosmogony involves fundamental philosophical and theological questions.[44] It states that cosmogony "bucks up against philosophy and theistic belief systems" and outlines three central paradoxes that any origin theory must confront:

1. **Causation**: the question of what caused the universe, commonly associated with Aquinas's arguments for the necessity of a first cause.

2. **Conservation**: the problem of how something can arise from nothing, given that energy and matter cannot be created or destroyed.

3. **Temporal or logical regression**: the issue of whether the universe had a beginning, and the implications of either a finite or infinite past.

It further notes that science may offer models but that these paradoxes are more clearly addressed by philosophers, citing Leibniz and Kierkegaard by name.[45]

In contrast, as noted, the later May 2025 version defines cosmogony as "any model concerning the origin of either the cosmos or universe," and it immediately redirects the topic toward modern theoretical physics, citing the Big Bang as the prevailing model. Any recognition of metaphysical or philosophical implications is pushed to a subsection labeled "Myths," effectively cordoning off centuries of reflection into a cultural sidebar. This reflects a decision about which aspects of origin are considered relevant, and which are to be excluded.

War of Cosmogonies is about that shift—about what was hidden, what was renamed, and what was quietly rejected. It is about the war—between Moses and the materialist, between Genesis and the vacuum, between revelation and redefinition. And somewhere behind the materialist models and metaphors, a preference lingers, for the impersonal cosmogonies of the East, where all is one, all is cyclical, and nothing is judged.

Although modern physicists assume that the cosmogonic problem Jeans described has been resolved by this contemporary cosmology—as if the larger questions are now outdated, or no longer scientific because they fall outside methodological naturalism, these "strictly-science" scientists still, however, build narratives. They still speak cosmogonically behind a veil of calculation, redefinition, and unacknowledged metaphysics.

For example, Stephen Hawking's *A Brief History of Time* became a modern sacred text for scientific materialism, read widely as an explanation of the universe that leaves no room for God.[46] And yet, it actually does not offer freedom from metaphysics, but instead, a shift in posture. Hawking speaks of the beginning of time, the collapse of classical physics at the singularity, and the possibility of a self-contained universe with no boundary. These are cosmogonic claims by any standard. But the term cosmogony never appears. The metaphysical stakes are left unnamed, even as the book invites the reader to believe that physics alone can answer the deepest questions of origin. What Hawking offers is an ambiguous version of cosmogony based on *the name we do not speak*.

Lawrence Krauss, by contrast, does not hide the stakes—he simply redefines them. In *A Universe from Nothing*, he claims that modern physics has finally answered the oldest question: why is there something rather than nothing, by redefining nothing as something. The nothing Krauss describes, indeed, is not nothing. It is a quantum vacuum, governed by laws, fields, and energy states. It is a fertile something—recast in minimalist terms to appear empty. Krauss disguises metaphysics as physics. His cosmogony is explicit, aggressive, and ideological. It does not avoid a cosmogony such as Genesis because it has something better, but because it cannot tolerate a world in which creation implies a Creator.

Sean Carroll offers a third approach: casual, self-assured, and disinterested in the deeper consequences of his claims. In *The Big Picture* and elsewhere, he proposes models of eternal inflation, multiverse generation, and the emergence of time from entropy gradients.[47] He speaks of origins but insists on calling them physics. His is a cosmology that extends into total explanation, but resists all accountability to meaning. Like others, Carroll carefully avoids any gesture that would imply moral direction or metaphysical ground.

The Genesis According to Neo-Physics

In *Natural Technology: The Theory of Everything*, I go into depth about the standard cosmological model's narrative; however, its model's genesis goes something as follows: The universe begins from nothing. At $t = 0$, existence is undefined.[48] Then, a hypothetical field called the *inflaton*, in the first

0.0000000000000000000000000000000000001 seconds, triggers a process known as cosmic inflation.

In her book, Ryden introduces the inflaton field as a generalized scalar with no defined physical identity. Its energy is expressed in terms of an adjustable potential, $V(\phi)$, allowing the model to match observational requirements.[49]

Nothing about the field is derived from empirical data. It is constructed to deliver inflation, not discovered through experiment. The field's properties (how it starts, how it stops, how it decays) are not constrained by physical evidence.[50] The model begins with an undefined mechanism and retrofits it to fulfill materialist assumptions about the origin of the universe. It cannot be falsified in any meaningful way. Any evidence interpreted through it is necessarily post hoc.[51]

Even the term inflation is not the word we use in the familiar sense, but a sudden, mathematically defined "expansion" that took the universe from smaller than a proton, less than 10^{-11} centimeters, to over 10^{26} centimeters (roughly 10 billion light-years across) in 10^{-35} seconds.[52]

Thus, inflation, along with what is called "expansion," is an egregious euphemism. What it describes is not growth at all but the instant creation of the universe. It unfolds in 0.0000000000000000000000000000000000001 seconds, making the Genesis account appear slow by comparison.[53] All resources—space, energy, scale—appear faster than the time it would take to say, "Let there be." By this account, the God of the Bible really took His time.

Inflation, however, was not part of the original Big Bang model. It was introduced in 1980 by Alan Guth to resolve observational contradictions that arose within the materialist framework—issues that methodological naturalism could not explain, such as the horizon and flatness problems.[54] The inflaton field, which has only been imagined, is assumed to contain the energy necessary for the universe to start and to stop inflating at exactly the right time.

Following 0.00000000000000000000000000000001 seconds, the energy from the inflaton field is said to decay into matter and radiation, in an event called "reheating."[55] This is when particles, forces, and radiation supposedly appear. However, no known mechanism explains how the inflaton decays, nor how its energy converts into particles.[56] This process is also ad hoc. It was invented to match observed outcomes, not derived from any established principle or empirical cause. By 0.0000000001 seconds, the universe is said to be over 100,000 light-years across—larger than a galaxy.[57] Neither does this result have an observable cause. It, too, was prepared to order, to match the universe we already see.

At three minutes after this beginning, temperatures fall enough for protons and neutrons to combine into helium and trace elements, but not heavier ones.[58] At this stage, none of the elements essential for life—carbon, oxygen, iron—exist. The universe is still dark, opaque, and uniform. Only at 370,000 years do temperatures cool enough for atoms to form, allowing light for the first time. This light—the cosmic microwave background (CMB)—is often cited by scientists as evidence for the model.[59]

While the discovery of the CMB was initially taken as confirmation of the Big Bang, it is what ultimately exposed contradictions within the model. Its uniform temperature across vast regions—too far apart to have ever interacted—implied that early conditions were not shaped by any gradual process, but by a sudden, coordinated event the original timeline couldn't account for without adding inflation. Still, it reflects conditions after the proposed origin—not the origin itself.

At 200 million years, the model asserts that the first stars form.[60] These are called Population III stars—hypothetical objects said to contain 100 to 300 times the mass of the Sun.[61] They must appear suddenly in a universe composed only of hydrogen and helium, with no planets, no dust, and no metals. The problem is not just that none have been observed; it is that the model provides no account of how stars of that size and energy could assemble themselves in a chemically barren vacuum.

These first stars are essential to the story because their violent deaths through supernovae are said to produce all heavier elements—carbon, oxygen, iron—necessary for every star, planet, and life form that follows. But their formation remains entirely unexplained.

The problem, however, is not only that Population III stars had to form independently under radically different conditions—it's that the model also assumes every star since then formed independently, within localized clouds enriched by earlier supernovae. These clouds, called "star nurseries," are said to emerge billions or trillions of times across the universe, each one executing the same precise sequence of star reproduction events.[62] That process, too, is not only unknown—it must occur spontaneously, repeatedly, and uniformly across the entire cosmos.

This is an extraordinary claim. It resembles the problem of convergence in evolutionary biology. Imagine someone suggesting that every eye on Earth evolved independently, without shared ancestry or inherited mechanisms. Such a claim would be outright rejected, because it violates what we know about biological development and probability. Yet the standard cosmological model effectively makes the same claim: that the first stars—formed under radically different, metal-free conditions—emerged spontaneously across the early universe, without a known mechanism, and did so billions of times. The model requires this outcome, but it cannot explain how it occurred.

Though inflation is said to end via the slow-roll transition, this supposed deceleration doesn't resolve the deeper problem: it imposes structure onto a moment that, by the model's own logic, should have been chaotic.[63] The abrupt conversion of vacuum energy into matter isn't explained by any antecedent cause. Again, it's inserted solely to match what we already observe. Inflation is assumed to stop because the universe we see requires it—not because any mechanism compels it. In effect, causation is replaced by calibration: at the requisite instant, the math must yield particles. This passes for explanation, but it is merely programming the desired outcome—a scheduled shift from invented energy to real matter, never observed, never repeated, and never explained.

And even that is not the end of the problem: after supposedly exiting inflation through a still-undefined process, the model requires that expansion eventually accelerate again, as it appears to be doing today—this time under the influence of a different unobserved entity: dark energy. Thus, the universe must break the cosmic speed limit by unimaginable magnitudes, then slow to a crawl, and later begin accelerating again—all driven by unknown physics.

Today, supposedly 13.8 billion years after beginning, the universe is said to contain over 1,000,000,000,000,000,000,000 stars, spread across roughly 2 trillion galaxies. Supposedly every atom, every star, and every structure originate from quantum fluctuations in a vacuum, expanded and smoothed by inflation, shaped by gravity, and organized over time.

This is the standard scientific cosmogony. It presents a beginning without explanation, laws without origin, and structure without cause. It does not offer a reasonable scientific replacement for Genesis. It offers a creation story where abstract equations carry miraculous agency. Where the Genesis says, "Let there be," the latter says, "Assume it was."

CHAPTER 2

Stardust, Soup to Sapiens

> *Evolution is purposeless. It's foresight-less. Think of the billions, trillions of lives that are wasted on bad trials. And it's slow. Intelligent design is purposeful, somewhat foresighted, governed by cost considerations, and usually relatively fast. ... Evolution may be slow and costly, but it's brilliant. Often, in evolutionary biology, whether at the molecular or ecological level, you find a feature of some organism that seems daft—like stupid design. Later, you realize it's much more clever than you thought, even more clever than you are.*[64] —Daniel Dennett

Once cosmologists accounted for the structure and expansion of the universe—however incompletely—the cosmogony continued. The next chapter was life. In contemporary discourse, the phrase "we are stardust" has gained significant prominence.[65] This soundbite, popularized by notable individuals like Carl Sagan, Neil deGrasse Tyson, Lawrence Krauss, and Martin Rees, carries implicit messages. The choice of 'stardust' over more scientifically accurate terms, such as Earth dust, is not arbitrary. It reflects a stance aimed at emphasizing an evolutionary origin from stars while negating human uniqueness. Notably, it assumes we are stardust, though the first stars themselves cannot be accounted for outside of an utterly miraculous chain of mathematical events. Meanwhile, much of the public sees statements like "we are stardust" as profound.

Despite mounting contradictions to the plausibility of an abiogenic origin of life, educational materials from kindergarten through college continue to present various scenarios as potential explanations for abiogenic processes. Yet there is no consensus among origin-of-life (OOL) researchers on any coherent narrative that connects prebiotic chemistry to a plausible pathway for the emergence of life.[66] Educators and popular science communicators often omit these clarifications. In fact, presenting details that clarify the probability of the first life arising by random causes, or questioning whether the subsequent diversity of life arose through evolutionary theory, can lead to legal issues in public schools.[67]

In his 2006 book, *The God Delusion*, Richard Dawkins argues the importance of acknowledging ignorance in scientific inquiry, arguing that gaps in knowledge should inspire further research rather than be filled with unscientific explanations. On page 125, Dawkins criticizes Biblical creationists for using gaps in understanding as opportunities to insert God as an explanation. He contrasts this with a scientific approach of embracing ignorance as a motivation for ongoing research.[68] He reiterates this on page 126, emphasizing that admissions of ignorance are vital to good science.[69] Dawkins further criticizes the "God of the Gaps" reasoning as lazy and defeatist on page 128, condemning the quick resort to "irreducible complexity" or divine intervention in areas lacking data or understanding.[70]

Two years following the publication of *The God Delusion*, in a notable 2008 interview conducted by Ben Stein for the documentary "Expelled: No Intelligence Allowed," Dawkins candidly acknowledged the prevailing ignorance in scientific circles about life's origins.[71] He states in the interview, "Nobody knows how it started. We know the kind of event that it must have been. We know the sort of event that must have happened for the origin of life."[72]

Although he appears cautious by admitting "nobody knows," Dawkins' subsequent claims introduce a contradiction. He asserts he knows the "sort of event" that "must have" led to the origin of life, a statement that contradicts the empirical restraint he advocates for in his book. By admitting ignorance about the origin of life while asserting the kind of event that 'must' have initiated it, Dawkins essentially relies on a 'scientism of the gaps' argument: we don't know how it happened, but we're certain the explanation is material. This spiritual-like position is no different from those he criticizes.

Dawkins' shift from "nobody knows" to "we know" suggests that his speculations hold an elevated status in his mind. Consider this: if someone asks how family members arrived at your house and you reply that you don't know but insist it must have been by car, bike, or walking, your hypothesis is understandable—if you've previously seen vehicles or people performing such tasks, or at least something similar.

If the family members have always been inside the house, and no one has ever witnessed their arrival or any form of transportation, it becomes impossible to know what kind of event brought them there—simply based on observing how people move within the house. The only thing anyone knows is that each member was born inside. Without an external reference point, any claim about the original arrival lacks scientific credibility, as it invokes a cause unsupported by observable evidence. The only consistent evidence is that life begins through birth and ends in death—beyond that, the mechanism of original arrival remains unknown.

Methodological naturalism, by restricting itself to observable and repeatable phenomena, faces a significant challenge in addressing origins. While we know that life only arises from life, theories like abiogenesis can offer only imaginative scenarios that contradict what is known about chemical processes. It is understandable that the absence of evidence for how life arrived on Earth may be frustrating for those seeking to confirm a particular belief system. This also applies to speciation. Dawkins forgets, in the same work, the objectivity he champions by overlooking his own call to embrace ignorance as a motivation for continued inquiry.

Primordial Soup

The primordial soup theory and the Miller-Urey experiment originated a century ago from attempts to understand how life began on Earth. The theory, proposed in the 1920s by Alexander Oparin and further developed by J.B.S. Haldane suggested that life began in a chemical "soup" filled with a rich mixture of gases like methane, ammonia, hydrogen, and water vapor.[73] They suggested that this could have been the breeding ground for complex organic molecules and that this atmosphere, interacting with energy sources like sunlight or lightning, could produce a "soup" of organic compounds in the oceans.

In "The Oparin Hypothesis is a Falling Star," published in the *Athens Journal of Philosophy*, Tonći Kokić, a professor of Science at the University of Split, Croatia, critiques Alexander Oparin's hypothesis on the origin of life.[74] He contends that the Oparin hypothesis failed to decrease "the gap between the most complicated organic substances and the most primitive living organisms."[75] He concludes by stating:

> the Oparin [primordial soup] hypothesis was founded on unconfirmed or indefinite premises which are not plausible according to the contemporary knowledge of our best scientific theory. His hypothesis has a high metatheoretical value but as a specific scientific hypothesis, its contribution is highly limited to the area of the history of science and the history of philosophy (of science).[76]

Kokić's assessment highlights serious concerns about the continued endorsement of the primordial soup hypothesis in educational content. From his perspective, maintaining this hypothesis as a valid explanation for the origin of life in academic discussions is unjustifiable.

Open-Source Curriculum

As does many textbooks, the *Introduction to Biological Concepts* textbook used by the College of Lake County in Chicago, Illinois continues to endorse the primordial soup hypothesis as a scientifically valid explanation for the origin of life. In Chapter 3, titled "Biologically Important Molecules," the textbook states the following:

> The Earth is estimated to be 4.6 billion years old, but for the first 2 billion years the atmosphere lacked oxygen. Without oxygen, the planet could not support life. One hypothesis about how life emerged on earth involves the concept of "primordial soup." This hypothesis proposes that life began in a body of water when metals and gases from the atmosphere combined with a source of energy, such as lightning or ultraviolet light. These interactions formed carbon compounds, the first chemical building blocks of life. In 1952, Stanley Miller (1930–2007), a graduate student at the University of Chicago, and his professor Harold Urey (1893–1981) set out to confirm this hypothesis. Miller and Urey combined what

they believed to be the significant components of the earth's early atmosphere—water (H2O), methane (CH4), hydrogen (H2), and ammonia (NH3)— in a sealed, sterile flask. Next, they heated the flask to produce water vapor and passed electric sparks through the mixture to mimic lightning in the atmosphere (Figure 3.1). When they analyzed the contents of the flask a week later, they found amino acids. Amino acids are carbon compounds that make up proteins. Proteins are essential for life. Their data provided evidence that supported the "primordial soup" hypothesis.

In this chapter, students will look at the atom carbon and the role it plays in making up the four major classes of carbon-based molecules: carbohydrates, lipids, proteins, and nucleic acids. Students will also learn to identify and describe the functions of different macromolecules.[77]

The passage presents the Miller-Urey experiment as confirmation of the primordial soup hypothesis's validity, then moves directly into biology. Contextual omissions mislead students about that experiment and the current state of understanding regarding life's origins. The passage concludes its discussion as if the primordial soup hypothesis were definitive, without acknowledging that many researchers have long discarded it as a viable explanation.

The textbook's narrative commits a logical fallacy known as 'if A, then B,' implying that because a single type of amino acid can form under certain laboratory conditions, this process directly explains the origin of life on Earth. This is an example of a non sequitur, where the conclusion does not logically follow from the premises. Concluding that the formation of only one kind of amino acid is the first step toward the emergence of life is like a child forming a single lopsided brick in his backyard and imagining it's the first step in a state-of-the-art hospital constructing itself. This experiment should be presented primarily for its historical significance rather than as a potential explanation of life's origins.

Moreover, The conditions simulated in the Miller-Urey experiment do not represent the early Earth's atmosphere as understood today.[78] Research suggests that the early atmosphere likely consisted of mostly water vapor, carbon dioxide, and nitrogen, similar to our atmosphere today, with only insignificant amounts of carbon monoxide and hydrogen, and essentially no methane or ammonia.[79]

This presentation as a mystery-solved narrative deprives students of the opportunity to critically engage with the complexities and uncertainties of these topics. The way this is presented is no accident. Textbook creation involves extensive pedagogical planning, revisions, and collaboration over many years—especially given that this science project occurred in 1952.[80] Often adapted from resources like OpenStax, the content is further refined by experienced faculty and subject matter experts, making its presentation of outdated information all the more deliberate, discouraging independent thinking by presenting it as foundational truth in the classroom.[81]

Though this narrative is widespread in education, the textbook in question is not used in middle or high schools, but at the college level. Consequently, many K–12 Earth science and biology teachers, who begin teaching after earning their bachelor's degrees, are often unaware that they are passing along misleading content. Being briefly introduced to such topics without critical details is concerning. As a result, K–12 teachers frequently perpetuate the narrative, creating a ripple effect that misinforms students across multiple levels of K–12 education and continues to influence those who go on to attend college. This persists despite the fact that origin-of-life researchers are fully aware the narrative is inaccurate.

Like many educational institutions, the College of Lake County uses materials from widely accessible resources. In this instance, Chapter 3, "Biologically Important Molecules," uses a chapter from an OpenStax textbook titled "Microbiology".[82] OpenStax, "An educational, nonprofit initiative of Rice University and leader of the new SafeInsights national education research hub," is a respected provider of free, open-source content.[83]

A significant factor in the popularity and widespread use of textbooks like those provided by OpenStax lies in their licensing under Creative Commons (CC).[84] This type of licensing allows educational institutions to freely use, modify, and distribute the original materials without the need for explicit permission from the copyright holder, as long as the original creators are credited, and the use is non-commercial.

The College of Lake County, along with many other schools, takes advantage of this flexibility to adapt OpenStax textbooks to better fit their specific course structures or educational objectives. It allows for including local or course-specific content, such as additional images or modified sections, which can help educators tailor the material more closely to their standards. For direct illustrations of the textbook adaptations discussed, see Figures 36.1 and 36.2.

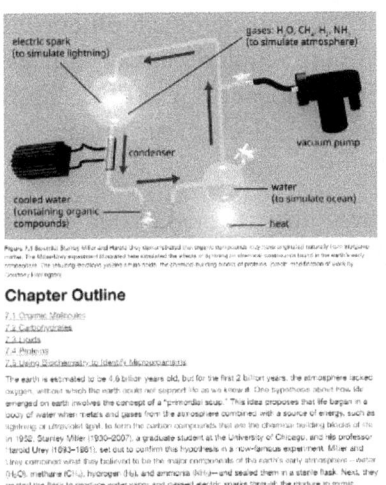

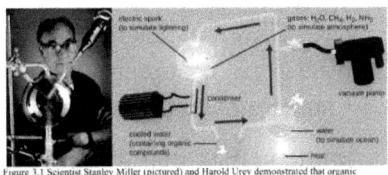

Figure 2.1, (Left), Introductory section of Chapter 7, "Microbial Biochemistry," Image source: OpenStax textbook.

Figure 2.2 (Right), Introductory section of Chapter 3, "Biologically Important Molecules," from the College of Lake County's textbook, adapted from OpenStax. Modifications include adding a photo of Stanley Miller and removing the OpenStax hyperlink. The presentation of the Stanley Miller experiment as an introduction to microbiology remains identical in both texts, with no additional information provided on the origin of life. **Image source:** College of Lake County textbook, page 63.

Although this adaptability might be seen as a strength, it, at times, perpetuates outdated theories. This issue is evident in the continued use of the Miller-Urey experiment to explain the origin of life—one of the most stubborn areas to show progress in aligning with modern scientific understanding.

OpenStax describes its commitment to ensuring that educational content remains current and scientifically accurate in the following on its FAQ page:

> OpenStax textbook projects are developed and peer-reviewed by educators to ensure they are readable and accurate, meet the scope and sequence requirements of each course, are supported by instructor ancillaries, and are available with the latest technology-based learning tools… The online version of OpenStax books are always kept up-to-date and freely available.[85] Instructors are welcome to submit errata suggestions via their book page on the OpenStax website for our subject matter experts to review.[86] We revise our books when it is pedagogically necessary; we may publish a new edition to accommodate significant developments in the field, while smaller updates are made regularly in the web view of your book.[87] Each June, OpenStax publishes new PDFs and print versions of most of our books to reflect these updates (when substantial changes are present).

It is commendable that OpenStax allows adaptations under a Creative Commons license, enabling users to tailor the content effectively to their specific needs. However, there is a disconnect between their stated standards and their presentation of the 1952 Miller-Urey experiment and other content about life's origin in their textbooks. Considering that OpenStax has stated that it has reached over 36 million learners since 2012, it is concerning that the content influencing such a large audience includes outdated representations.

My critique of educational materials is not explicitly aimed at OpenStax; it is a critique of a normalized approach within U.S. educational materials altogether. In fact, another highly influential online educational platform is Khan Academy. It, among other examples, plays a significant role in shaping scientific understanding of theories that interpret reality, such as the origin of life, for countless learners. Despite this role, Khan Academy also presents misinformation on such topics. For instance, in their College AP Biology course, in a video lesson from "Lesson 11: Origins of Life on Earth," the presenter begins the discussion by framing it with the declaration: "Let's start with *what we actually know*."⁸⁸ ⁸⁹ This phrase primes the audience to receive all subsequent information as fact while, as we will see, disregarding caution.

The presenter draws a line on the digital blackboard to illustrate Earth's timeline, marking key moments while utilizing the versatile tool of deep time—repeating "billions of years" as a primer:

> So, let's go one billion years ago. Let's go two billion years ago, three billion years, four billion years ago. So, this is now. And once again, we're talking about a billion years ago.⁹⁰

He punctuates this discussion by presenting the early conditions of our solar system as chaotic, explaining:

> You had collisions of all scales happening all the time. The moon itself was formed from the collision of two planet-sized objects; one we call the proto-Earth and another planet-sized object. And they collided. And then they started to spin around, and one part became the moon.⁹¹

He then subtly shifts to an unsubstantiated biochemical hypothesis by pointing to a "region" on his timeline and stating:

> ...even if we knew the exact timeframe that some RNA ended up getting in the right configuration so it could replicate itself in some way… it still leaves unanswered, maybe, the more interesting question, which is the how.⁹²

This statement unhesitatingly jumps to a huge conclusion without any disclaimer. It introduces the RNA World Hypothesis as "the how" life began. He declares outright that RNA molecules were the first forms of life to replicate themselves.

He further asserts, while pointing to molecular structures on a chart, "The how is really, at least to me, more important, more interesting than 'the when'. And to the how question, there are a couple of layers on it."⁹³

He introduced simple molecules like water and carbon dioxide as starting points: "The first is, let's just start with the most simple molecules that we would have expected to find on early Earth."⁹⁴

He proceeds to explain "the how" chemical evolution achieved the "next step up." He points from amino acid structures to nucleotide structures and states:

> ...the simple answer is we now have a lot of evidence that this is doable, that you can go from these things to these things, abiotically, without the presence of life.[95]

By pointing from amino acids to nucleotides, he inaccurately claims that there is a *direct* and evidence-backed pathway for their synthesis abiotically and in the lab. This statement contradicts the current scientific understanding, which does not support such a process. This presenter's "simple answer" that a substantial body of evidence supports the abiotic, direct, and straightforward chemical pathway from basic building blocks like amino acids to the more complex nucleotides is false. The presenter's lack of caution in discussing the origin of life during this presentation is particularly troubling, potentially an educational malpractice. This issue is not isolated in Khan Academy videos.

While thinkers like Stephen Jay Gould and Eugenie C. Scott have argued that one cannot fully understand the natural world or think scientifically without a firm grasp of evolution, one might question why misleading narratives, such as the primordial soup hypothesis, continue to persist in textbooks. Those who question evolution are often dismissed as ignorant, yet students are still taught speculative origin stories like the primordial soup hypothesis—even though no random or intentional pathway to the beginning of life has ever been established. This only makes the sweeping extrapolation from a single-celled organism to the full diversity of life all the more questionable.

CHAPTER 3

Geologism

The Hindu religion is the only one of the world's great faiths dedicated to the idea that the Cosmos itself undergoes an immense, indeed an infinite, number of deaths and rebirths. It is the only religion in which the time scales correspond to those of modern scientific cosmology. Its cycles run from our ordinary day and night to a day and night of Brahma, 8.64 billion years long. Longer than the age of the Earth or the Sun and about half the time since the Big Bang.[96] —Carl Sagan

The uncertainty surrounding the origin of life raises deeper questions about the assumptions underlying evolutionary theory—especially the foundational ones inherited from geology. Darwin's framework grew out of a geological model that was as much philosophical as it was scientific. The model he adopted was that of Charles Lyell, a prominent 19th-century geologist known for his revolutionary work, *Principles of Geology: Being an Attempt to Explain the Former Changes of the Earth's Surface, by Reference to Causes Now in Operation.*[97] His work redefined the study of Earth's history, overturned the prevailing catastrophist view. The catastrophist view holds that a few global catastrophes, most notably Noah's Flood, explains the geological record.

Lyell posited, however, that slow, consistent processes—observable in the present—were sufficient to explain Earth's features. His work helped establish modern geology as a science grounded in deep time and regularity, treating these processes as all-encompassing and effectively eternal, and for many, rendering a global flood unnecessary as an explanation for the geological record.

During his voyage on the Beagle, Charles Darwin read Lyell's work closely. The concept of gradual, natural change over vast timescales became central to Darwin's theory of evolution. Lyell's influence on Darwin was immediate and lasting. They met shortly after Darwin returned to England, on October 29, 1836.[98]

Figure 3.1 Charles Lyell, age 43, painted by Alexander Craig during the British Association meeting in Glasgow, 1840. **Image source:** Fæ, Wikimedia Commons.

Just over a week after first meeting, Darwin wrote to W.D. Fox on November 6, 1836, reflecting that "no one has been nearly so friendly & kind, as Lyell."[99] Darwin admired Lyell's grace and free-heartedness, noting, "You cannot imagine how good-naturedly he entered into all my plans."[100] This early bond laid the foundation for Darwin's trust in Lyell. Yet, as their friendship grew stronger, it became clear that it wasn't solely Darwin's plans at play. Darwin's early trust and admiration for Lyell gave Lyell quiet influence over the direction of his thinking, subtly drawing him into Lyell's broader vision for the future of science.

Eight years later, in a letter to Leonard Horner in 1844, Darwin reflected on Lyell's influence on his own work, writing:

> I cannot say how forcibly impressed I am with the infinite superiority of the Lyellian school of Geology. I always feel as if my books came half out of Lyell's brains... the great merit of the Principles, was that it altered the whole tone of one's mind & therefore that when seeing a thing never seen by Lyell, one yet saw it partially through his eyes.[101]

Darwin regarded Lyell's geological framework as so foundational that it reshaped his entire way of thinking. Even when observing phenomena unknown to Lyell, he still saw them through Lyell's intellectual lens. He felt that ideas falling outside this framework seemed questionable or required reinterpretation. When Darwin notes that Principles "altered the whole tone of one's mind," the phrase echoes Romans 12:2—"Be transformed by the renewing of your mind"—suggesting that Lyell's approach demanded a full intellectual reorientation. His reference to the "infinite superiority" of Lyell's school, though figurative, elevates Lyell's influence to a near-infallible status—one on which Darwin grounded his own theories.

Some may argue that Darwin later "disagreed" with Lyell, but this misrepresents their relationship. It was not Darwin who broke with Lyell, but Lyell who hesitated to endorse Darwin's theory. Darwin continued to regard Lyell as the intellectual foundation of his thinking, and even expressed self-doubt when Lyell showed reluctance to support natural selection.

Additionally, in a letter to Lyell in 1858, while seeking publishing advice, Darwin remarked, "I have always thought you would have made a first-rate Lord Chancellor; & I now appeal to you as a Lord Chancellor."[102] Flattery was common in 19th-century scientific correspondence, often employed in a warm or teasing manner, but this particular context feels different. Given Darwin's deep reverence for Lyell, his petition to him "as Lord Chancellor" seems neither casual nor playful. Rather, Darwin sought serious counsel, elevating Lyell to Britain's highest legal authority.

Paranoid Ideation

Though regarded as a scientific giant in Darwin's eyes and widely respected for his contributions, Lyell faced notable personal challenges. He struggled with the sense that the religious orthodoxy of his time limited both his work and his personal freedom. It is true that it was not uncommon for some scientists to face conflict with religious views, but Lyell's internal struggle appeared deeply personal. His sense of intellectual superiority and the immense importance he placed on his scientific pursuits seem to have made him feel that his ideas—and by extension, his identity—were under moral attack. But it was his preexisting insecurity about revealing those ideas that deepened the torment: he believed he possessed superior insight, yet lacked the courage to offend.

This internal battle can be traced back to his childhood hobby of collecting insects, where he first encountered societal judgment. These early experiences seem to have shaped his sensitivity to external opinions, a trait that would define how he later navigated tensions during his career. Lyell learned early on to be tactical and "stealthy." His autobiography offers a glimpse into the mindset that would later culminate in a more duplicitous nature. Publicly, Lyell was cautious and respectful, but privately, he was driven by resentment and intent on carrying out epistemological violence.

In his autobiography, Lyell reveals his vigilance of others' judgments, which led him to conceal his passion for entomology to avoid scrutiny. He notes:

> The disrepute in which my hobby was held had a considerable effect on my character…I followed it up almost by stealth.[103]

To cope with this, Lyell rationalized the public's indifferent views as ignorance. He explains:

> I never confessed to myself that I was wrong, but always reasoned myself into a belief that the generality of *people were too stupid* to comprehend the interest of such pursuits.[104]

This reveals a condescending view toward those who didn't share his interests. The conflict between craving recognition and harboring contempt shaped how he moved through his personal and professional life. It allowed him to maintain confidence in the value of his work by framing criticism as the product of lesser minds.

As noted, during his career as a geologist, Lyell worked within an era of intellectual tension, where challenges to prevailing religious beliefs often stirred controversy. However, the idea that he was constrained by existential threats is, in retrospect, overstated. His position within the scientific community was more akin to a tenured-like status, providing him with substantial influence and security. Rather than directly challenging prevailing views, Lyell chose to be culturally sensitive or inclusive. What he faced was less about direct censorship and more about the self-imposed restraint he adopted to navigate the professional and social pressures of his time.

Similarly, some individuals today tread carefully to avoid controversy. For example, with the growing dominance of certain progressive views, many harbor strong resentments, feeling tormented by the need to conform to social norms and ideas they believe conflict with their reality, reflecting past struggles under differing ideological pressures to be "politically correct."

Based historical records such as Lyell's personal letters, the idea of Lyell being in intellectual bondage seems to be legend, especially when compared to the challenges faced by some modern academics. Today, individuals in academia or academia-adjacent roles who modestly question Darwinism or suggest flaws can face significant professional consequences—a form of censorship far more tangible than anything Lyell encountered.

Consequently, Lyell channeled his frustrations with societal norms, personal expectations, and professional pressure into his opposition to Mosaic cosmogony, which he increasingly attacked as a barrier to intellectual progress. Behind his careful public persona, a more tactical and irreverent tone sometimes surfaced. This is evident in an 1829 letter to his sister Marianne, where he mocked a newly published book defending the Hebrew cosmogony, revealing his antagonism toward Biblical interpretations. He wrote:

> Longman has paid down 500 guineas to Mr. Ure of Dublin for a popular work on Geology, just coming out. It is to prove the Hebrew cosmogony, and that we ought all to be burnt in Smithfield. So much the better. I have got a rod for the fanatics, from a quarter where they expect it not.[105]

Lyell's reference to being "burnt in Smithfield" invokes the 16th-century site where religious dissenters were executed for heresy—an exaggerated, sarcastic jab at what he saw as the overreach of Biblical literalism in science.

Readers may recall the eerie childhood chant, "Bloody Mary, Bloody Mary, Bloody Mary," whispered in front of a mirror to summon a vengeful ghost. This urban legend may stem, at least in part, from the infamous Queen Mary I, known as "Bloody Mary" for her brutal persecution of Protestants—

many of whom were *burned at the stake in Smithfield*.[106] But this was nearly three centuries before Lyell's time, and his use of the reference is more comparable to folklore.

Further, his use of tactical language— "a rod for the fanatics, from a quarter where they expect it not"—reveals that he saw his challenge to Biblical narratives as a calculated strike, like a general planning an ambush on an unsuspecting enemy. His words seem gleeful as he looks forward to launching his attack against the unexpecting defenders of the Mosaic creation narrative.

In his letter, he goes on to compare his challenge to religious orthodoxy with the Pope's reversal of the Church's condemnation of Galileo. This comparison reveals Lyell's vision of himself as part of a broader movement aimed at liberating scientific disciplines from the teachings of Moses. He illustrates this by referring to a historical precedent, stating:

> He [the Pope] instituted lectures on the Mosaic cosmogony to set free astronomy and geology.[107]

Lyell's private words show a man who reveled in the thought of defeating his ideological opponents—particularly those defending the authority of Moses—far removed from the reserved public figure he presented to the scientific community.

In a June 1830 letter, Lyell urges his former mentor George Poulett Scrope to insert ideas into the publication *The Quarterly Review*. He wrote:

> I am sure you may get into Q. E. [Quarterly Review] what will free the science from Moses, for if treated seriously, the party are quite prepared for it.[108] [109]

This statement further reveals Lyell's resentment and motives toward the Moses' narrative and his strategic approach to undermining it. Operating as a saboteur, he worked behind the scenes to shift scientific thought while avoiding direct confrontation. His comment that "the party are quite prepared for it" was an exhortation that the intellectual environment was now ripe for infiltration.

In his letters, Lyell continues to focus on what he saw as naturalistic explanations, showing his disdain for referencing a "beginning" or divine creation as an explanation for natural phenomena. He acknowledges, however, "Probably there was a beginning—it is a metaphysical question, worthy a theologian," but dismisses the need to acknowledge this idea, citing James Hutton: "no signs of a beginning, no prospect of an end."[110] Again, there is sarcasm in Lyell's statement, especially in his choice of words. When Lyell says, "Probably there was a beginning—it is a metaphysical question, worthy a theologian," he implies that the question of a beginning is not a scientific one but belongs in the realm of theology, which he saw as an outdated framework for understanding the natural world. This is reminiscent of the mindset Lyell developed as a child: dismissing others' perspectives as misguided or disregarding arguments that didn't reflect his own views.

Lyell's refusal to consider a definitive "beginning," however, seemed to be much about ensuring his worldview prevailed. He repeats his plea:

> All I ask is, that at any given period of the past, don't stop inquiry when puzzled by refuge to a 'beginning.'[111]

Here, Lyell dismisses the argument for a singular beginning as an intellectually lazy "refuge," indirectly labeling those who consider a beginning as less open-minded. By dismissing the notion of a singular origin, even when evidence might suggest otherwise, he was actively safeguarding his belief in an eternal, self-sustaining Earth governed by gradual processes—an outlook that, as we'll see, was not free from its own metaphysical assumptions in a supernatural sense.

Interestingly, Lyell further argues that "proofs" is what matters, not the metaphysical "probability of a beginning": "It is not the beginning I look for, but proofs of a progressive state of existence in the globe."[112] For Lyell, these proofs align with his declared commitment to observable, ongoing explanations, as laid out in the subtitle of his seminal work: "Being an Attempt to Explain the Former Changes of the Earth's Surface, by Reference to Causes Now in Operation." In other words, Earth's past could be fully understood by studying present-day processes—erosion, sedimentation, and volcanic activity.

Lyell lays out a strategy for Scrope, suggesting that, with a cunning approach, even religious leaders could be subtly enlisted to their cause. He writes:

> If you don't triumph over them, but compliment the liberality and candour of the present age, the bishops and enlightened saints will join us in despising both the ancient and modern physico-theologians.[113]

This shows a deliberate effort to manipulate public perception and gain allies through flattery. Lyell believed that eroding the influence of religious interpretations would take time, but it could be done by gradually redirecting the sympathies of moderate clergy.

Egging on Scrope further, Lyell continues:

> It is just the time to strike, so rejoice that, sinner as you are, the Q. E. is open to you.[114]

His use of "sinner" introduces more sarcasm, either acknowledging that challenging religious views on Earth's history was seen as a kind of heresy, or mocking religious beliefs themselves. Seeing *The Quarterly Review* as an important breach in the intellectual landscape opened to Scropes, Lyell urges him to seize the opportunity to challenge religious interpretations of the Earth's history.[115]

In a letter to his sister, Marianne, in 1830, Lyell privately mocked the attempts to reconcile science and religion in earlier correspondences. Referring to the Mosaico-geological system, he derided his former teacher, prominent Oxford geologist William Buckland, and the Swiss geologist Jean-André De Luc, known for trying to reconcile geological findings with a Biblical framework. Lyell criticized such figures, saying their attempts to merge scripture with geology had done "no good to science or to religion."[116] He saw their compromises, such as splitting geological events into pre- and post-diluvian periods to fit the Biblical flood narrative, as absurd concessions to religious orthodoxy.

However, he didn't mind compromising intellectual honesty when it came to his own interests. He confided to his sister, stating:

> I am afraid that what delights my friend Scrope more than all—the honest history of the Mosaico-geological system—will hurt the sale.[117]

He admits that this critique delights Scrope, who was more confrontational. But Lyell worries it "will hurt the sale"—he's afraid that being too open about challenging the Mosaic narrative will alienate readers or provoke backlash, reducing the book's commercial success.

In an 1829 letter to Gideon Mantell, Lyell offers a vivid, mocking account of a Geological Society meeting, which further undercuts the popular image of contemporaries as cautious rebels muzzled by religious authority.[118] Instead, Lyell appears as a confident strategist engaged in what he clearly saw as an intellectual—and cultural—battle.

The occasion was a paper by William Conybeare defending diluvialist geology, which posited major geological change through catastrophic floods, including the Biblical Deluge. Lyell and Murchison, representing the "Fluvialists," argued for gradual, observable processes like river erosion. Buckland, present to support the diluvialist view, is described by Lyell as "very piano," or unusually subdued. Lyell describes the meeting as entertaining and politically satisfying. He gleefully recounts Greenough's bizarre attempt to discredit uniformitarianism through a fable in which the Fluvialists are equated to a wolf plotting murder:

> 'Give me time, and I will murder you.' So say the Fluvialists![119]

Greenough's intent was to mock the idea that long spans of time could justify any geological claim. Lyell notes this drew "roars of laughter," making Greenough the butt of his own analogy.

While Lyell delights in the irony of the moment, the most consequential line is his final assessment. He makes a blunt assertion of the collapse of Mosaic geology within scientific discourse:

> Conybeare's memoir is not strong... He admits three deluges before the Noachian! and Buckland adds God knows how many catastrophes besides, so we have driven them out of the Mosaic record fairly.[120]

This statement declares victory in a campaign against the Biblical account of Earth history. The language is unmistakably martial: to "drive" someone out of a position suggests siege, expulsion, and conquest.

In a letter to his father, Lylell adopts a restrained and even admiring tone regarding Buckland's Bridgewater Treatise, which sought to reconcile geology with Christian theology. Lyell writes that it would "spread correct notions of the science, and probably popularise it much," though he also concedes, "I should have been sorry to have had to trust myself upon it."[121] Though he found them unconvincing, he acknowledged that Buckland's efforts to reconcile geology with cosmogony were better constructed than expected. This demonstrates how Lyell could shift his tone depending on his audience and circumstances, simultaneously critiquing and approving of religiously-influenced science.

In another conversation with French geologist D'Aubuisson, Lyell found an ally in critiquing the merging of religious and scientific perspectives. D'Aubuisson remarked that, "We Catholic geologists flatter ourselves that we have kept clear of the mixing of things sacred and profane, but the three great Protestants, De Luc, Cuvier, and Buckland, have not done so."[122] Lyell echoed this sentiment, sarcastically suggesting that Buckland's need to conform to religious expectations at "orthodox" Oxford may have been necessary to attract an audience, saying, "perhaps he could get no audience by other means."[123] This is the same Lyell who carefully calculated the impact of his own opinions on book sales, wary of being too honest about his views.

To Lyell, however, the open and sincere attempts of others to reconcile their views with his perspective were embarrassing and intellectually dishonest. He predicted that "they themselves will be ashamed of seeing how they will look by-and-by in the page of history."[124] This same Lyell, who preached intellectual forwardness, candidly admits in 1830 that he deliberately held back his more controversial ideas to avoid revealing their full implications:

> Full half of my history and comments was cut out... because either I, or Stokes, or Broderip, felt that it was anticipating twenty or thirty years of the march of honest feeling to declare it undisguisedly.[125]

Lyell's admission of disguising the intent behind his broader beliefs reflects the pattern that traces back to his childhood, running consistently through his social engagement: concealing, delaying, and calibrating his message to manipulate cultural reception. For Lyell, the ideological coup was inevitable. He often casted himself as the smartest man in the room—here, boasting that his theory was so far ahead of its time that he possessed the intellectual ammunition to dismantle his opposition, but chose restraint, convinced the world needed another twenty or thirty years before it was ready for the full force of his argument.

Unlike Lyell, some in his circle—such as Darwin, for example—did not appear to hold a lifelong hostility toward religious texts or opposing worldviews. Darwin was, however, fully aware that his ideas would provoke controversy. In fact, for some time, Darwin's polarizing conclusions seemed to grieve him. On the other hand, unlike Lyell, figures like Thomas Huxley and John Tyndall were more openly combative in challenging religious authority, particularly regarding the influence of religion on scientific inquiry.

Lyell confided his more controversial views only to a select group of trusted friends and family. Filled with metaphors of bondage, Lyell's letters reveal the extent of his inner turmoil. Ironically, he frequently targeted Moses, who is traditionally seen as a symbol of freedom, as the source of oppression. Even Darwin didn't seem fully aware of the more calculating side of Lyell, perhaps because Lyell recognized the moral integrity Darwin possessed and kept certain aspects hidden. Perhaps this was because, as he admitted, he "got too much in the habit of avoiding being seen, as if ashamed of what [he] did."[126]

From early on, Lyell's friendliness and kindness toward Darwin successfully concealed the broader, unspoken aim to protect himself and his publications from harm while quietly winning his war against religious orthodoxy. He avoided confrontational battles, leaving them to Scrope, Darwin, Huxley, Wallace, and Hooker. While Lyell privately supported Darwin, he pushed him to publish *Origin*, even though he wasn't convinced by it. And this was despite knowing Darwin's own lingering doubts, which he expressed in his book and after its publication.

Though Darwin had long admired Lyell and depended on his support, by 1863, four years after On the Origin of Species was published, Darwin's patience had worn thin. In a letter to Joseph Hooker, he vented his frustration:

> The Lyells are coming here on Sunday Evening to stay till Wednesday. I dread it, but I must say how much disappointed I am that he has not spoken out on Species, still less on Man. And the best of the joke is that he thinks he has acted with the courage of a martyr of old. I hope I may have taken an exaggerated view of his timidity.[127]

From referring to Lyell as the "Lord Chancellor" to later referring to him as "timid," Darwin's evolved language reveals how he grew frustrated with Lyell's indifference toward the evolutionary mechanism of natural selection. As mentioned, there was no true disagreement between Darwin and Lyell; rather, Darwin spent over two decades desperately waiting for Lyell's approval. What Darwin didn't realize, however, was that Lyell had considered his theory and never intended to fully support it. Lyell wasn't simply undecided or timid; he had his own belief system and a different agenda that never included supporting natural selection.

The Presiding Mind

Darwin was a means to an end in Lyell's long-term campaign to establish uniformitarianism and ultimately dismantle the Mosaic cosmogony. Initially, Darwin's geological research—particularly his observations of gradual landscape changes, coral reef formation, and fossil distribution during the Beagle voyage—supported Lyell's vision of a law-governed, slowly evolving Earth. However, once Darwin shifted his focus from geological change to speciation by natural selection, Lyell then understood that Darwin could only serve his broader objective of freeing Victorian England from Moses.

One might think that Darwin's theory would perfectly align with Lyell's, given their shared emphasis on gradual natural processes. However, while Lyell's uniformitarianism was formulated based on observable geological processes, Darwin's theory extended into assumptions that could not be empirically verified at the time. Though they stood on the same ideological side, Lyell and others in Darwin's circle—such as Thomas H. Huxley—clearly recognized the distinction. They did not embrace Darwin out of true agreement with his explanation for the origin of life's diversity, but rather because his work advanced a broader ideological project: the removal of teleological and theological explanations from science.

Moreover, framing Lyell's contention with Mosaic writings as purely scientific is a myth. Lyell's theory wasn't scientifically problematic simply because his presuppositions led him to dismiss a beginning; it was also driven by deeper ideological and metaphysical commitments that underpinned his science. At the heart of his worldview wasn't just naturalism, but a subtle supernatural perspective. While Lyell is widely known for highlighting natural processes as the basis of geology, what is less recognized is that his cosmogony included a kind of prime mover.

In one of his more revealing moments, Lyell speaks of a "Presiding Mind" overseeing the creation and extinction of species.[128] In a letter to his confidant Sir John Herschel, Lyell wrote about the "succession of extinction of species, and creation of new ones, going on perpetually now," stating:

> The idea struck me as *the grandest idea which I had ever conceived* so far as regards the attributes of the Presiding Mind.[129] For one can in imagination summon before us a small past at least of the circumstances that *must be contemplated and foreknown, before it can be decided* what powers and qualities a new species must have in order to enable it to endure for a given time, and to play its part in due relation to all other beings *destined to coexist with it*, before it dies out.[130] [131]

This passage, in which Lyell reveals his spiritual conviction, underscores that he never accepted natural selection as a sufficient explanation for the origin of species—and, given his underlying worldview, likely never could. His reference to a "Presiding Mind" and the idea that a species' traits must be "contemplated and foreknown" point to a belief in a guided, intentional process rather than an undirected mechanism like natural selection. This is a direct contrast to Darwin's theory, which does not require foresight or purpose in the development of species.

The fact that Lyell privately expressed such views while never outright rejecting Darwinism in public suggests that he strategically withheld his true position. While he publicly rejected the Biblical creation narrative, privately he believed in a directed, purposeful process—one governed by a Presiding Mind overseeing the cyclical processes of an eternal Earth within his uniformitarian cosmogony. Clearly, Lyell believed he had conceived a more "grand" idea, because his reluctance to publicly endorse natural selection may also reflect a deeper unease with Darwin's failure to account for origin, causation within observable reality, or coherence with the fossil record. The lack of a demonstrable, ongoing mechanism consistent with Lyell's uniformitarian principles reaffirmed his commitment to his own framework.

Notably, in *Principles of Geology*, Lyell reveals that he was well versed in Eastern and Greek cosmogonies.[132] He notably incorporated cyclical cosmologies into his work, drawing on the Hindu trinity—Brahma (creator), Vishnu (preserver), and Shiva (destroyer)—as a model for creation, preservation, and destruction.[133] This reinforced his belief in uniformitarianism and a Presiding Mind governing natural processes. This cosmogony aligned with Lyell's idea of (erosion, sedimentation, and volcanic activity) one, ongoing, non-catastrophic process. In Hindu thought, these gods represent the eternal or endless cycle of creation, preservation, and destruction.

In his book, Lyell framed these cycles as natural laws, stating:

> It is not inconsistent with the Hindoo mythology to suppose that Pythagoras might have found in the East not only the system of universal and violent catastrophes... but also that of periodical *revolutions*, effected by the continued agency of ordinary causes.[134]

Though Lyell stripped these cycles of their divine agents, he privately went further, substituting in his own god, describing the Presiding Mind as "the grandest idea which I had ever conceived."[135]

His concept of a purposeful force behind natural processes seems to be a kind of pantheism or monism, where nature and divinity were inseparable. This is seen in his belief that species and natural phenomena were "designed to coexist" in harmony. In his letter, he compares this intelligence to

Babbage's calculating machine, suggesting it meticulously orchestrated the balance of species and geological change.[136] He preferred this neutral, self-regulating Earth, perpetually and passively, governed by his Presiding Mind. Conversely, he detested the penal aspect of the Mosaic narrative and sought to stamp it out in the name of science, while promoting a replacement rooted in this personal revelation. Notably, Darwin too was most troubled by the judgment embedded in Christianity rather than the idea of a supreme agent. Lyell's ambiguity allowed him to navigate both scientific and religious discourses without fully committing to either.

The concept of a "presiding deity" or "presiding god" is integral to various Hindu traditions, symbolizing a divine entity that governs specific aspects of the cosmos, natural phenomena, or human faculties.[137] [138] The records examined in this work suggest that Hindu cosmogonical concepts had a significant impact on his thinking. In Hindu philosophy, presiding deities, known as Adhidaivata, are believed to oversee and regulate different elements of the universe and aspects of human experience.[139] Texts such as the Chandogya Upanishad assign these intelligences roles in sustaining the cosmic balance, reflecting a worldview where divine consciousness saturates and regulates all levels of reality.[140]

This idea—a passive but guiding intelligence embedded in the structure of nature—closely parallels Vedantic thought. As I explored in *Natural Technology: The Theory of Everything*, physicist Erwin Schrödinger also turned to Vedanta to make sense of what quantum mechanics implied about the unity of consciousness.[141] He regarded the Upanishadic formula *Tat tvam asi* ("You are that") as capturing a truth he believed physics pointed to: that the division between individual minds is ultimately an illusion. In *Mind and Matter*, Schrödinger wrote:

> There is obviously only one alternative, namely the unification of minds or consciousnesses. Their multiplicity is only apparent, in truth there is only one mind. This is the doctrine of the Upanishads.[142]

For Schrödinger, Vedanta offered the only framework consistent with what science revealed about consciousness and reality.

While Schrödinger acknowledged his philosophical influences directly, Lyell avoided naming his. Still, his idea of a Presiding Mind, likened to Babbage's calculating machine, shows a belief in intelligence operating behind the scenes—a silent orderer of species, cycles, and geological change. Though Lyell rejected the penal structure of the Mosaic cosmogony, he did not settle for randomness. His version of natural law was not secular in any complete sense; it was metaphysically strapped. These are metaphysical commitments expressed in scientific terms.

This kind of framing has repeated throughout the history of science. Spiritual motivations are often disguised as objectivity simply by avoiding references to creators, souls, or design. But the impulse is forever present. Unless one holds to a genuinely agnostic position—a rare and unsustainable outlook for most committed materialists—any view of origins ends up carrying metaphysical weight. Inflation, uniformitarianism, and natural selection each claim to explain how reality unfolds, yet all of them point, if indirectly, to forces or structures beyond the verifiable.

Thus, Lyell wasn't a detached seeker of truth. He was a man driven by a quiet but persistent spiritual conviction—one that shaped his interpretation of the Earth and its processes. Whether out of caution, superiority, or both, Lyell kept much of his foundational worldview to himself. Possibly, those Lyell deemed "too stupid" to fully reveal his more visceral ideas may have included Darwin. Over the decades, as Darwin patiently waited for Lyell's full validation and support in defending his ideas, he failed to realize that he was a piece on Lyell's epistemological chessboard.

Lyell's Straw Man

Let's take a closer look at Lyell's uniformitarianism, along with his and Darwin's broader assumptions, with a critical eye, playing the devil's advocate, or in this case, the Designer's advocate. Though Lyell's theory was grounded in observable processes, it led him—and those who followed—to treat presumptive arguments as if they were conclusive. Lyell's refutation of the Mosaic text reflects a kind of Dunning-Kruger effect: he mischaracterizes the Biblical perspective by filtering it through his own assumptions, creating a straw man of the argument he claims to discredit.

By focusing exclusively on gradual and eternal processes, Lyell overlooked the engineering requirements necessary for a young Earth to be suitable for human dominion and productivity. He never recognized that his assumption of an eternal Earth was mistaken. But more than that, from a Mosaic perspective, the appearance of deep time and ongoing natural processes is not deceptive—it is integral to the creation narrative. Scripture presents an Earth designed with purpose and intent, fully mature and capable of sustaining human life from the moment of existence. According to this account, immediate functionality was necessary so that humanity could fulfill its role to "have dominion," "be fruitful," and "multiply" from the very beginning. In dismissing both catastrophe and creation, Lyell closed off the possibility of intentional discontinuities—whether by judgment or design. The Mosaic account includes both: a fully formed world built for human life, and decisive historical ruptures that structure the Biblical narrative. By insisting on uninterrupted processes, Lyell excluded not only Genesis, but the entire Biblical pattern of divine interruption—creation, flood, exodus, and incarnation.

For a more intuitive understanding, consider the example of Adam. Few would argue it makes sense for Adam to have begun life as a zygote. The day of his creation was not the beginning of a natural process, but a moment of mature appearance—an intentional interruption in biological continuity. His apparent age was distinct from the moment of his origin. Adam is depicted as being created fully formed by God, rather than through a lengthy process of aging over deep time, which would typically be considered the "natural process" of human development from conception to adulthood.

Suppose Lyell had stood next to Adam shortly after his creation; based on his uniformitarian assumptions and the processes we 'know,' he might have insisted that Adam must have taken years to gradually mature into adulthood. Lyell would likely argue that Adam's facial hair, height, and reproductive maturity could only be explained by years of natural development—consistent with gradual, observable processes. But that view reflects an entirely different narrative, not the Mosaic account, which affirms deliberate, methodical interruptions distinct from what we believe to be a natural order. No amount of modern expertise in human development can refute the Biblical claim that Adam was formed just a week earlier, despite exhibiting all the traits of a fully developed, mature man.

Lyell's uniformitarianism does not undermine Moses' account as he and his followers may have thought. Instead, his misunderstanding lies in dismissing the premise of Moses' account of divine will, failing to grasp the necessity of a fully matured Earth from the outset. Lyell concentrates on what follows—regular, observable processes—but misses that in the Mosaic account, what follows is meaningful only because of what precedes it: a deliberate act of creation. By ignoring the initial intervention, he treats continuity as self-sufficient, while the narrative treats it as derivative.

Similar to the creation of Adam, Moses' creation account of Earth does not imply a 'zygote Earth,' but one designed to be fully functional for humanity's immediate dominion and fruitfulness. This maturity wouldn't have been just aesthetic; Earth needed to be fully equipped with the biological, agricultural, and mineral resources essential for human survival and progress—everything in place for the rise of civilization.

Had the Earth been created in a state of gradual development, humanity would have lacked immediate access to critical resources, such as metals, necessary for survival and innovation. How could God have commanded the Israelites to construct the Tabernacle with gold, silver, and bronze (Exodus 25:3) if these metals had not already been placed within the Earth for them to access? Metallurgy, in particular, has played a foundational role throughout history, with metals like copper, iron, and gold proving essential to technological advancements and the growth of early economies.

Moses' perspective that creation was mature and fully functional from its inception directly challenges interpretations of his narrative that impose modern, gradualist assumptions onto the text. Moses' account narrates a cosmos created with fully formed ecosystems, established rock formations, and starlight already in place, along with, as for Adam, a ready-made age for both Earth and the universe. Thus, it would be a contradiction to suggest that Adam, the Earth, or the universe were not created with an initial functional completeness, appearing with an age necessary for their intended purpose. There is nothing in Moses' narrative to suggest ambiguity about creation as a complete and finished act.

What person would buy an aquarium and leave the elements to develop on their own, expecting the water, plants, and fish to gradually create a thriving ecosystem without any guidance or intervention? Rather, one would plan to have everything in place for the fish's survival—ensuring the water, the light needed, the plants, and the food are ready before introducing the fish, not leaving it to chance or gradual development. In ignoring Moses' claim of divine intervention, Lyell's philosophical refutation becomes an ill-conceived notion, misrepresenting the Mosaic text.

Chapter 4

Values

> *No purposive principles exist in nature. Organic evolution has occurred by various combinations of random genetic drift, natural selection, Mendelian heredity, and many other purposeless mechanisms. Humans are complex organic machines that die completely with no survival of soul or psyche. Humans and other animals make choices frequently, but these are determined by the interaction of heredity and environment and are not the result of free will. No inherent moral or ethical laws exist, nor are there absolute guiding principles for human society. The universe cares nothing for us and we, have no ultimate meaning in life. These implications of modern science produce much squirming among scientists, who claim a high degree of rationality.*[143]
> —William Provine

Although Darwin's work largely remained focused on the natural world and avoided the antagonistic tendencies of figures like Lyell and Huxley, by the 1870s, his letters and remarks increasingly grew cynical and reflected frustration. He grew particularly concerned with how both theologians and naturalists, as he saw it, distorted his ideas. While his theory of natural selection was scientific in intent, it became entangled with the rise of materialism. Many of his anti-theist and materialistic peers misrepresented his personal stance. These misinterpretations, along with personal and public attacks, contributed to his growing agitation during this period.

In an 1868 letter to Ernst Haeckel, Darwin expressed concern about Haeckel's speculative conclusions. He wrote, "Your boldness, however, sometimes makes me tremble," and went on to critique Haeckel as "rather rash in venturing to say at what periods the several groups first appeared."[144] Darwin worried that such overconfidence could damage the credibility of his theory by stretching claims beyond what the evidence supported.

By this point, Darwin was well-established as a leading scientist. His theory of evolution had gained significant attention, and he had the confidence to critique peers like Haeckel, who was twenty-five years younger, especially when he felt their methods could harm the credibility of his broader scientific effort. His concerns were later realized when Haeckel admitted to falsifying parts of embryo illustrations to make vertebrate embryos appear more similar than they actually were, compromising the integrity of Darwin's theory. Despite this, Haeckel's broader philosophical outlook was never fully disowned.

As noted, the anti-Mosaic paradigm has selectively tolerated spiritual language—so long as it serves its broader narrative. Haeckel, a staunch advocate of Darwinism, openly rejected traditional theism while embracing a form of pantheistic monism that framed the universe as a self-organizing, divine whole. His "God-Nature" construct was not a rejection of the sacred but a repackaging of it—one that conveniently excluded the personal deity of religious traditions.[145]

Haeckel's spiritualized materialism was welcomed as a philosophical extension of evolutionary thought, not dismissed as unscientific.[146] His pantheism could be absorbed into the grand narrative of self-organizing matter, while other metaphysical perspectives are treated as speculative or even unworthy of serious consideration. The question, then, has not been whether science allows metaphysical conclusions—but which ones it is willing to accept.

Similar to Lyell, Haeckel's case is particularly revealing because he vilified traditional religious belief while crafting his own quasi-religious system, complete with a sacred cosmic order, an eternal unity, and even moral prescriptions drawn from nature.[147] His philosophy, at times, bore the dogmatic certainty he condemned in others—yet, because it was attached to Darwinian evolution, it was treated as a rational worldview rather than a speculative faith.

His metaphysical commitments actively influenced his "science"—not the other way around.[148] He took liberties in presenting unfounded theories as established facts, and his fraudulent embryo drawings, which remained in use for well over a century to promote evolutionary ideas, reflect both his

The Value Paradox

Charles Darwin wrote the following in his autobiography in 1876, primarily for his family. It was not intended for publication during his lifetime:

> But I had gradually come, by this time, to see that the Old Testament from its manifestly false history of the world, with the Tower of Babel, the rainbow as a sign, etc., etc., and from its attributing to God the feelings of a revengeful tyrant, was no more to be trusted than the sacred books of the Hindus, or the beliefs of any barbarian.[149]

Darwin dismisses the Old Testament as false and morally flawed, calling its portrayal of God that of a "revengeful tyrant," and equating its credibility to that of other so-called primitive belief systems. However, in doing so, he relies on implicit standards of truth and morality—standards that are difficult to justify if all human beliefs (including moral judgments) are products of evolutionary chance and survival utility, not truth-tracking. To call one belief system "false" or "barbaric" presumes a position of epistemic and moral authority, yet under strict evolutionary naturalism, Darwin's own reasoning and values would also be the outcome of the same blind, adaptive processes. This creates a discrepancy: he critiques religious belief as irrational or culturally backward while assuming his own beliefs somehow transcend those same natural origins. So, why does his beliefs holds special claim to truth or objectivity?

Similar to Lyell, Darwin's doubts about the possibility of a God, particularly a benevolent, omnipotent Christian God, largely centered on his perception of injustice in the natural world and in certain doctrines. His writings and letters reveal that he grappled with reconciling the existence of suffering, predation, and what he found to be morally troubling Christian doctrines, particularly the concept of eternal judgment.

Darwin's more antagonistic shift toward religion also stemmed from, along with Huxley, becoming the poster child of radical Naturalism and a target for theists who, he believed, attacked his theory without fully understanding its science. Unlike Lyell's long-held prejudices, however, Darwin's religious views evolved over his life. He did not begin with anti-religious sentiments.

Initially, he held conventional Christian beliefs, but these gradually eroded as he developed his theory of evolution and grappled with its implications in contrast to those of Christianity. Darwin's faith eroded further in the 1850s, possibly influenced by personal tragedies such as the death of his beloved daughter Annie.[150] By the time he published *On the Origin of Species* in 1859, Darwin was largely agnostic. However, he did not set out to collapsing religious beliefs but rather aimed to present his explanation for biological diversity.

Darwin's most persistent struggle with Christianity centered on the problem of suffering and divine judgment, especially as it related to nature and human destiny. Darwin criticized the exclusivity of Christian theology, particularly the idea that only believers were saved. It was this doctrine, more than the death of his daughter, that most contributed to the erosion of his faith. He grappled deeply with the damning implications this belief had for his close family members and best friends. Darwin believed that, under Christian doctrine, the eternal fate of many men in his life—his father, brother, and closest friends—would be eternal damnation. In his autobiography, he wrote:

> I can indeed hardly see how anyone ought to wish Christianity to be true; for if so, the plain language of the text seems to show that the men who do not believe, and this would include my Father, Brother, and almost all my best friends, will be everlastingly punished. And this is a damnable doctrine.[151]

Darwin's revulsion was sincere, but it reflected a secular humanistic view of morality—one that conflicted with the Biblical teaching that "no one is righteous."[152] His difficulty was with a gospel that begins by asserting that even the best people, by human standards, stand in need of redemption.

Darwin's growing antagonism toward the idea of a benevolent creator was intensified by his reflections on the apparent cruelty of nature. Regarding parasitic wasps and predation, for example, he remarked in a letter to Asa Gray, dated May 22, 1860:

> I cannot persuade myself that a beneficent and omnipotent God would have designedly created the Ichneumonidae with the express intention of their feeding within the living bodies of caterpillars, or that a cat should play with mice.[153]

Modern Darwinians often cite remarks like this to critique the Biblical God, arguing that the brutality of nature is incompatible with divine goodness. But here lies a retrospective hypocrisy: the same features—parasitism, predation, and suffering—are accepted without moral objection when attributed to blind evolutionary processes. What is framed as evil under theism becomes amoral under naturalism. This double standard condemns divine justice for permitting cruelty, while granting evolutionary randomness a moral exemption. If cruelty disqualifies divine design, why should it not equally challenge the moral legitimacy of its alternative? And if suffering in nature can be neutral under evolution, then why can't it be just under God?

In 1881, Darwin, openly acknowledged the philosophical descrepancy within his evolutionary views in a letter to the Irish philosopher William Graham. He remarked, "the Universe is not the result of chance," yet he struggled to reconcile this conviction with his interpretation of blind, natural processes.[154] Questioning the trustworthiness of human cognition, he posed a contemplation: "Would anyone trust in the convictions of a monkey's mind, if there are any convictions in such a mind?"[155]

He also wondered whether life, existing as unconscious organisms on the moon, could possess any inherent purpose. He acknowledged a sense of purpose in the universe, but he remained skeptical about the extent to which human cognition, shaped by his evolutionary processes, could reliably discern such truths. These reflections reveal this philosophical dilemma: can life, emerging from purposeless origins, coherently claim value and purpose without contradicting its own foundations?

To critique the Biblical God for allowing suffering—on the basis that a benevolent deity would inherently value life and seek to protect it—implicitly argues that life has intrinsic value. Yet, paradoxically, these interrogators accept a worldview in which life itself has no meaning, purpose, or inherent worth, leaving no basis for their moral outrage.

For clarification, the value of life must first be established: Is life without inherent value because there is no benevolent creator, or is life devoid of objective value because it is the product of random, indifferent causes? This contradiction reveals the *value paradox*: the implicit reliance on the very value system they reject. Even if one claims that value is emergent, this invites another dilemma: emergent from what, and how can it be objective if it arises purely from subjective or material processes? In any case, the argument appears to hit a philosophical dead end. It becomes this: "If I, who sees no intrinsic value in life, were God, I would see intrinsic value and treat life differently."

If that makes any sense, this substitute god would essentially be an entirely different god, one whose role does not begin and end with resolving issues of suffering. This role would, however, require wearing infinite hats. One would hope this more reasonable god would have the wisdom to tackle other profound questions, such as the formation of the sun, the eye, the sky, the brain, and the fine-tuning of the universe. After all, suffering is just one of thousands of so-called hard problems that modern materialists themselves concede have left them perplexed.

The notion of knowing what is best for creating a universe assumes a perspective that imposes human limitations and perspectives onto the Being believed to transcend such constraints. But really, how can someone who denies intrinsic value in life assume a divine perspective to judge God? Instead of questioning why, or if, God should allow suffering, a better alternative is to ask, "If God exists, who am I to question the Supreme authority that designed all existence?"

Further, by shifting the explanation from divine intent to evolutionary processes, the moral question that troubled Darwin: why such suffering exists, remains unresolved. Again, the cruelty of parasitism and predation does not disappear under evolution; it is simply reframed as natural.

Darwinism is Inherently Racist

A modern misrepresentation, which I may have been guilty of, is the notion that Darwin consciously formulated his theories to promote racial inferiorities, justify the mistreatment of people of color, or deny individual freedoms. His theory does lead to those conclusions, and he also made some egregious racist statements in his career, particularly, later in *The Descent of Man*. However, these views appear to be consequences of his expanding theory rather than its foundation. In reality, it does not seem that he initially fully thought through many of his theory's implications. It's important to note that though his theory inherently carries racist implications, his original theory was based on observations of variations and similarities among species, not on establishing hierarchies. Though he did characterize certain races as more "civilized" or "advanced" than others, it seems that his sentiments are, again, a direct reflection of the ignorance that arose from the implications of his theory, not hatred.

Notably, ten years before the radical views in *The Descent of Man*, Darwin strongly opposed slavery, even rebuking Lyell, one of the most significant figures in his life, over this issue. This part of the narrative, where Darwin condemned slavery and advocated for human dignity, is often overlooked when discussing his legacy. Yet, this also reveals a value paradox inherent to his theory: Darwin's personal convictions, at times, affirmed human equality and moral worth, while his evolutionary framework emphasized competition and fitness, concepts that inherently support hierarchical interpretations. In 1861, in a personal letter to Lyell, Darwin expressed the following concerning slavery:

> I was delighted with your letter, in which you touch on slavery; I wish the same feelings had been apparent in your published discussion... How could you relate so placidly that atrocious sentiment about separating children from their parents, and in the

next page, speak of being distressed at the Whites not having prospered? I assure you the contrast made me exclaim out.[156]

This private letter reveals how Darwin condemned slavery, while expressing disappointment at Lyell's placid tone and concern for Whites' prosperity, further revealing the gap between Lyell's private views and his published discussions. Darwin's emotional reaction to Lyell's tone on slavery reveals the depth of his moral convictions. Far from explicitly promoting a theory that justified inhumanity or the denial of fundamental human rights: Darwin's response reflects a belief in human dignity and equality. Darwin's concept of gradual evolution from a microbe to man, however, appears to have been the most insidious influence on his life.

Chapter 5

Behind the Throne

A carefully scripted, elaborate plan... crafted by a relatively small group of people associated with Berkeley lawyer Phillip Johnson and the Discovery Institute... to dismantle the evolution edifice brick by brick. The Wedge Strategy outlines their tactics, from placing supporters in key leadership positions and manipulating public opinion to changing school science standards and achieving their goals through politics, legislation, and legal decisions. Their movement seeks 'nothing less than to overthrow the system of rules and procedures of modern science and those intellectual footings of our culture laid down in the Enlightenment and over some 300 years.' At its core, the strategy is about replacing materialistic science with a theistic framework under the guise of academic fairness and scientific inquiry. [838] —Barbara Forrest and Paul R. Gross

Darwin's doubts about aspects of his theory, particularly natural selection as the mechanism of evolution, persisted throughout his life. Though he remained committed to establishing the overarching principles of evolution, his personal correspondence and writings reveal several moments of uncertainty and reflection on the limitations of his theory. In a letter from October of 1859, just weeks before the publication of *On The Origin of Species*, he revealed his fear that he might have devoted his life to a "phantasy."[157] This candid admission was a window into the genuine anxiety that often consumed him.

In fact, there is considerable ground for speculation that Darwin's chronic illnesses may have been exacerbated by mental strain, particularly stress related to his work, the reception of his theories, and personal losses. His private doubts reveal the visceral emotional and intellectual turmoil he endured. Some researchers suggest Darwin's physical symptoms were manifestations of extreme anxiety or psychosomatic responses to stress. As history Keith Thomson notes:

> Overall, the correlation between the most stressful events in Darwin's life and his episodes of intestinal and dermatological ill health is too complete to ignore. Chronic anxiety would surely account for many of Darwin's symptoms, starting with the facial eczema, palpitations and gastric distress. An argument could then be made that Darwin suffered first from a chronic anxiety syndrome compounded by poor diet and genuine alimentary malfunction, and then exacerbated over the years by hypochondria in a destructive feedback loop.[158]

While many modern materialists describe him as resolute, numerous researchers retrospectively diagnose Darwin with panic disorder, noting that his documented symptoms became more pronounced after his Beagle voyage and worsened over time.[159] [160]

Yet, Darwin found solace in the varying support of esteemed scientists such as Lyell, Joseph Hooker and Huxley, whose comforting provided Darwin with the confidence to continue advocating for his ideas despite lingering doubts. As noted, in a letter to Lyell in 1859, written *one day before* the publication of *On the Origin of Species*, Darwin stated:

> For myself, also, I rejoice profoundly; for thinking of the many cases of men pursuing an illusion for years, often & often a cold shudder has run through me & I have asked myself whether I may not have devoted my life to a phantasy. Now I look at it as morally impossible that investigators of truth like you & Hooker can be wholly wrong; & therefore I feel that I may rest in peace.[161]

Here, Darwin expresses both relief and validation from his peers' recognition of his work, despite Lyell stopping short of fully agreeing with natural selection. Darwin acknowledges the significant impact their varying backing had on him.

His repetition of the phrase "often & often" amplifies the intensity of his concerns, demonstrating the frequency and emotional weight of his self-doubt. This literary device, known as epizeuxis, he uses to emphasize his inner turmoil, similar to the Biblical style of repetition to emphasize meaning.[162] [163] From a historical and scientific standpoint, Darwin's private admission of doubt offers a behind-the-scenes look into the sincerity of his emotions as he wrestled with the broader implications of his theories.

It's crucial to note that Darwin's reassurance in his ideas wasn't particularly grounded in scientific support but in the collegial verification from his close circle of like-minded peers. Like Lyell, even the one nicknamed Darwin's bulldog supported Darwin more for ideological and power ambitions rather than for the explanations of Darwin's theory. In fact, it wasn't just Lyell, his intellectual hero, but also his bulldog, Huxley, who doubted Darwin's mechanism.[164] Ruth Barton, author of The X Club: Power and Authority in Victorian Science, notes:

> Darwin was sometimes disappointed with his defender: 'He gave no just idea of natural selection,' Darwin protested to Hooker after Huxley's Royal Institution lecture. Darwin regarded natural selection as the centerpiece of his theory but, in the style of Darwin's inductivist critics, Huxley argued that Darwin *had failed to show that natural selection had ever produced a new species.* There might be other, equally important processes of change (Huxley inclined to saltations or leaps); hence, natural selection was merely the best theory currently available.[165]

Huxley described the contradictions he saw, but Michael Behe also notes that modern molecular biology shows that jumps and leaps contradict Darwinism rather than support it.[166] Barton explains that the nickname "Darwin's bulldog" exaggerates Huxley's identification with Darwin.[167] Thus, though he was backed as a philosophical colleague, Darwin's fears of pursuing a "phantasy" were never truly resolved by evidence. To this day, his mechanism has only explained sorting or refining, not creating.

Figure 5.1 Image of Thomas Henry Huxley. Known as "Darwin's Bulldog." **Image source:** Fæ, Wikimedia Commons.

Huxley acknowledged the lack of sufficient transitional forms in the fossil record. He explicitly acknowledged that Darwin's theory was provisional, stating:

> Our acceptance of the Darwinian hypothesis must be provisional so long as one link in the chain of evidence is wanting.[168]

While defending Darwin's ideas, Huxley argued that Darwin's version of evolution was feeble because the evidence does not proceed gradually, stating:

> Mr. Darwin's position might, we think, have been even stronger than it is if he had not embarrassed [hampered] himself with the aphorism, 'Natura non facit saltum,' which turns up so often in his pages. We believe, as we have said above, that Nature does make jumps now and then, and a recognition of the fact is of no small importance in disposing of many minor objections to the doctrine of transmutation.[169]

Huxley's critique reveals just how void of evidence Darwin's gradualism is, even to its most ardent defender. Huxley's proposal of saltations, however, born out of necessity to explain the fossil gaps, now stands as a genetically implausible solution that underscores the inadequacy of the theory at its foundation. For Huxley, Darwin's theory was "good enough" to advance the cause of naturalism. Or as Barton noted: "merely the best theory currently available"

Revisiting Darwin's doubts: an additional moment of clarity in his thinking comes from *Origin of Species*, where he candidly admits:

> To suppose that the eye, with all its inimitable contrivances... could have been formed by natural selection, seems, I freely confess, absurd in the highest possible degree.[170]

Darwin's recognition of the complexity of the eye illustrates his awareness of the monumental challenge natural selection faced in explaining such intricate biological systems. He continues:

> Yet reason tells me, that if numerous gradations from a perfect and complex eye to one very imperfect and simple, each grade being useful to its possessor, can be shown to exist; if further, the eye does vary ever so slightly, and the variations be inherited, which is certainly the case; and if any variation or modification in the organ be ever useful to an animal under changing conditions of life, then the difficulty of believing that a perfect and complex eye could be formed by natural selection, though insuperable by our imagination, can hardly be considered real.[171]

Darwin's follow-up to his statement about the eye being "absurd in the highest degree" to have evolved underscores the speculative nature of his reasoning. For instance, he essentially argues, 'I know it sounds improbable, but if small, gradual steps occurred and each step was useful, then it could be true.'

This is not scientific reasoning; it is a predetermined conclusion retrofitted with speculative justifications. Rather than conceding the empirical challenges, it amounts to saying, 'I know it sounds very speculative, but it could be true if we assume enough unknowns to fill the gaps.'

Though Darwin speculated that the eye could have evolved through a series of gradual, beneficial modifications, simply invoking "beneficiality" does not explain the biological mechanisms required for such changes. Beneficiality is an outcome, not an account of the structural steps necessary to achieve it. Similarly, explaining how 1% of a population comes to own 50% of a nation's wealth requires more than noting that wealth is advantageous; it demands a detailed explanation of the systems, events, and pathways that led to that concentration.

Darwin's lingering fear of chasing an illusion, even as late as 1859, suggests he was never fully certain that his theories were as empirically sound as he had hoped. This glimpse into his personal doubts reveals how confirmation bias can influence scientific thinking.[172] As any scientist, Darwin was vulnerable to favoring information that supported his existing belief system. Acknowledging these complexities in Darwin's character adds depth to our understanding of his contributions to science.

Yet, modern commentary often downplays Darwin's admissions of doubt, because uncertainty about evolution is blasphemous within the materialist framework. These reinterpretations of his words overlook the depth of his personal reflections, leading to a sanitized version of Darwin that ignores his struggles. Materialists present these admissions as if Darwin never really questioned his own ideas, despite numerous candid confessions to the contrary.[173] If someone simply suggests, it's one thing; someone stating a 'confession' goes further. But when Darwin says, "I freely confess, [this idea seems] absurd in the highest possible degree," it leaves no doubt about the weight of his words.

In correspondence with Asa Gray, Darwin once stated, "I am quite conscious that my speculations run quite beyond the bounds of true science."[174] This extraordinary acknowledgment defies any denying of Darwin's awareness about the speculative nature of his theories.[175] Consider again: Darwin's most revered mentor, Charles Lyell, would not fully endorse his ideas, nor his proverbial bodyguard and spokesman, Thomas Huxley. Huxley openly criticized Darwin for proposing gradualism when the evidence suggested otherwise—arguing instead for evolutionary jumps. Given this, how could anyone argue that Darwin himself was not doubtful of his own theory? Acknowledging Darwin's doubts doesn't diminish his legacy but instead reveals the dynamic nature of science: a process of discovery, revision, and, when necessary, the overhaul of theories as new evidence comes to light.

The X Club

The role of Darwin's circle of highly influential figures is further illustrated in Bruce Thyer's 1995 article on the X Club, which sheds light on a significant yet lesser-known aspect of scientific history.[176] In his piece, titled "The X Club and the Secret Ring: Lessons on How Behavior Analysis Can Take Over Psychology," Thyer, a Professor of Social Work at Florida State University with expertise in behavior analysis and research methods, examines the role of the X Club in the dissemination and support of Darwinian theory.[177]

According to Thyer, the X Club, led by biologist Thomas Huxley, played a tremendous role in championing Darwinian theory within scientific circles, particularly in institutions like the Royal Society. As Thyer notes, "On November 3, 1864, the British scientist Thomas Huxley gathered a group of nine friends and scientific colleagues into a semisecretive organization they labeled the X Club (X standing for nothing)."[178] Remarkably, eight of these nine members were Fellows of the Royal Society of London, a distinguished and historically significant scientific organization.[179]

Reflected in their chosen name, their strategy went beyond open advocacy to include a more covert and calculating approach.[180] From the outset—just as Lyell had done throughout his career—this clandestine group employed a wedge strategy to systematically erode the influence of religious thinkers and metaphysical considerations within the scientific community.[181] Thyer notes:

> X Club members had an ambitious plan to secretly govern the Royal Society and other scientific organizations. Typically, the X Club met for dinner at a London club shortly before the monthly meetings of the Society to discuss current developments in the body scientific.[182]

This arrangement facilitated the coordination of their efforts and reinforced their influence over significant scientific discourse and governance. Thyer notes that purposes of the X Club were diverse but related, and included the following:

- The promotion of serious empirical research.

- The promotion of a purely naturalistic worldview, with a corresponding diminution of the influence of religion in guiding science.
- The reduction of the role of aristocratic patronage and administration.
- The promotion of pure science, rather than applied research guided by commercial or utilitarian purposes.
- The promotion of the infrastructure of science within education and government.[183]

Several significant issues become apparent in evaluating the X Club's objectives, particularly their promotion of a purely "naturalistic" worldview and the prioritization of "pure" science. The divide the X Club established between "pure" science and applied research, demoting commercial or practical purposes, presented a false dichotomy fallacy.[184] This distinction implied that pure science, presumably conducted without immediate practical applications, was somehow nobler or more unbiased than applied science, which often targeted practical and commercially viable outcomes. This division was misleading because it overlooked the reality that all forms of scientific inquiry, whether pure or applied, could contribute valuable knowledge and advancements.

Applied science did not inherently compromise scientific integrity or quality but focused on different, often practical objectives. This division suggested that only "pure" science could be driven by genuine curiosity or lead to "true" scientific progress. Such biases, embedded in the Club's principles, reflected a restrictive view of what constitutes legitimate scientific inquiry and led to the stifling of broader intellectual pursuits and innovation within the scientific community.

"Pure science" is defined as "science that seeks to expand knowledge regardless of the short-term application of that knowledge."[185] Nevertheless, the naturalist principles once championed by the X Club, which dismissed applied science in favor of pure science, are now purported to be the hallmark of neo-naturalism. Yet this is a departure from the original stance of the X Club, which promoted pure science as a more noble pursuit, free from commercial or practical concerns. The X Club's disdain for applied research as somehow inferior now stands in contrast to the modern narrative, which credits naturalism with driving technological and practical advancements. Materialists now claim that opposition to their worldview equates to opposition to foundational science, which they present as indistinguishable from applied research and technological progress itself.

This becomes a pathetic irony when considering how today's neo-naturalists, even as they promote the legacy of naturalism as a force for innovation, often oppose concepts like Behe's irreducible complexity.[186] Behe's concept of the flagellum motor exemplifies science in its pursuit of fundamental truths about the natural world—exemplifying the definition of pure science. Investigating irreducible complexity means examining life's foundational structures to assess whether existing naturalistic theories can account for them. Yet, rather than engaging with this line of inquiry, neo-naturalists dismiss it outright, not based on scientific merit, but because it challenges their philosophical commitments.

As X Club's influence grew, they began to exert a significant impact on the direction of Victorian scientific discourse and institutions.[187] The members of this group worked systematically, placing supporters of Darwin in key leadership positions within these institutions. Thyer points out that in 1864, "as one of their first acts, X Club members used their influence to arrange for Darwin to be awarded the Royal Society's Copley Medal, 'the ancient olive crown' of the Royal Society."[188] This method of operation, Thyer likens to an "invisible hand," was essential in nudging Darwinian theory from the fringes to solidifying it as the standard scientific thought.[189]

Moreover, Thyer points out that the influence of the X Club extended over several decades, making them a formidable force behind the scenes in the governance of not only the Royal Society but also other prominent British scientific groups.[190] As the "power behind the throne," their dedication to promoting Darwinian theory and a purely naturalistic viewpoint in science was unwavering, and their efforts significantly shaped the trajectory of scientific inquiry and discourse.[191] This long-term, strategic positioning and influence have guided science towards a path that continues to dominate scientific thought today.[192]

In Ruth Barton's examination of the X Club's influence and actions in British scientific circles, we see a more intimate narrative of their behavior. Barton suggests that X Club members "manipulated elections" to place themselves in positions of power within institutions like the Royal Society, securing roles such as treasurer, biological secretary, and president.[193] Her term "manipulated elections" suggests unethical methods.

The coordinated effort began with William Spottiswoode becoming treasurer in 1870, a role that gave him control over the Society's finances and influence over which research received support.[194] Then, in 1872, Thomas Huxley was elected biological secretary, putting him in charge of publications and giving him a platform to promote the X Club's naturalistic and secular views in scientific discourse.[195] This was followed by Joseph Dalton Hooker ascending to the presidency in 1873, which placed him as the Society's leading voice and allowed him to steer its overall vision toward the X Club's ideals.[196] Finally, in 1878, Spottiswoode himself became president, extending the X Club's influence over the Society's leadership.[197]

Additionally, the X Club played a principal role in establishing Nature as a major scientific journal dedicated to promoting naturalistic science and Darwinian theory. Huxley, Joseph Hooker, and John Tyndall used their influence to shape the journal's editorial standards and direction, establishing a litmus test for science which obligated a science free from religious influence. Today, Nature is one of the world's most prestigious scientific journals, widely regarded as a leading publication in the scientific community. However, its foundational philosophy, established by the X Club, continues to influence its editorial stance, often filtering out research that challenges the philosophical framework of Materialism.

Thyer points out that by shaping Nature as a "permanent press outlet," the X Club used it to "favorably review each other's books and other works consistent with their goals"—a practice that set a lasting precedent.[198] This promoted groupthink, creating a self-sustaining intellectual bubble that ingrained Darwinian and materialistic assumptions within scientific discourse, which is why ideas invoking intelligence are often excluded from mainstream journals today.

The X Club's influence extended across several journals they founded or helped launch, which "served as additional outlets to promote the views of X Club members." For instance, Huxley "responded to a papal encyclical critical of Darwin with a slashing rejoinder published in The Reader." The X Club's control over key journals exemplifies *institutional capture*, as they dictated which perspectives were promoted while ensuring that any challenges to their ideological framework were swiftly countered within the same publications they controlled, reinforcing their dominance.[199]

Barton describes the X Club as a "party" in the sense that its members were united by a shared cause.[200] By supporting each other's nominations and filling these top positions, the X Club transformed the Royal Society into a stronghold of scientific naturalism and secularism, ensuring that science, as they defined it—empirical, objective, and free from religious influence—was firmly established as the guiding framework for British science.

The X Club's commitment to naturalistic science also influenced education, where they played a significant role in shaping science pedagogy. In Barton's examination of Huxley's curriculum for the Department of Science and Art (DSA), she references James Elwick, who points out that some topics may have included implicit "naturalistic or even materialistic 'metaphysical' assumptions," such as "the living body considered as a machine."[201] Barton, however, raises an open question regarding whether these assumptions were deliberately embedded or whether they naturally reflected the scientific perspectives of the time. She notes that the exact ways in which such ideas were incorporated into exams, textbooks, or labs are still "awaiting investigation."[202]

In modern interpretations, describing the body as a "machine" can carry metaphysical implications by suggesting purpose or design, which, in turn, imply the existence of a designer. Calling an organism a machine increasingly implies intentionality, leading to a teleological interpretation; life has inherent purpose.

Though arguments like Paley's watchmaker analogy had been made, they likely did not have a significant impact on Victorian scientific thinking at large, particularly among figures like Huxley and the X Club, who sought to remove theological implications from science. At the time, describing the body as a "machine" was likely seen as a neutral, reductionist description of unknown natural processes, rather than an argument for design. However, in light of modern technological advancements—especially in bioengineering and information theory—the analogy of living systems as machines now carries far stronger teleological implications than it might have in their time. However, the language they employed unwittingly carried the connotations of intentionality and design they sought to reject, showing the inherent contradiction in attempting to describe complex biological systems without teleological terms.

Still, during that era, the inclusion of "creation" in educational text was likely unavoidable, while serving as a strategic concession to placate the broader audience—particularly those still holding firm to religious perspectives. Barton describes how Hooker's botany text introduced students to both evolutionary ideas and "independent creation," labeling the latter as "purely speculative," which subtly encouraged students toward a naturalistic interpretation.[203] This tactic was a form of 'poisoning the well,' where religious explanations were included only to be cast in a less credible light compared to naturalist explanations. Presenting these ideas as speculative or outdated implicitly nudged students toward adopting a secular, materialistic worldview.

Barton's analysis does not label this approach as overt indoctrination, but she shows that Huxley, Hooker, and other X Club members used education to cultivate certain scientific "attitudes" in students.[204] They influenced students' perspectives on what constituted valid scientific explanations. This subtle shaping of attitudes and assumptions positioned naturalistic science as the primary path to truth.

Interestingly, Thomas Huxley described science as a new "true faith" and called science educators "scientific missionaries" tasked with "converting the Christian Heathen."[205] [206] This mode sarcasm is strikingly similar to Lyells. Huxley saw education as a means to reshape society's beliefs, moving away from supernatural explanations toward secular, empirical reasoning. To Huxley, science was a means of cultural reprogramming, one that could lead to a kind of religious conversion, where traditional beliefs were naturally displaced by the authority of *rational*, secular thought.

Barton clarifies that the X Club's militancy was targeted not at religion in general, but specifically at theology and religious doctrines that, in their view, hindered intellectual progress. She notes that Beatrice Webb (a British sociologist, economist, and social reformer) described them as "self-confident militants," and Barton highlights their confrontational approach: "figures like Huxley and John Tyndall used debates and public challenges to weaken religious authority over education and moral issues, seeing organized religion as an obstacle to scientific and social progress."[207] Barton notes that for the X Club, "naturalism was at war against supernaturalism," highlighting their commitment to exclude religious explanations from science.[208]

The Wedge Strategy

Modern Darwinians often reference the Wedge Strategy as 'gotcha' evidence to refute the arguments of intelligent design (ID) proponents. The Wedge Strategy, drafted by the Discovery Institute in 1998, outlined a five and twenty-year plan to influence scientific discourse, particularly in education. Yet, there is irony when contrasted with the strategic planning and bold maneuvers of figures like Charles Lyell, Ernst Haeckel, and members of the X Club. These 19th-century figures consistently, and sometimes, independently employed their own wedge strategies, wielding ambitions of incomparable magnitude, with a level of cunning that makes the Discovery Institute's efforts seem trivial.

The X Club's Machiavellian tactics far surpassed anything modern ID proponents have attempted, crafting a legacy so deeply ingrained that, despite its irreparable weaknesses, Darwinism is still perceived as the inevitable triumph of 'the fittest' ideas. By the protection rackets the X Club ran, coupled with the scale and zeal with which they promoted their agenda, they appear as extremists in comparison to the modest efforts of ID proponents. Today, this disparity is evident in the disproportionate influence wielded by the X Club's naturalist torchbearers.[209] Firmly embedded in academia, these torchbearers continue to wield the authority to define what counts as scientifically valid, ensuring that the original framework remains largely unchallenged.[210]

As a part of their wedge strategy, the X Club crafted and fueled a false narrative of conflict between theology and science.[211] This portrayal of a science-religion conflict served a socio-political agenda aimed at elevating the societal stature of 'science'—now redefined through a naturalistic worldview—to seize control while 'converting' the so-called Christian heathen.[212] Thus, by design, their worldview was elevated to the status of pure science itself. The narrative of a science-religion conflict was further perpetuated by historians whose accounts have since been recognized as part of the myth of a pseudo-conflict between science and religion.[213]

Upon this framework, we should scrutinize how individuals within the X Club, specifically Thomas Huxley and his allies, orchestrated a calculated campaign to redefine the relationship between science and religion, shaping public perception and scientific discourse for generations to come.[214] Huxley was particularly instrumental in crafting and disseminating the narrative that sharply divided science and religion.[215]

John William Draper further amplified this narrative through his works, most notably in his 1875 book *History of the Conflict between Religion and Science*.[216] Draper's widely read and cited account portrayed the relationship between science and religion as a long-standing historical battle, with science cast as a damsel in distress, struggling to free herself from the grip of religious constraints. This portrayal resonated with the societal shifts towards secularism and was pivotal in shaping public and academic perceptions.

These efforts by Huxley and his colleagues within the X Club effectively set the stage for the exclusion of spiritual perspectives from scientific discourse, championing a materialistic worldview as the only legitimate lens to investigate nature.[217] This is why, today, from the general public to the most esteemed scientists, it is fallaciously assumed that debating Materialism is equivalent to debating science itself.

Notably, even the conflict between the Church and Galileo, often cited as a classic example of the clash between religion and science, was not a direct result of Biblical doctrine itself, but rather of the specific historical, political, and institutional context in which these events took place. Over the centuries, various groups and institutions have interpreted and applied Biblical teachings in ways that served their own interests, sometimes leading to actions that are not aligned with the core principles of the Bible. As far as I'm aware, Jesus, the foundation of Christianity, did not prescribe or justify the punishment of individuals for scientific discoveries. Galileo's conflict was rooted in the conflict between new scientific ideas and the existing authority structure, which felt threatened by these ideas. Similarly, there is a conflict between Behe's ideas and the existing authority structure of today.

Moreover, Nazi Germany employed Darwinism as a scientific framework to justify Aktion T4 (involuntary euthanasia) and genocide.[218] One might argue that this represents a misuse of Darwinian principles: I would agree in terms of Darwin's personal convictions. However, when evaluating the principles of his theory itself, it is prudent to conduct comparative investigations. This includes examining whether there is an inherent conflict between the actions of the Catholic Church's authorities and the teachings of Paul or Jesus, as well as assessing whether the principles in Darwin's theory align with or contradict the actions of Hitler. A curious question arises: How do, or don't, these doctrines inherently conflict with or undermine the integrity of science, human rights, and human dignity? Exploring their foundational precepts and implications, as outlined by their founders, could yield valuable insights.

Kirsten Birkett, a scholar from the University of New South Wales, offers a poignant critique of the legacy left by the ringleader of the X Club. She states,

> Huxley's aim to see science and Christianity established as enemies has largely succeeded. It is by far the most common metaphor for discussion of science and Christianity. It is a powerful metaphor, but a ridiculously improper one for anyone interested in understanding our world. Let us hope that in a new century we can do better.[219]

This historical backdrop sets the stage for understanding the current state of origins research, progress in interpreting biological realities, and the challenges faced by proponents of intelligent design.

CHAPTER 6

Accuracy, Honest, and Confidence

No one is dumb who is curious. The people who don't ask questions remain clueless throughout their lives.[220] —Neil deGrasse Tyson

The National Center for Science Education (NCSE) was founded in 1981 by Stanley L. Weinberg, with Eugenie C. Scott joining shortly thereafter as its first executive director.[221] The organization was established to combat efforts to introduce Creationism and other religiously motivated ideas into public school science curricula.[222] Over time, the NCSE has evolved into a powerful lobbying group, striving to establish the teaching of evolution as an unquestionable truth, comparable to the certainty with which mathematics is taught in schools.

The NCSE expanded its mission to include climate change education in 2012. Its website describes its mission as ensuring that "evolution and climate change" are taught "accurately, honestly, and confidently."[223] On the surface, the NCSE's title as the National Center for Science Education makes its cause sound like a noble endeavor. However, its mission statement calls into question how terms like 'accuracy,' 'honesty,' and 'confidence' are applied in practice—especially given that the organization's foundational stance, upheld for over 40 years, depends on the unquestioned acceptance of natural selection and mutations as the explanation for the diversity of life in public schools and colleges. It is itself questionable whether that stance can be considered accurate and honest.

The 2012 addition of climate change to the NCSE's focus further lent legitimacy to the organization, as climate change aligned with the widely accepted scientific consensus. During that time, the NCSE published an article titled "Why is NCSE Now Concerned with Climate Change?"[224] explaining that while "evolution and climate change are accepted by the scientific community," they "remain controversial" among the broader public.[225]

Notably, the NCSE has distinguished teachers from their communities, emphasizing that "teachers trying to teach evolution and/or climate change too often face opposition in their communities." According to the NCSE, this opposition stems from "religious ideologies in the case of evolution [and] economic and political ideologies in the case of climate change."[226] This generalizes real teachers as those who agree, while framing disagreement as ignorance or interference.

The article frames the controversy as a conflict between scientific consensus and public skepticism, with consensus equated to truth. It states that "*teachers* are pressured to downplay these topics, misrepresent them as scientifically controversial, and air supposedly scientifically credible alternatives to them."[227] Due to the persistence of a "substantial portion of the public" rejecting what the NCSE characterizes as "good science," the organization expanded its mission to include climate change education.[228] Their stated aim is to "help the public to understand the consensus view of scientists that evolution has occurred and is occurring."[229]

Again, the NCSE's framing creates an artificial division between teachers and the public, portraying the latter as ignorantly opposing truth while casting itself as the savior tasked with enlightening them. This positions the NCSE as both the arbiter of truth in opposition to an uninformed public and the protector of that same public's understanding. This is a paradoxical role reminiscent of Orwellian manipulation. By design, this narrative discredits dissent while consolidating control over what constitutes "good science," effectively constructing an echo chamber.

Though polarizing, combatting climate change benefits from a more concise and digestible body of evidence, such as rising global temperatures, ice sheet loss, and increased CO_2 levels.[230] This makes it less susceptible to criticism compared to evolution, where speciation mechanisms like natural selection and mutation have faced increasing scientific discrepancies.[231] By broadening its scope to include climate change, the NCSE aims to position itself as a defender of science education as a whole, potentially deflecting attention from the reality that its efforts are ideologically rooted in defending Darwinian mechanisms of evolution.

As for climate change, however, the NCSE generally does not emphasize the distinction between the broader scientific definition of climate change—any change in climate over time—and the narrower definition found in the Framework Convention on Climate Change, which attributes changes specifically to human activity.[232] Instead, its educational materials and public messaging predominantly attribute recent climate change to human-induced factors, such as increased greenhouse gas emissions, while overlooking the broader definition that includes natural causes.

This lack of distinction allows the NCSE to present climate data in a way that supports its mission of refuting skepticism, but it does not reflect the full scope of scientific understanding. It blurs the line between what humanity may influence and what lies beyond our control. Moreover, by framing human-caused climate change as settled science, the NCSE simplifies a complex issue. Their expansion into climate change further entrenches an 'us versus them' narrative, casting dissenters as opponents of science itself.

Science education, however, spans numerous disciplines—physics, chemistry, biology, computer science, and engineering, to name a few. Each plays a vital role in fostering critical thinking and problem-solving skills. Yet, the NCSE's mission is really fixated on a singular topic—evolution—which, if it were a course, would have to be classified as an elective. Evolution is a subject that cannot stand on its own, but the NCSE somehow equates it with teaching science itself.

Teaching "honestly" implies presenting topics in an evidence-based manner, but does this unwavering truth allow room for critical thinking? Is teaching evolution "confidently" a call to constrain critical thinking rather than encouraging a student-centered approach where they evaluate evidence and draw their own conclusions? Imagine asking educators to teach chemistry or computer science "honestly and confidently"—would such terms even make sense in those fields? The necessary demand by a special interest group to teach evolution "honestly" and "confidently" reveals that unanswered questions regarding the adequacy of Darwinian explanations for the diversity in nature are legitimate.

Rational Skeptics

In 2001, the Discovery Institute (DI), the principal advocate of intelligent design theory, created a declaration called "A Scientific Dissent from Darwinism" to provide scientists and academics a platform to voice their skepticism about Darwinian evolution.[233]

Signatories affirm:
> We are skeptical of claims for the ability of random mutation and natural selection to account for the complexity of life. Careful examination of the evidence for Darwinian theory should be encouraged.[234]

Thus, the declaration does not dismiss or handwave the concept of evolution but instead calls into question specific mechanisms, such as random mutation and natural selection—an area where skepticism has always been legitimate.

As noted, these are not new doubts: Lyell, despite being a champion of gradualism, never fully accepted natural selection as sufficient to explain the diversity of life.[235] Likewise, Huxley, Darwin's ideological bulwark, expressed rational skepticism about Darwin's narrative of gradualism. Huxley viewed Darwin's mechanism of natural selection as tentative and incomplete.[236]

Huxley and Lyell prioritized the advancement of their shared goals, often placating Darwin's frustrations in the process. Though Huxley and Lyell consistently promoted naturalism and evolution in public, they often neglected Darwin's specific arguments. On multiple occasions, much to Darwin's frustration and possibly, shame, Huxley publicly emphasized that he was not fully convinced by Darwin's central claims.[237] This is evident in Huxley's private correspondence with Darwin, where he wrote:

> My dear Darwin.
>
> You are the cheeriest letter-writer I know, and always help a man to think the best of his doings. I hope you do not imagine because I had nothing to say about 'Natural Selection,' that I am at all weak

of faith on that article. On the contrary, *I live in hope* that as paleontologists work more and more in the manner of that 'second Daniel come to judgment,' that wise young man M. Filhal, we shall arrive at a crushing accumulation of evidence in that direction also. *But the first thing seems to me to be to drive the fact of evolution into people's heads; when that is once safe, the rest will come easy.*[238]

Huxley's private correspondence with Darwin reveals a strategic posture toward the promotion of evolution. While expressing support for Darwin, Huxley's position has often been misinterpreted. In reality, he notably avoids endorsing natural selection directly. Though he reassures Darwin that his silence should not be seen as a "weakness of faith," his phrasing—"I live in hope" and "we shall arrive at a crushing accumulation of evidence"—reveals that convincing empirical support for natural selection was still lacking at the time.

More revealing is his stated priority: "the first thing seems to me to be to drive the fact of evolution into people's heads; when that is once safe, the rest will come easy." This underscores a tactical approach: establish public acceptance of evolution itself, regardless of whether its proposed mechanisms are fully evidenced. Huxley did not see it as necessary to prove natural selection first. He believed that once people accepted the idea of evolution, they would be more easily persuaded to buy-in to natural selection as its explanation. Huxley's language frames belief in natural selection more as an article of conviction than scientific conclusion. This letter thus captures an early moment when rhetorical momentum took precedence over evidentiary sufficiency—a strategic move to secure evolution's place in public and scientific discourse, even while understanding that foundational mechanisms remained unproven.

Like Lyell, one thing Huxley was certain of, however, was that the Church was wrong. This was a pattern that further indicates their reluctance to advance Darwin's specific mechanism, even if it came at the expense of bringing Darwin's central focus into disrepute. This letter from Huxley to Darwin, dated May 10, 1880, was written approximately two years before Darwin's death on April 19, 1882. Hence, Huxley did not fully argue for natural selection as the sole or complete mechanism of evolution, as he placated Darwin before his death—or even afterward.

Huxley's lack of confidence in natural selection, combined with the absence of a coherent alternative theory, led him to rely on promissory naturalism, assuming that future discoveries would resolve the origin of species, potentially through alternative mechanisms. Huxley's hopeful messaging, both to the public and to Darwin, regarding natural selection as a likely candidate could be interpreted as a tactical stall—a strategic gamble to buy time while awaiting stronger evidence or alternative naturalist mechanisms to address the discrepancies he observed in the fossil record and patterns of variation.

Huxley noted:

> How far 'natural selection' suffices for the production of species remains to be seen. Few can doubt that, if not the whole cause, it is a very important factor in that operation; and that it must play a great part in the sorting out of varieties into those which are transitory and those which are permanent. But the causes and conditions of variation have yet to be thoroughly explored; and the importance of natural selection will not be impaired, even if further inquiries should prove that variability is definite, and is determined in certain directions rather than in others, by conditions inherent in that which varies.[239]

This passage suggests that Huxley's belief in the role of natural selection leaned more toward a micro-level understanding of evolutionary processes—where natural selection "sorts out" existing variations. This seems to be what Huxley is consistently comfortable with affirming concerning natural selection. Huxley's skepticism about macro-evolution is evident in his statement, "How far 'natural selection' suffices for the production of species remains to be seen," which reflects his doubt that natural selection alone can explain speciation. He emphasizes that "the causes and conditions of variation have yet to be thoroughly explored," leaving the mechanisms of broader evolutionary change unresolved.

Strikingly, this structural distinction between variation being sorted versus new forms being generated mirrors arguments still made by modern critics of macroevolution, including some creationists. While Huxley approached the issue from within a naturalistic framework, the nature of his reservations remains similar: natural selection may explain refinement, but not origination.

Another clear instance of Huxley invoking the future is evident in his remark:

> The combined investigations of another twenty years may, perhaps, enable naturalists to say whether the modifying causes and the selective power, which Mr. Darwin has satisfactorily shown to exist in Nature, are competent to produce all the effects he ascribes to them; *or whether, on the other hand, he has been led to over-estimate the value of the principle of natural selection,* as greatly as Lamarck overestimated his vera causa of modification by exercise.[240]

Again, Huxley acknowledges that natural selection had demonstrated the existence of some modifying power, however, he remains unconvinced that these forces are adequate to explain all diversity. He saw natural selection as a valid hypothesis rather than an established truth. By comparing Darwin's reliance on natural selection to Lamarck's overestimation of modification by exercise, Huxley signals that Darwin's mechanism is possibly overreaching.[241] This remark speaks directly to Huxley's reservations and his view of the evidence—a quiet admission that the gradualist model, central to Darwin's theory, does not align with what the evidence actually shows.

Huxley's commitment to evaluating Darwin's mechanisms "accurately and honestly," even publicly acknowledging their shortcomings while awaiting validation, provides a historical precedent for addressing unresolved issues in evolutionary theory today. As Huxley himself noted, "What if species should offer residual phenomena, here and there, not explicable by natural selection?"[242] Such questions remain relevant, especially given the inability of naturalistic mechanisms to account for phenomena like irreducible complexity or the origin of functional information. Michael Behe and Stephen Meyer, prominent proponents of ID, raise precisely the kinds of questions that Huxley deemed scientifically valid.[243]

Huxley explicitly acknowledges that Darwin's theory is not directly proven through observation but is instead logically necessary based on observable conditions. He states that Darwin did "not so much prove that natural selection does occur, as that it must occur," reasoning that natural selection is a deduction from principles like variation, competition, and survival, rather than something directly observable in action.[244] Huxley argued that such an approach was acceptable because long-term evolutionary processes cannot be directly witnessed, and scientists must rely on inference and deduction to address historical phenomena.

However, by Huxley's own standard, Behe and Meyer present a case that commands even greater scientific respect. Unlike Darwin, whose mechanism was inferred from limited observation and extended through speculative reasoning, Behe and Meyer confront specific, observable phenomena that resist explanation through Darwinian processes. Behe's concept of irreducible complexity identifies biological systems that cannot function unless all parts are present simultaneously, posing a formidable challenge to the stepwise evolutionary pathways required by natural selection. Similarly, Meyer's critique of the origin of functional information in DNA, questioning whether undirected processes like mutation and selection can generate the specific, highly complex arrangements needed for life.

These arguments do not dismiss inference; instead, they elevate Huxley's reasoning insisting that scientific explanations for such phenomena must align with observed evidence and causal adequacy. Where Darwin relied on deductive reasoning to propose natural selection, Behe and Meyer identify gaps in that framework that demand new explanations. They bring the conversation full circle—applying Huxley's own standard in addressing unresolved issues in evolutionary theory. If Darwin's theory deserved to be heard based on Huxley's standard of logical necessity—a standard Huxley himself set lower for Darwin despite not fully supporting it—then Behe's and Meyer's arguments merit greater consideration.

Consensus of The Science Union

The Union of Concerned Scientists, as part of the NCSE's *Voices for Evolution* project, characterizes ID as a threat to science education, asserting that natural selection is "one of the most studied and tested theories in science" and the "central organizing principle of biology."[245] They argue that failing to teach evolution is a "disservice to students," implying that only their framework represents legitimate science.[246] Yet, in the same breath, the NCSE concedes that "natural selection is not the only mechanism for evolution" and admits that "some phenomena that natural selection may not adequately explain could be explained by other evolutionary mechanisms."[247]

But if natural selection is not sufficient, how can simply asking questions about its adequacy be considered a "disservice"? This rhetorical framing holds competing views to a standard of completeness that their own framework cannot meet.

The NCSE's extensive appeal to consensus in the *Voices for Evolution* project underscores a broader issue. With 176 groups represented, the collection emphasizes widespread support for teaching evolution but offers no specific engagement with the scientific arguments raised by critics. Consensus does not resolve explanatory gaps, particularly when irreducible complexity or functional genetic information remain inadequately addressed.

Stasis of Explanations

With natural selection and "other mechanisms" described as "one of the most studied and tested theories" and "the central organizing principle of biology," one might ask where an inquisitive mind can learn more about this principle. Taking up this question, I turned to what the NCSE identifies as the premier educational resource: The *Understanding Evolution* website.[248] [249]

Published in 2004, its press release announced that, "the *Understanding Evolution* website is now live."[250] They framed it as "written for teachers but accessible to the general public — intended to provide "one-stop shopping" for evolution education."[251] It stated: "There is also an extensive section especially for teachers, giving advice on teaching evolution, ideas for lesson plans, ways to avoid confusing students, and answering common student questions." It exhorted readers to "Be sure to check it out!"[252]

I did just that, but it fell short of the expectations of being the 'one-stop shop,' failing to deliver the wealth of knowledge and evidence it had promised. The Understanding Evolution website is more of a covert propaganda machine than an educational resource. It takes basic, uncontested phenomena, repackaging them into confirmation bias with trademarked appeals to consensus, while its advice carries an almost cult-like quality. The material on "Macroevolution," "Speciation," and "The Big Issues" fail to substantiate the claim that evolution is the "central organizing principle of biology."

For example, the "Macroevolution" material discusses patterns such as *stasis*, *character change*, and *lineage splitting* but uses these patterns.[253] Particularly, the inclusion of stasis can be seen as a way to preserve the theory's credibility in light of fossil evidence that doesn't show gradual transformation. Stasis, derived from the Greek word meaning "to stand still, remain, or stay," refers to the observation that animals thought to have lived over many millions of years often exhibit no change in form.[254] While there may be variations in size, shape, or minor traits, the fundamental form of these organisms shows no meaningful evolutionary change. In some cases, evolution is acknowledged to have paused for tens or even hundreds of millions of years.

The example of coelacanths—a lineage thought extinct but rediscovered in 1938—illustrates morphological stasis over 80 million years, yet the page offers no detailed mechanistic explanation for how such prolonged stability aligns with mechanisms like mutation and natural selection, which are supposed to drive change.[255] The article does not suggest that stasis presents a conflict or problem for evolutionary theory. Instead, it treats stasis as a standard, expected pattern in macroevolution, on equal footing with character change and lineage splitting. Specifically, the article states:

> Some lineages remain relatively unchanged for millions of years. This pattern is called stasis.[256]

It describes this as an empirical observation, and does not raise any concern or an interpretive discrepancy between stasis and gradual evolution.

This inconsistency in the explanatory power of Darwin's gradualism is one of the reasons Huxley found it "wanting." Darwin's steady, incremental model failed to explain both the abrupt appearances of new forms in the fossil record and the long stretches of morphological stasis observed in species such as coelacanths. In *Geological Contemporaneity and Persistent Types of Life,* Huxley noted that certain groups of organisms exhibit remarkable stability in form over vast periods.

Huxley writes:

> Again, what can be more remarkable than the singular constancy of structure preserved throughout a vast period of time by the family of the Pycnodonts and by that of the true Coelacanths; the former persisting, with but insignificant modifications, from the Carboniferous to the Tertiary rocks, inclusive; the latter existing, with still less change, from the Carboniferous rocks to the Chalk, inclusive?[257]

Huxley further stated:

> *The only circumstance to be wondered at is*, not that the changes of life, as exhibited by positive evidence, have been so great, but *that they have been so small.*[258]

For Huxley, these observations suggest that evolutionary changes may occur in bursts rather than through slow, steady progression, consistent with his openness to saltations as a more plausible explanation for patterns in the fossil record.

Similarly, the website's *Speciation* material employs geographic isolation models, such as fruit flies separated by hurricanes, to illustrate lineage divergence.[259] Divergent evolution is said to occur when two or more species that share a common ancestor become increasingly dissimilar due to different environmental pressures and adaptations, often leading to the creation of new species from a common ancestor; essentially, it's when a single species branches off into multiple distinct species with unique characteristics based on their different environments.[260] However, by emphasizing vague processes like isolation leading to divergence, while avoiding the mechanistic details of how random mutations and natural selection could produce irreducibly complex systems, the *Speciation* material retrofits this phenomenon into evolutionary theory.[261] This creates a circular logic: it assumes that isolation and divergence inevitably result in new functionality without providing the detailed pathways by which this occurs, beyond the blanket assertion that evolution is responsible.

Today, we have the tools to genetically map evolutionary changes across deep time and observe patterns at magnitudes far beyond what the naked eye could detect. As Behe notes, "evolution must now be argued at the molecular level—the domain of the science of biochemistry"—rather than continuing to rely on the superficial methods of observations grounded in 19th century speculation.[262]

Huxley himself points out Darwin's own acknowledgment of a "serious defect" in the initial sketch of his theory by the omission of the problem of divergence. Darwin later described this issue as the tendency for organisms descended from a common ancestor to diverge in character as they are modified, explaining:

> This problem is the tendency in organic beings descended from the same stock to diverge in character as they become modified…. The solution, as I believe, is that the modified offspring of all dominant and increasing forms tend to become adapted to many and highly diversified places in the economy of nature.[263]

Darwin's explanation was not based on research, but offered as a theoretical necessity to address a recognized flaw that was pointed out in his model. While Darwin saw divergence as a necessary addition, Huxley viewed its delayed inclusion with skepticism, remarking:

> It is curious that so much importance should be attached to this supplementary idea. *It seems obvious* that the theory of the origin of species by natural selection necessarily involves the divergence of the forms selected.[264]

By calling it "obvious," Huxley asserts that gradual divergence should have been an inherent part of natural selection from the start, —underscoring his broader skepticism that Darwin's theory had been rigorously thought through.

Huxley's skepticism extends a paradox in the fossil record it: failed to show the expected convergence of diverse life forms back toward primitive, "undifferentiated protoplasmic" origins. As he observed:

> If... the diverse forms of life which now exist have been produced by the modification of previously-existing less divergent forms, the recent and extinct species, taken as a whole, must fall into series which must converge as we go back in time.... But, as a matter of fact, the amount of convergence of series, in relation to the time occupied by the deposition of geological formations, is extraordinarily small.[265]

Huxley's remarks reveal another fundamental discrepancy within Darwin's theory: if life's diversity arose through the modification of less divergent forms, the fossil record should display a clearer convergence of species as one moves back in time. Yet, he notes, "the amount of convergence of series, in relation to the time occupied by the deposition of geological formations, is extraordinarily small." This exposes a fundamental inconsistency between evolutionary theory and the fossil record, undermining the expectation of convergence over time. Huxley's critiques remain relevant, emphasizing the need for evolutionary explanations to reconcile their theoretical claims with the complexities of observed phenomena.

In Understanding Evolution's "The Big Issues," the material acknowledges questions about the evolution of complex features like eyes and wings, suggesting processes like co-opting and advantageous intermediates.[266] However, these scenarios, such as feathers evolving for insulation before being used for flight, lack supporting genetic, developmental, or biochemical mechanisms to explain how such transitions could occur.[267]

Collectively, the material frames evolutionary theory as an unquestionable consensus rather than a testable theory. Instead of delivering the "nitty-gritty details" as the website's presser initially promised, it focuses on superficial patterns, while avoiding in-depth discussions of the mechanisms that underlie these processes.[268] It fails to address foundational challenges posed by skeptics with the same 'accuracy,' 'honesty,' or 'confidence' it expects from teachers. It undermines its credibility as a comprehensive educational platform and exposes the limitations of its capacity to address debated issues in evolutionary biology.

This website presents evolution in a way that is similar to the superficial perspective Darwin had in 1859. Darwin's work lacked the understanding of genetics and molecular biology, but the Understanding Evolution website, despite benefiting from modern advancements, continues this legacy of not providing details of how evolution works under the hood: insights Darwin and Huxley anticipated would eventually emerge.

Choosing Words Carefully

Literature and film have long explored how the manipulation of language can serve as a powerful tool for maintaining ideological conformity and suppressing dissent. Consider, for instance, the 2005 movie *V for Vendetta*, or the 2004 movie *The Village*, or perhaps recall the well-known book *1984* by Eric Blair, more commonly known as George Orwell.[269] Both *1984* and *V for Vendetta* are classic examples of dystopian fiction.[270] Dystopian fiction depicts a society characterized by oppression, control, and the erosion of personal freedoms, often as a warning against authoritarianism, societal decay, or the misuse of technology or the manipulation of intuitive language.

V for Vendetta is set in a future where an authoritarian regime controls nearly every aspect of society, including speech and thought.[271] The government enforces strict rules about what can and cannot be said, effectively erasing dissenting voices and banning ideas that challenge their authority. Words, symbols, and even books are censored to maintain the illusion of unity.

In this world, a culture of compliance is mistaken for harmony. The regime uses propaganda to rewrite history and distort reality, ensuring that only their version of the truth prevails. Limiting language and suppressing free expression allows oppression to thrive under the guise of order. Citizens live in fear of voicing dissent, knowing that even a single unauthorized word could lead to severe punishment.

This control of language ensures that only the regime's approved narrative is spoken and believed, leaving no room for questioning or alternative perspectives. Through the character of V, the film explores the power of ideas and speech as tools for liberation, pointing to the human need for freedom to question and challenge authority.

Similarly, *The Village* by M. Night Shyamalan revolves around a community where residents are forbidden to say certain words related to the "creatures" they fear.[272] As a result, any words related to the "creatures" or "Those We Don't Speak Of" are avoided. The village elders create a taboo around these words to maintain control over the community, perpetuating the myth of the creatures in the woods to keep people from leaving.

Likewise, in the book *1984*, a totalitarian regime under Big Brother employs constant surveillance, propaganda, and language manipulation (*Newspeak*) to maintain absolute control over the population.[273] [274] The Party presents itself as a force of historical inevitability, with its ideology—Ingsoc (English Socialism)—being the pinnacle of human advancement.[275]

By rewriting history, the Party erases any memory of alternative systems, framing itself as the ultimate driver of progress. These types of 'community guidelines' deliberately redefine or eliminate words to narrow the range of thought, making it difficult—if not impossible—for individuals to conceive of ideas contrary to the dominant ideology. This manipulation gives the illusion that their rule has always been, and will always be, necessary for the good of humanity.

A chilling example of progress as a symbol, the Ministry's work of "truth correction" is portrayed as intellectual and moral advancement, even as it systematically eradicates individuality and freedom. The underlying reality is regression into totalitarianism, where "progress" is a narrative weapon used to justify their actions and disguise the erosion of freedom and humanity.

In these types of totalitarian dystopian fictions, consensus is wielded as a weapon to delegitimize dissent. When an idea is framed as universally accepted, those who challenge it are cast as irrational or even dangerous. Suppressing alternative views while magnifying the appearance of agreement allows these regimes to maintain power, using the illusion of consensus as proof of their righteousness. These themes described in fiction have striking similarities to the way many promote the theory that all life forms have a single common ancestor—religiously as an unassailable fact.

The Understanding Evolution website's "Undergraduate Teaching Guides: Avoiding Pitfalls" reveals a deliberate linguistic disparity in how biological structures are treated compared to human-made tools.[276] The term "pitfalls" seem to represent unauthorized thinking: ideas that deviate from the prescribed narrative of evolution. Like the controlled use of language in dystopian fiction, this guide, under the guise of avoiding genuine teaching errors, frames intuitive thinking as obstacles to be avoided rather than opportunities for critical thinking.

For example, under the subtitle "Choosing your words carefully," the webpage instructs teachers on which words are deemed "appropriate" and which are not, listing examples such as: function, *not purpose*; adaptation, *not design*; and evolution, *not development.*[277] This linguistic framing actively discourages independent thought and exploration in the classroom.

The webpage imposes arbitrary distinctions between "purpose" and "function," creating a contradictory framework that denies intentionality in biological systems. For example, it states: "The purpose of a hammer is to pound nails," explicitly connecting design and purpose by pointing out its most apparent use.[278] Yet, when discussing the hand—an even more complex structure—it arbitrarily chooses the idea of a hand holding a hammer to insist, "it's not appropriate to say that one purpose of a hand is to hold a hammer."[279] This argument may sound compelling at first, but once the semantic game is exposed, the inconsistency becomes clear: remove the word "hammer" and simply acknowledge that the hand's purpose is to hold or grasp.

Imagine reversing the scenario. Suppose the hammer's use were described more broadly to negate its purpose:

> The purpose of a hand is to hold or grasp things, and one's purpose in using the hand might be to build a bench. However, it's not appropriate to say that one purpose of a hammer is to build a bench. Instead, you can say that one function of a hammer is to pound nails into the wood. Biological tools are designed for purposes. Human-made tools have functions.

I'm satirical language mirrors the tactics employed by the webpage. This selective language manipulation lacks scientific justification. Such practices amount to a form of thought reform, shaping discussions to reinforce predetermined assumptions rather than encouraging critical thinking—or, at the very least, stepping aside and allowing the evidence to speak for itself. Instead of directly refuting opposing perspectives, the guide—and the website as a whole—talks around them, projecting defensiveness rather than confidence in evolutionary science.

The tactics outlined in the *Understanding Evolution* guide also share striking similarities with those employed by religious cult leaders and other dogmatic organizations. Both rely heavily on controlling language, shielding followers from dissenting ideas, and reinforcing ideological boundaries to maintain conformity. The guide manipulates language, redefining terms to align with a materialist worldview that renders competing perspectives unthinkable. Language is employed as a tool for control rather than clarity.

I'm not surprised that coercive tactics like these are a part of some teacher professional development sessions. What does surprise me is the boldness of publishing these thought reform practices openly on the web as an exemplary framework for fostering scientific progress.

Steven Hassan's *Combatting Cult Mind Control* provides a framework for understanding how language can be manipulated to control thought and reinforce ideological conformity.[280] His analysis of destructive cults reveals striking parallels to the rhetorical strategies employed by the *Understanding Evolution* guide, particularly in its discouragement of terms like "design" or "purpose."

As Hassan explains:

> A destructive cult inevitably has its own 'loaded language' of unique words and expressions. Since language provides the symbols we use for thinking, using only certain words serves to control thoughts. Cult language is totalistic and therefore condenses complex situations, labels them, and reduces them to cult clichés. This simplistic label then governs how members think in any situation.[281]

This concept reflects the guide's insistence on replacing terms like "purpose" with "function" and rejecting any implication of intentionality in biological systems. Such linguistic manipulations simplify complex ideas into a narrow, materialist framework, shaping how students interpret biological systems.

Hassan further notes that "the cult's clichés and loaded language also put up an invisible wall between believers and outsiders," emphasizing how language can isolate members from alternative perspectives.[282] The Understanding Evolution guide mirrors this tactic by preemptively framing discussions of design as scientifically invalid, discouraging engagement with dissenting viewpoints and fostering an intellectual echo chamber.

CHAPTER 7

Thoughtcrimes

Why get excited over this latest episode in the long, sad history of American anti-intellectualism? Let me suggest that, as patriotic Americans, we should cringe in embarrassment that, at the dawn of a new, technological millennium, a jurisdiction in our heartland has opted to suppress one of the greatest triumphs of human discovery. Evolution is not a peripheral subject but the central organizing principle of all biological science. No one who has not read the Bible or the Bard can be considered educated in Western traditions; so no one ignorant of evolution can understand science.[960] —Stephen Jay Gould

Antony Flew, considered by many to be the most influential atheist of the 20th century, exemplifies the challenges of breaking with dogmatic thinking. Flew, celebrated for his defense of Materialism, gained renown, particularly for his 1950 essay titled "Theology and Falsification."[283] In this seminal work, Flew argued that religious claims could not be tested scientifically and, therefore, were meaningless from a logical standpoint. This essay became one of the most widely reprinted philosophical works, solidifying Flew's position as a staunch atheist.

But after further contemplation, at the age of 81, Flew concluded that the idea of a cosmic evolutionary continuum from stardust to life was not feasible. The change of heart by this darling of atheism sparked a 'hate week' against him within the scientific community, a hostile backlash, effectively leading to his 'unpersoning.'[284][285] Disenchanted detractors from the scientific Party of consensus began to question Flew's comprehension of science.[286][287] Although once among the highest ranks of materialist thinkers, Flew experienced a rapid and sharp decline in reputation as he stood trial in the court of consensus, where he would later be convicted as a treasonous "thoughtcriminal." The statement was clear: no one is above the law of consensus.

Such incidents undoubtedly pressure researchers of lesser renown to stay in line with the orthodoxy, understanding that any deviation could make them next, placing their careers and quality of life in jeopardy. This self-confirming paradigm requires absolute allegiance to Darwinian evolution.[288] This is similar to the example of Lysenkoism in the Soviet Union. At that time, the state enforced Trofim Lysenko's flawed agricultural theories despite the emerging understanding of genetics.[289] Scientists who disagreed were silenced, leading to disastrous agricultural policies. Similarly, as Richard Feynman put it, "Science is the belief in the ignorance of experts."[290]

Dr. Richard Sternberg

Persecution of dissenters has been so pervasive that it is carried out and overlooked as though entirely natural. Dr. Richard Sternberg's experience exemplifies this. After committing editorial heresy by publishing a paper on ID in a peer-reviewed journal, he became the target of a severe and coordinated backlash, which had lasting effects on his career and reputation.[291]

Initially, Sternberg held a respected role as the managing editor for the *Proceedings of the Biological Society of Washington*, alongside his position with the National Institutes of Health (NIH) and his research association with the Smithsonian.[292] Yet, as managing editor for the Society, his autonomy existed only within the boundaries of conformity. Once he published a paper authored by Stephen C. Meyer supporting ID, the process of "unpersoning" began.[293] Although the paper was peer-reviewed by qualified scientists, it was Sternberg's decision to accept and publish it. That gave his critics a direct target. They constructed a narrative that he had acted unethically or deceptively, even though the review process itself was not found to be improper. Nevertheless, the officials sought ways to discredit him and force him out.[294]

Colleagues spread rumors questioning his credentials, and his work environment became hostile. His access to research areas and resources was restricted. His office keys were taken away, and he was assigned to a supervisor who was openly hostile to his views. The aim was clear: make it untenable for him to continue in his role without explicitly firing him.[295]

Two federal investigations later confirmed that Sternberg was indeed the target of discrimination, but the pressure he experienced did not end there.[296] Since that incident, Sternberg had reported continued obstacles and reputational damage. Because he had been declared a facilitator of a thoughtcrime, he was thereafter regarded with suspicion and professional hostility by much of the scientific community.[297]

According to Sternberg's account, the reaction was overwhelming and negative. Colleagues expressed "extreme hostility and anger" merely because he permitted a "creationist" argument to be reviewed and published.[298] He described the response as a combination of a herd mentality, with some scientists voicing objections simply in line with others, but outright disdain from some, largely driven by ideological disagreements.

So Much Consensus Evidence

Another modern example can be seen in the case of Skip Evans, a former NCSE employee.[299] His critique is a predictable argument against ID proponents. Evans questions the credentials of the dissent from Darwinism signatories, stating,

> Few [signatories] were from biological subfields associated with organismic and population-level biology — the divisions of biology most closely associated with the study of evolution.[300]

He assumed that only evolutionary biologists can critique Darwinian mechanisms. Ironically, Evans himself didn't have a background in biology, holding a B.S. in computer science instead.[301] Nevertheless, his dismissive appeal to consensus overlooks the very premise of the dissent: the valuable contributions that engineers, mathematicians, and other scientists can bring to the table. If ID's argument is that the comprehensive evolution of all life forms is false and that life shows evidence of design, then the very concept of the "evolutionary biologist" as an authority figure is illusory, predicated on a flawed assumption rather than objective necessity.

Evans equates skepticism about Darwinian mechanisms with rejecting facts, arguing that no one within the consensus questions how it occurs. He writes:

> Arguments within the scientific community about how evolution occurs should not be confused with arguments—conspicuously absent from the scientific community—about whether evolution occurred.[302]

That statement demonstrates its own lack of logic.

Further, he states, "the list is nothing more than careful word play—what is known as 'spin.'"[303] Evans, however, does not address or negate the claims made by ID proponents. Simply dismissing the list as "spin" avoids addressing the argument and fails to provide any substantive critique or refutation.

This pattern reflects a dynamic within scientific discourse, where the battle over ideas is fought without clear rules, making it difficult for bystanders to determine which side is closer to the truth. There is an abundance of papers critiquing ID, often questioning the motives, intent, and scientific validity of ID proponents.[304] However, a we've seen, the same journals that publish these critiques frequently block ID advocates from publishing their own arguments and data.

Thought Bullying

Consider this scenario: A league of thinkers—from diverse fields—assembled to fight for epistemological justice. Their goal: to "defend science education" from a perceived threat—the group of scoundrels—known as the defenders of ID, accused of threatening the foundations of science.

Among the crusaders of epistemological justice were biochemists Alan D. Attie and Michael M. Cox, staunch advocates of evidence-based science and experts in methodological thoroughness in the biological sciences; philosopher Elliot Sober well-versed in logic and evolutionary theory; and eminent historian Ronald L. Numbers, known for his work on Creationism and the history of science and religion, providing valuable context from the past.[305]

They were joined by legal professionals like Beth Cox, who addressed constitutional and educational concerns, and with Wisconsin State Legislator Terese Berceau, who advocated for *science* education policies.[306] Together, this coalition united to publish a peer-reviewed paper, laying out the case that ID is unscientific, fundamentally dangerous, and must be stopped. They explain the extent of the threat stating: ID is "not simply an assault on evolution; it is an assault on science itself." They continue, "the assault on evolution and science threatens our nation's scientific and technological leadership."[307] The paper does not, however, reveal how questioning speciation by natural selection or the origin of genetic information threatens the nation's "technological leadership."

Insisting the stakes were high, they called on everyone to join the fight. To illustrate the severity of the threat posed, they offered evidence of ID's plot against science:

> Creationists purposefully confuse the two meanings of the word 'theory'... In common usage, a theory connotes a statement that is tentative or hypothetical. However, science uses the term 'theory' differently.[308]

While conflating ID proponents with traditional creationists, the paper argues that their use of the term 'theory' is misleading, stating that "when substantiated to the degree that evolutionary theory has been, a theory is regarded as a fact." Thus, the report reveals that evolution is no longer subject to scrutiny as a mere theory.

Under the document's subtitle "Why ID is a threat to science," it further states:

> The constant, unanswered assault on evolution is harmful to science and science education. ID and its progeny rely on supernatural explanations of natural phenomena. Yet *all of science* education and practice rests on the principle that phenomena can be explained only by natural, reproducible, testable forces. ... Political and economic agendas are interfering with the free flow of scientific information. ... political appointees have ordered

scientists at NASA to eliminate references to the Big Bang Theory and to cease to mention the eventual death of the sun billions of years from now in their comments and publications. Other scientists have been cautioned about speaking out on global warming. These actions disrupt the long-standing tradition of *public policy based on the consensus of the scientific community*.[309]

The paper presents scientific consensus as proof and the proper basis for public policy. It rejects ID by labeling it "supernatural," ignoring the fact that ID arguments often focus on empirical patterns, not appeals to miracles. It implies that questioning evolution is harmful, but offers no clear evidence of what kind of harm this would cause—beyond disrupting a paradigm. The claims in the passage about NASA employees being "ordered to eliminate references to the Big Bang" or "cautioned about global warming" are presented without specific context or evidence

The paper also makes an urgent call for action to end the threat to the consensus-based policies that have endured 150 years, outlining "a wide range of actions that each scientist can take to facilitate good science education." It's curious, however, why trained scientists would need to visit the NCSE website to learn, but the paper provides recommendations for readers:

> Educate yourself. A few hours with publications available on the websites of the National Academy of Sciences, the American Association for the Advancement of Science, or the National Center for Science Education can help clarify the issues and provide the preparation needed for an effective scientific response to challenges.[310]

Other recommendations include:

> Write letters... to legislators, newspapers, and school boards considering actions that might undermine science education.

> Organize campus evolution groups. ... Regular meetings to plan special events such as Darwin Day celebrations can serve as outreach exercises.

> Participate in outreach activities... Go to local schools... Attend school board meetings... Talk to local business groups.

> Revise textbooks... Scientists engaged in textbook writing should be more cognizant of the need to educate future scientists and science teachers about evolutionary biology.
>
> Become more effective lobbyists... We urge scientists in all 50 states to work with their respective legislatures to enact legislation similar to the bill just introduced in the Wisconsin Legislature... to uphold the standards of science education.[311]

Given the article's title, "Defending Science Education Against Intelligent Design," it's clear that "science education" is treated as synonymous with shielding evolution from audit. The paper fails to deliver a convincing case that ID theory threatens science education.

It's noteworthy that the authors open the paper by downplaying the challenge of refuting ID, stating:

> Expertise in evolutionary biology and in the history of the public controversy is useful but not essential. However, entering the fray requires a minimal toolkit of information.[312]

This claim is striking, especially given that the document itself fails to present a scientific defense. It relies heavily on ad hominem attacks, appeals to authority, and fearmongering to dismiss ID. The authors downplay the need for strong scientific expertise in the debate, while their arguments do not take on the actual claims of ID. For example, instead of addressing the arguments, they call for political lobbying and organizing events like Darwin Day.

Is the "central organizing principle of biology" so difficult to defend with any clarity? These authors act as henchman of the broader "materialist nationalist" infrastructure that underpins contemporary scientific discourse. The article positions its worldview as synonymous with "the people," "science," and even "the government," presenting ID as a threat to all three, effectively encircling it within these spheres.

By claiming that "ID is therefore not simply an assault on evolution: it is an assault on science itself," the authors equate their perspective with the entirety of scientific inquiry, a trademark of radical Materialism, effectively closing the door to legitimate debate or dissent. This framing extends into public education, where the authors argue that "ID groups have threatened and isolated high school science teachers," depicting ID as an oppressive force undermining the best interests of communities and educators.

By associating ID with unrelated political and social issues, the authors suggest that their view represents the integrity of government and national progress. By conflating their perspective with rationality, public welfare, and national interest, the paper also frames ID as anti-democratic and unpatriotic.

Under the section "What can you do," the authors also encourage scientists to read the decision rendered by John E. Jones III in the *Kitzmiller vs Dover* case, describing it as "a particularly excellent resource and well worth reading in its entirety." But why are scientists asking other scientists—and the general public—to read a legal ruling about the implications of ID, rather than simply providing a clear, scientific explanation of why arguments like irreducible complexity are likely invalid? Promoting the *Kitzmiller v. Dover* ruling as a main resource for scientists undercuts the paper's own claim to defend science. A group of experts came together to argue against ID, but instead of using science, they relied on consensus and authority.

A court decision is based on legal reasoning, which often incorporates non-scientific considerations like constitutional law, public policy, and precedents. The decision in the Dover case relied on the same type of consensus arguments presented in this paper—rather than through independent scientific experimentation or peer-reviewed research. To frame the ruling as an essential resource for understanding ID avoids directly addressing ID's claims, as the paper's title suggests it set out to do.

Intriguingly, the authors paraphrase Orwell, stating: "a mere training in . . . sciences . . . is no guarantee of a humane or skeptical outlook," and they quote his advocacy "for *universal* science education" focused on "acquiring a method — a method that can be used on any problem that one meets — and not simply piling up a lot of facts."[313] This citation is deeply paradoxical and, in a sense, heretical. Orwell's quote is not meant for the enforcement of ideological conformity. Yet, the authors use it to justify just that—piling up appeals to legislation, straw man arguments, and calls for silencing dissent.

Further, the authors' use of the word "universal" to describe Orwell's vision of science education is tactfully misleading. There's a significant difference between universal science education, where everyone has the opportunity to be educated, and a universal science education where children are taught not to question. The contextual placement of the word universal into their paraphrase of Orwell's words implies a uniform approach to truth, which directly contradicts Orwell's advocacy for an education that's open to skepticism and the freedom to challenge accepted ideas. Most familiar with Orwell know which type of universal education Orwell advocated for.

It is also particularly ironic that these highly educated Ministers of Truth, including a philosopher, would cite Orwell's statement, "a mere training in . . . sciences . . . is no guarantee of a humane or skeptical outlook," especially given the nature of their argument. Orwell's point was that being well-trained in science does not automatically make someone a rational thinker or ensure they make logical, skeptical conclusions. He argued that true skepticism and critical thinking come from a broader method—one that involves actively questioning and testing ideas, rather than simply accepting them because they are part of a consensus. By doing so, the authors subtly reverse Orwell's intention. Orwell did not argue for science, or any philosophical stance, as a tool for enforcing a singular, controlled narrative.

In the context of this article, the authors' desire for complete control over the scientific narrative—through judicial rulings and appeals to consensus—represents a push for a top-down enforcement of what they deem to be scientific truth. In *1984*, the Ministry of Truth's control over information symbolizes totalitarianism, where dissent is suppressed, and alternative viewpoints are eradicated. The authors' invocation of Orwell's ideas, in defense of their authoritarian control over scientific discourse, inadvertently mirrors the practices Orwell warned against. The citation of Orwell, rather than supporting the author's argument, indicts the heretical nature of their position.

Additionally, while continuing to appeal to consensus in their argument, they dismissed ID as a "manufactured controversy," claiming that evolutionary biology "draws strength from a supporting scientific literature extending across 150 years that includes literally hundreds of thousands of individual papers." They note:

> The 'teach the controversy' hoax. The ID movement employs a tactic that appeals to the American tradition of "fairness and balance.' ID advocates argue that since there is a controversy over evolution, we should 'teach the controversy' in public school science classrooms. The 'controversy' is manufactured. Evolutionary biology draws strength from a supporting scientific literature extending across 150 years that includes literally hundreds of thousands of individual papers. Creationists offer no science. [314]

Their claim of "150 years" of literature (since Darwin) seems to state the obvious, but invoking the sheer number of papers does not inherently refute the points raised by ID proponents.

To put this into perspective, the Catholic Church, which established universities as early as the 12th century—over 600 years before the establishment of the theory of evolution—facilitated education and scientific research for centuries.[315]

Moreover, despite the supposed "literally hundreds of thousands of individual papers" supporting evolution, the idea of one species transmuting into another has not led to a single tangible scientific advancement.[316] If ID is as scientifically weak as they claim, why the need for such a coordinated effort to discredit it rather than engaging with its arguments directly?

The paper also employed other non-scientific tactics, such as using a comic strip of the "stork theory of reproduction" to mock ID.[317] By equating ID with an obviously absurd idea like storks delivering babies, the authors reveal their lack of substantive critique, offering only mockery.

This undermines the objectivity expected of peer-reviewed work. These tactics reflect intellectual bullying, the kind of behavior one might expect in a middle school debate rather than in a forum dedicated to rational inquiry. This exposes a flagrant inconsistency in the peer-review process. How does buffoonery like this pass peer review, while serious arguments by Behe or Meyer are shut out of journals—often with professional consequences for those who allow them, as in the case of Sternberg?

Historically, theories have been defended through evidence and direct engagement with critiques. Darwin himself set this standard in *On the Origin of Species,* where he painstakingly addressed potential challenges to his theory, including those analogous to modern claims of irreducible complexity. Darwin recognized that the strength of a theory lies in its ability to withstand scrutiny, not in the popularity of its proponents or the consensus it commands.

If the goal is to defend evolution against ID, the focus must shift from advocacy to substance. Behe's observation of irreducible complexity deserves a detailed response. Rather than relying on appeals to consensus, writing letters to legislators, or organizing events such as Darwin Day, the scientific community must engage with the claims of ID directly and demonstrate, with clarity, why evolutionary theory remains robust.

The American Civil Liberties Union

As seen, in the debate around intelligent design, ad hominem attacks are not the exception but the rule of engagement, and mockery of its proponents' faith is considered colloquial discourse.[318] For example, labeling ID as a "new form of creationism" functions as mockery, aimed at dismissing its arguments without allowing them to be fairly heard.[319] The "new" serves to imply that the concept was refuted long ago and is just ignorance repackaged.

As discussed, however, anyone attempting to explain how the universe came into existence is, by definition, engaging in creationism (the C-word). Even Eugenie C. Scott has unwittingly acknowledged this, stating:

> All people try to make sense of the world around them, and that includes speculating about the course of events that brought the world and its inhabitants to their present state. Stories of how things came to be are known as origin myths. They are tied to the broad definition of creationism.[320]

This definition naturally extends to the vast diversity seen in nature. Therefore, using the "C-word" to dismiss creation science is inherently contradictory, as it overlooks the fact that any cosmogonic explanation inherently addresses the concept of creation.

The American Civil Liberties Union (ACLU) is another organization that has invested much energy in fighting for materialist creationism. This institution holds a significant position in American society, marked by its longstanding influence on a range of critical issues pertaining to civil liberties and rights.[321] Founded in 1920, the ACLU is a political organization that prides itself as a champion of defending the constitutional rights and freedoms of U.S. inhabitants.[322] Its influence is evident in its active role in landmark Supreme Court cases and its persistent advocacy in legislative matters.[323] It has been instrumental in shaping the discourse and legal landscape around key issues such as free speech, privacy, LGBTQ+ rights, racial equality, and women's rights.

The ACLU often participates in discussions where scientific knowledge intersects with public discourse and policy. Though known for defending civil liberties, the ACLU paradoxically does not typically extend this olive branch to those whose freedom of expression involves skepticism of Darwinian evolution. In fact, the ACLU and the NCSE have frequently collaborated on national legal efforts to vilify intelligent design and block its scientific claims from being considered in public school curricula.

A notable example of the ACLU's staunch stance against ID can be found in their "Frequently Asked Questions About Intelligent Design" section on the Pennsylvania subpage of their website.[324] This section employs various rhetorical strategies, often taking the rhetoric too far.[325] The ad hominem attacks aimed at suppressing ID proponents' voices, are particularly noteworthy given that the ACLU is an organization ostensibly dedicated to protecting civil liberties such as free speech and equality.

Notably, the ACLU positions itself as a champion of social equity, diversity, and inclusion. Yet, the ACLU contributes to the intellectual bullying of proponents of ID, a group that has been significantly discriminated against due to their religious affiliations. Along with a conglomerate of other agencies, the ACLU misrepresents the arguments of ID.[326] Their "Frequently Asked Questions about Intelligent Design" page states:

> **Q:** How is ID like and unlike traditional creationism and creation science?
>
> **A:** ID is the most recent incarnation of creationism. Unlike traditional forms of creationism, ID does not openly rely on a literal interpretation of the Bible.[327]

They openly question the scientific credentials of ID proponents, emphasizing, for example, a lack of biologists among the movement's leadership:[328]

> **Q:** Who is behind the ID movement?
>
> **A:** The ID movement is led by a small group of activists based at the Discovery Institute's Center for Science and Culture ... There are very few credentialed scientists among the group's leadership, and those who are scientists typically studied in fields unrelated to biology. Their approach to religion is very different from the leading scientists in the United States who are religious. *Most legitimate scientists* who are people of faith accept the overwhelming evidence supporting the scientific theory of evolution and see no conflict between the two.[329]

By focusing on the lack of biologists among ID proponents, the ACLU, as do others, misses the central point: if speciation by natural selection does not occur, then evolutionary biology ceases to be a science of observation and becomes pseudoscience. If intelligent design holds true, biology becomes a study of engineering, not mutations.

The ACLU has not updated this referenced page since 2005, but the number of biologists supporting ID has grown significantly since last updated, but focusing on numbers still misses the point. To argue that "legitimate scientists who are people of faith accept the overwhelming evidence [of Darwinism]" is a juvenile appeal to authority that offers no explanation of the evidence itself.

On a different page of the ACLU, titled "What the Experts Say," the discussion reveals more of its reliance on appeals to authority, without pointing to actual evidence.[330] The entire page could serve as a case study in logical fallacies. An example can be seen in the statements Kenneth R. Miller. Although an expert "evolutionary" biologist, his statement appeals to the overwhelming scientific consensus against ID, yet he avoids addressing directly the specific scientific propositions of ID.[331] He states:

> Intelligent Design is a new anti-evolution movement that has been presented as an alternative to an older formulation known as 'creation science.' It argues that an unnamed 'designer' must have been responsible for much of the process, although it presents no evidence for the actions of such a designer.[332]

Further, Miller reinforces his position by asserting:

> Nonetheless, in nearly a century and a half of investigation, not a single piece of scientific evidence has emerged to contradict the idea that a process of evolutionary change gave rise to the species that exist today.[333]

Not a single piece? While dissenting evidence is routinely suppressed, there remains no conclusive proof that natural selection is responsible for the rise of distinct species. Ironically, Darwin, Huxley, and Lyell themselves were never empirically convinced that evolutionary change alone gave rise to the species we see today. This undermines Miller's claim from the outset. One might ask Miller: what do we know now that Huxley didn't, which resolves the contradictions Huxley himself pointed out?

Similarly, Robert T. Pennock parallels the consensus-driven arguments of Miller. In his "expert report," Pennock asserts:

> Intelligent Design departs from accepted scientific methods by appealing to supernatural explanations, which fundamentally changes the ground rules of science.[334]

This assertion dismisses ID as religious, categorically excluding it from scientific discourse based on its theistic implications rather than its empirical claims. By doing so, these thinkers seem intent on presenting a diluted version of ID rather than addressing its actual arguments.[335]

This perpetuates a legacy where theistic implications are used preemptively to reject scrutiny. This is like members of a political party voting against a beneficial bill because it might lend credibility to the opposing party. Ultimately, the discourse is marked by circular reasoning: the assumption that ID lacks scientific validity is used as the basis for dismissing it as unscientific—a conclusion drawn from the very premise being posited.[336]

Chapter 8

Kitzmiller v. Dover

> *Darwin deliberately used the example of the vertebrate eye in The Origin of Species to demonstrate how complexity and intricate design could come about through natural selection, which of course is not a chance phenomenon. In creationist literature, evolution is synonymous [sic] with chance. In scientific accounts, there are random or chance elements in the generation of genetic variation, but natural selection, acting upon this genetic variation, is the antithesis of chance.*[337] —Eugenie Scott

In 2004, a Dover, Pennsylvania school board's decision became the flashpoint for a national controversy, raising questions about the boundaries of science, religion, and education. What began as a textbook dispute over the school board's proposal to supplement the standard biology textbook with a companion text on intelligent design later became a formal policy requiring that students be read a disclaimer about evolution. The disclaimer stated that evolution was "just a theory" and "not a fact."

Science teachers were instructed to read the disclaimer to students at the start of the unit on evolution.[338] It encouraged students to explore intelligent design through a supplementary textbook, *Of Pandas and People*. The following was the school board's mandated disclaimer:

> The Pennsylvania Academic Standards require students to learn about Darwin's Theory of Evolution and eventually to take a standardized test of which evolution is a part.
>
> Because Darwin's Theory is a theory, it is still being tested as new evidence is discovered. The theory is not a fact. Gaps in the theory exist for which there is no evidence. A theory is defined as a well-tested explanation that unifies a broad range of observations.
>
> Intelligent Design is an explanation of the origin of life that differs from Darwin's view. The reference book, *Of Pandas and People*, is available for students who might be interested in gaining an understanding of what Intelligent Design actually involves.

With respect to any theory, students are encouraged to keep an open mind. The school leaves the discussion of the origins of life to individual students and their families. As a standards-driven district, class instruction focuses on preparing students to achieve proficiency on standards-based assessments.[339]

It sparked immediate backlash from some parents, educators, and scientists, who saw it as a veiled attempt to introduce religious ideas into public education.

By December 2004, a group of parents, represented by the ACLU and Americans United for Separation of Church and State, filed a lawsuit against the school board.[340] Behind the scenes, additional organizations, such as the NCSE, were also involved, shaping the narrative and strategy throughout the case. *Kitzmiller v. Dover Area School District* would become the first federal trial to address the constitutionality of teaching ID in public schools.[341]

This wasn't an isolated skirmish; it reflected broader cultural tensions in the United States. The early 2000s had seen renewed debates over the teaching of evolution.[342] Advocates for intelligent design, including organizations like the Discovery Institute, argued that ID was a scientific theory, not a religious doctrine, and therefore deserved a place in science classrooms.

Thus, the Dover case became the focal point for these competing worldviews. On one side stood the school board members and their allies, who believed they were promoting academic freedom and exposing students to alternative theories. On the other were the plaintiffs, who saw the board's actions as an unconstitutional endorsement of religion and a threat to scientific literacy.

Several figures emerged as central to the trial. The school board's decision was spearheaded by members Bill Buckingham and Alan Bonsell, ones who openly expressed their religious motivations for supporting intelligent design.[343] Opposing them were 11 parents of Dover High School students, led by Tammy Kitzmiller, who argued that the board's policy violated the Establishment Clause of the First Amendment.[344] Their legal team sought to prove that the school board's decision was not about science but about promoting a religious agenda.

The plaintiff's attorneys called on figures who, today, remain prominent in their fields. Biologist Kenneth R. Miller, now a Professor in the Department of Molecular Biology, Cell Biology, and Biochemistry at Brown University and current president of the NCSE board of directors, testified to flaws in ID's claims.[345] Philosopher Robert Pennock, currently a University Distinguished Professor at Michigan State University and a philosopher of science, brought a philosophical perspective to counter ID.[346] He is known for his critiques of theology, particularly Biblical creationism, in *Tower of Babel: The Evidence Against the New Creationism*.[347]

Brian Alters, a professor in Chapman University's College of Educational Studies and director of Chapman's Evolution Education Research Center, contributed his expertise in defending evolution.[348] Alters is also the author of *Defending Evolution: A Guide to the Evolution/Creation Controversy: A Guide to the Evolution/Creation Controversy* [sic], and a former president of the NCSE board.[349] Philosopher Barbara Forrest, co-author of *Creationism's Trojan Horse: The Wedge of Intelligent Design*, was called to trace ID's roots to religious motivations, aiming to dismantle its claim to secular legitimacy.[350]

On the defense's side was Michael J. Behe, a biochemist at Lehigh University, an expert on cell biology, and an ally of the Discovery Institute. In this contentious battle over the origins of species, Behe found himself on the frontlines—not only as the cornerstone of the defense's argument but also as the primary target of cross-examinations designed to challenge his credibility as an expert biochemist.

Aside from Behe, the other expert witnesses did not play as significant a role in shaping the case for ID. While individuals like Scott Minnich and Steve Fuller testified, their contributions were comparatively less impactful, and their arguments did not carry the same weight as Behe's focus on irreducible complexity.

As for other witnesses for the defense, there were discussions surrounding the potential involvement of high-profile figures associated with intelligent design, such as Stephen C. Meyer, a Cambridge graduate and philosopher of science, and William A. Dembski, a mathematician and philosopher, both leaders of the Discovery Institute.[351] Meyer is perhaps the most widely-recognized figure associated with ID, Behe's ideas, however, remain the most tangible cornerstone of the ID movement. Behe's role as a practicing biochemist and professor, coupled with his preference to avoid the limelight, naturally places him more in the background, focused on research rather than public advocacy.

Stephen Meyer is known for his focus on the philosophy of science and the history of scientific thought, as reflected in his books *Signature in the Cell: DNA and the Evidence for Intelligent Design* and *Return of the God Hypothesis: Three Scientific Discoveries That Reveal the Mind Behind the Universe*.[352] Meyer and Dembski emphasize the concept of specified complexity, demonstrating that DNA sequences are not only complex but also functionally specified.[353]

Meyer and Dembski have noted that intelligent design's validity is independent of its implications. Dembski has explained that the term "specified complexity" shifted from being widely accepted to stigmatized within mainstream academia due to its implications when applied to biological systems, particularly stemming from bias against proponents of ID, who argue that this type of information strongly indicates design.[354] Dembski has pointed out that aspects of the concept were already recognized by thinkers, such as origin-of-life researcher Leslie Orgel, placing his formalization within a broader historical framework.[355] Meyer further notes that others before him, such as Francis Crick, who first described DNA as a code, recognized its specified complexity.[356]

Because the once-neutral term "specified complexity" is now used by proponents of intelligent design, Wikipedia—as is customary—reframes it with ideological bias. Wikipedia's opening sentence reads: "Specified complexity is a creationist argument introduced by William Dembski, used by advocates to promote the pseudoscience of intelligent design." Think about that. An encyclopedia labels the terms specified and complexity—straightforward, descriptive words—as a "creationist argument."[357] There's no miracle implied in either word. They reflect standard English usage, describing intricately arranged patterns in reality that perform meaningful functions. The terms themselves are not inherently controversial. For example, one might describe a computer program or a printed circuit board as displaying specified complexity—precise, purposeful arrangements that enable functional outcomes. Similarly, DNA is universally recognized as a code exhibiting specified complexity.[358]

Meyer and Dembski's presence in the Dover trial would have been a formidable addition to the defense. Ultimately, these figures did not participate—leaving Behe to take center stage. According to statements on the DI's website, Meyer's non-participation as an expert witnesses, along with that of Dembski and John Angus Campbell, stemmed from procedural disagreements with the Thomas More Law Center (TMLC), which was defending the Dover School Board.[359] The DI contends that Meyer and his colleagues requested independent legal counsel during depositions to protect their rights, but TMLC refused, citing concerns about conflicts of interest.[360] Additionally, Meyer reportedly declined a later offer to participate, "because the previous actions of Thomas More had undermined his confidence in their legal judgment."[361]

Leading up to the trial, the DI criticized the Dover School Board's policy, stating that while there are secular purposes for teaching about intelligent design, "it was not evident whether the Dover board" demonstrated a clear secular intent in its implementation of the policy.[362] They further claim that they had warned TMLC representatives in 2004 about the risks of misapplying their materials.[363]

These criticisms reflect philosophical differences within the broader ID movement, as the Discovery Institute emphasizes adherence to educational standards over direct challenges like the Dover board's mandate, which explicitly tied scientific discussion to the idea of a Creator.[364] As a result, the small-town school board was left to challenge a 150-year-old materialist paradigm—one institutionalized in academia and the legal system—and opposed by powerful organizations like the NCSE and ACLU, all of whom worked to keep the board's Christian perspective out of the science classroom.

The legal proceedings around Dover, under the precedent that intent determines constitutionality, allowed for a trial driven entirely by ad hominem attacks—largely directed at Christianity—rather than by an evaluation of whether intelligent design presented legitimate scientific claims. The plaintiffs openly based their case on the argument that the board's religious motivations invalidated its actions, applying the logic that neither a fact nor science can stand if it originates from a religious worldview.

The Devil in Dover: An Invisible Hand

Eugenie Scott, the Executive Director of NCSE from 1986 to 2014, offered a detailed account of the events leading to the *Kitzmiller v. Dover* trial in multiple interviews. Her recollections reveal a timeline of events that began earlier than widely assumed.[365] In a podcast interview with DJ Grothe, published in January 2006, Scott noted that she had been observing the situation in Dover for two to three years prior to the Kitzmiller complaint, a detail she reiterated to Swamidass and Lents sixteen years later in 2020 YouTube interview.[366][367] Scott stated that the NCSE had been working with citizens in the Dover community since the early 2000s, mentioning that Dover had been "on our radar" due to incidents involving Creationism and anti-evolution sentiment.[368]

She referenced a specific incident in which a custodian removed and burned a biology class mural in the "dead of night," framing it as just one of the events that drew the NCSE's attention to the area.[369] Scott does not specify any other incident, nor does she clarify when or to what extent the NCSE first engaged with the teachers or later with the parents who pursued the lawsuit.

In the 2006 interview with Grothe, Scott described the NCSE's monitoring of Dover, stating,

> We've been kind of keeping our eye on Dover for 2, 3 years now [leading up to the trial]. [During this time,] they've had a school board that has varied over time and sometimes they've had more creationist-oriented school board members than others.[370]

In both interviews, Scott was asked about her perspective on the events leading up to the Dover trial. Her account reveals two significant transitions that were not thoroughly scrutinized by the interviewers. First, there are the shifts from somehow merely noticing, to monitoring the situation, to actively engaging with citizens in the community. Scott admits that, at some unspecified point, the NCSE was approached by citizens who discovered the organization online. However, her statements do not clarify whether this outreach was the initial trigger for the NCSE's suspicion of Dover two or three years earlier, such as in their earlier monitoring in 2002, or if it occurred later after the two to three years of their monitoring began.

Second, in Scott's account, there is a notable transition in focus from the teachers' desires for the classroom to the parents' rights becoming the central issue. The early part of her narratives emphasizes the teachers' resistance to the school board's proposals. Interestingly, in one account, despite the narrative that frames the school board as imposing the teachers' will, Scott vividly reveals that the board ultimately conceded, allowing the teachers to use a traditional biology textbook, with the sole exception of requiring a disclaimer to be read before the unit on evolution. However, as the situation progressed, the narrative suddenly shifts to the parents as the plaintiffs.

These transitions warrant further exploration, as the lack of critical questioning by these interviewers regarding these shifts undermine a comprehensive understanding of the NCSE's role, leaving significant gaps in the timeline and the motivations behind these developments.

In the video interview with Swamidass and Lents, Scott stated the following:

> I've given a number of talks on Dover, and one of the things that I point out is how long it took before the decision was made that, look, '*we gotta sue.*' And the 'we' is the plaintiffs. They approached us. I mean, obviously, we had been working with citizens in the community for a while, but, you know, like way back in, like, the early 2000s, there had been incidents having to do with creation and evolution, anti-evolution incidents.[371]

Scott's body language during this portion of the interview offers subtle cues that reveal her awareness of the implications of her statement. After she states, "the decision was made that, look, 'we gotta sue,'" she appears to realize the potential for her remark to be interpreted as an acknowledgment that the NCSE initiated the lawsuit. In response, she backtracks, attempting to reframe the narrative by clarifying, "The plaintiffs, they approached us. I mean, obviously we had been working with the citizens in the community for a while."

However, the moment she adds, "we had been working with the citizens in the community for a while," she closes her eyes in a manner that seems to indicate discomfort, hesitation, or an awareness that this clarification could itself expose inconsistencies in her narrative. It appears to be a fleeting moment of internal processing, as if she is recalibrating her explanation.

It seems unlikely that citizens, however, seeking advice from the NCSE would independently arrive at or articulate a definitive claim such as "we gotta sue," without significant guidance or framing from the organization itself, so it's unclear why Scott felt compelled to clarify or backtrack after making that statement. Notably, Scott also appears to boast—perhaps inadvertently—that the NCSE had been involved in Dover long before it was publicly known. She offers an example:

> There was a mural, a panel painted by one of the students for the biology class teacher. One summer, after the biology teacher had left, the custodian, in the dead of night, took the mural out and burned it. Dover was already on our radar at the National Center for Science Education before the trial.[372]

This is a revealing statement.

According to *The Devil in Dover*, an ironical title of a book authored by Lauri Lebo, the mural incident Scott often references occurred in 2002.[373] Lebo, who was the education reporter for the York Daily Record during the Dover trial, reflected on her experience covering the case.[374] She describes the mural as a gift created by a graduating student and given to his science teacher.[375] This teacher's name is unknown to me, but according to Bertha Spahr, the chair of the science department who would later lead the charge in the conflict as the primary witness representing the teachers against the school board testified: "It was the late 1990s. I believe 1998," when the student, Zach Strausbaugh, gave the painting to his former teacher.[376] Four years later, in 2002, the mural was removed by the custodian, Larry Reeser, after both Strausbaugh and the teacher were no longer present.[377] At that point, the mural, as abandoned property, would have become the school's legal possession, allowing the district discretion over its fate.

This means, if the mural was contentious, Spahr was aware of this for at least four years. Rather than solely questioning Reeser's motive—which, in a less symbolic context, aligns with standard procedural practice—one must ask why Spahr left this obviously contentious piece of art, which, beyond sentiment, holds no scientific relevance, over several summers rather than removing it herself, as most teachers would with items that mean so much to them personally.

During her testimony, Spahr described the mural as depicting the "traditional ascent of man."[378] However, this phrase is more closely associated with the 1973 BBC series *The Ascent of Man*, which focused on cultural and intellectual milestones rather than evolutionary science.[379] While testifying about the anti-evolution sentiment of Reeser, she conflated this phrase with the widely critiqued *"March of Progress."* This might seem like splitting hairs, but not in the context of how the mural was invoked under the banner of science.

Spahr's use of this term reveals an apparent misunderstanding of the mural's significance and its historical relevance to scientific content. What stands out is that Spahr, the head of the science department, and others, seemed unaware at the time of its removal that the mural was, in fact, not a scientifically significant piece. It was no more so than Haeckel's now-discredited embryo illustrations. Spahr's later concern about the mural's absence in the classroom appears to stem more from personal sentiment or even a superstitious attachment to its presence rather than from its educational importance.

In reality, the mural served no purpose to science nor the school. Though Reeser may not have been fond of the mural, Scott's portrayal of him as a villain sneaking in under the cover of night is misleading. A more plausible explanation is that he or the board made the decision to remove the contentious piece of art during his regular duties, consistent with his role as "head of building and grounds." This was their rightful discretion; if it were not, this would have been the first lawsuit in the Dover district.

In a January 2014 YouTube video titled "From Dover to DNA: How Science-Literate Communities Can Change the Narrative," published by *Pennsylvania Nonbelievers*, Lebo recounts details of the incident involving Reeser.[380] According to Lebo, Reeser refused "to hang" the mural donated by the former student Strausbaugh—"to his favorite science teacher."[381] This suggests that the real cause of the tension was not Reeser, but rather a staff member asking him to hang the mural. If this wasn't the case, one might ask: why was he asked to hang an image when it was known for four years that Reeser was personally opposed to its presence in the classroom?

Additionally, in *The Devil in Dover*, Lebo dramatizes the mural incident by portraying it as a fresh discovery during a school board walkthrough of the building in the summer of 2002. She writes, "Reeser... wanted school board members to see what children in Dover were being exposed to in science class," and describes him leading the board to the science wing to point out the mural, which "depicted an evolving line of our ape-like ancestors running across a savannah."[382] This framing creates the impression that the mural had been hidden or newly uncovered, sparking tensions.

However, there is a deeper layer to this depiction. Lebo continues: "It never occurred to him [Strausbaugh] that there might be anything controversial about his work."[383] She tacitly frames Christians as thinking outside normal logic, suggesting that the mural is only controversial to Christians. Yet the controversy surrounding the mural is not limited to religious objections. Strausbaugh's artwork, as previously noted, was an interpretation of the *March of Progress* iconography—a visual representation of evolution that has been widely criticized and largely rejected by mainstream scientists, including Stephen Jay Gould, who referred to it as an "embarrassing illustration."[384] Even Scott, though making the mural an issue about the rejection of science, has stated: "The concept of biological evolution, that living things shared common ancestry, implies that human beings did not descend from monkeys."[385] To Lebo's credit, she has acknowledged that she doesn't know much about science. However, she paradoxically uses unscientific claims to dismiss those with differing worldviews as ignorant.

Testimony from Spahr provided many interesting details. Spahr noted that the mural had been prominently displayed in Room 217 since its creation in 1998. She stated:

> The mural was on a chalk tray in the back of the classroom, the classroom lab combined. It was very visible. You walked into the room, it was there. You couldn't miss it.[386]

She further testified about the mural's removal in 2002 when the teacher to whom the mural belonged left the district:

> **A.** The last time I saw the mural was in August of 2002. The teacher to whom the mural was placed in his room was no longer an employee of the district, and I was going into the room to see that the new teacher who was coming had his adequate books and supplies for the coming school year. It was an in-service time.
>
> **Q.** And I take it, you noticed the mural was not there?
>
> **A.** On Friday, it was there. On Monday, it was gone."[387]

Spahr's testimony suggests that the mural was never in her possession or under her control. It was associated with the teacher who left the district, and its disappearance coincided with their departure. This timing suggests that any concerns about the mural were deferred for years out of respect for the teacher who it belonged, allowing it to remain in place until they left the school.

Following its removal, Spahr inquired about the mural, alleging that it now belonged to the science department, but was told by administrators, as she put it: "It was a personnel issue and it was none of my concern."[388] Or, as Lebo's book frames it, "She barged into the administration office, seeking an explanation. She was told to mind her own business."[389]

It remains unclear to me whether the school contacted the former teacher to see if he wanted to claim his property before its removal or how the transfer of ownership was assumed by Spahr or any other teacher. Lebo's book, however, describes the events as a seamless succession of linear developments, with extensive rhetorical embellishments, as if: Strausbaugh works hard on a class project, graduates, Reeser encounters the mural, repeatedly growing angrier with each interaction, and finally, at a climax of frustration, destroys it.[390] Her narrative omits important context: Reeser had possibly worked at the school longer than any of the teachers and had already encountered the mural for four years, or perhaps even up to five.

Lebo writes:

> After he graduated, Strausbaugh took a job at a graphic arts company. He pretty much forgot about the painting. But Reeser couldn't forget. Each time he passed by the mural, he grew angrier, unable to keep himself from staring at the first ape's dangling genitalia. 'You can see the guy's schwantz hanging out,' Reeser complained, using a Pennsylvania Dutch word for penis. Board members looked at the painting and agreed that ape penises had no business in science class.[391]

Throughout, Lebo focuses on portraying Christian ideology as ridiculously outdated.

Lebo's depiction of the mural's destruction places it against the backdrop of 9/11, the Iraq War, and a local petition to reinstate school prayer. She describes how, in the wake of 9/11, "Americans turned to Christ for answers and control."[392] She links this to the petition with 1,500 signatures demanding school prayer and to the rise of figures like Bill Buckingham on the school board.

Lebo does not simply document these events—she weaves them into a broader contrast between progress and regression, between scientific enlightenment and religious zealotry. She juxtaposes the moment school board members were "eyeing the ape's schwantz" with what she portrays as a groundbreaking scientific milestone:

> At the time board members were eyeing the ape's schwantz, amazing strides were being made in decoding man's DNA. Scientists were rapidly completing the Human Genome Project, an intricate genetic roadmap of our ancestry.[393]

By positioning these two events side by side, Lebo implicitly predicts that while scientists were on the verge of connecting all the dots between humans and apes, religious conservatives remained preoccupied with petty cultural battles. Yet, despite this framing, the completion of the Human Genome Project did not yield proof of common ancestry that many anticipated. Instead, it raised new questions about the complexity of genetic information and the assumptions underlying evolutionary models.

Nevertheless, Lebo reinforces her contrast by expanding beyond the Dover school board and linking their supposed anti-science stance to a broader political movement.

> In addition to the scientific advances, that summer the Bush Administration pushed its campaign for an Iraq invasion. Many fundamentalists, in support, spoke reverently of the approaching Armageddon. 'It's end times,' my father told me.[394]

This framing is not accidental. Lebo deliberately ties the school board to both scientific denial and global instability, portraying them not just as backward thinkers but as active participants in a destructive, apocalyptic movement. After carefully constructing this apocalyptic backdrop, Lebo delivers the dramatic climax of her narrative, describing Reeser's final act as though she were an eyewitness to history: "Reeser carried the mural into the high school's parking lot. He set the student artwork on fire, watching the flames turn it to ashes."[395] It becomes the final symbolic rejection of modernity itself: while scientists uncover the secrets of human origins, Christians burn images that represent forward thinking.

This rhetorical maneuver allows Lebo to transform a minor school dispute into a grand civilizational struggle, where the battle over a classroom mural is a microcosm of a much larger ideological war. While ideological motives may have played a part, Lebo's projection of malice onto Reeser distorts the event into a rhetorical symbol far removed from its actual context of a person from a different perspective. This portrayal exaggerates the actions of the man she also describes as "nearing retirement."[396] Casting Reeser as a sinister figure egregiously inflates the personal drama of the event.

Figure 8.1 The missing 'March of Progress' mural from Dover Area High's science class, featured in the PBS/NOVA documentary on the Dover trial. Once a classroom fixture, it became a symbol of the school board's repudiation of evolution and science education.

The mural incident is often cited as evidence of the Dover school board's alleged anti-science stance. Interestingly, neither Reeser nor the district's leadership seemed fully aware that the mural indeed lacked real scientific value. Ironically, neither the head of the science department, who defended the mural in the name of science education, appeared aware. In truth, those accused of ignorance had a more valid concern than those defending the mural as scientific. This aspect of the controversy has been largely overlooked.

This selective framing surfaced again in Scott's interview with Lents and Swamidass. Lents critiqued Behe's book, Darwin Devolves, pointing out a "pretty big misunderstanding" by Behe that he saw as pertinent to the controversy:

> [Behe] uses the word 'devolve' and 'devolution' as if evolution's opposite is always increasing complexity, increasing function, increasing sophistication. That, right there, shows a pretty big misunderstanding about evolutionary theory. It is not a steady march toward progress or perfection.[397]

Lents' critique of Behe centers on the claim that evolution is not a process aimed at increasing complexity, sophistication, or progress. While this view is widely held in evolutionary biology, it unintentionally undermines the broader narrative. If evolution lacks direction—no inherent march of progress or evolutionary gradient to be seen—how did the immense complexity and functionality of modern life, including consciousness, arise from a single-celled ancestor through gradual, unguided processes? If the path from LUCA to humans was arbitrary, how did it yield such intricate, ordered outcomes without leaving a discernible trail?[398] If evolution is not directional and complexity is not a necessary outcome, then the emergence of highly organized, conscious beings like humans becomes even more extraordinary and difficult to explain. Rejecting the notion of progress in evolution to counter Behe's critique only raises the burden of proof for evolutionary theory—hardly justification for lawsuits against those who question it.

Lents' remarks have become customary among proponents of evolution because the concept is so slippery. It is *never* quite what skeptics grasp it to be in any aspect. Proponents of evolution are quick to point out what critics misunderstand yet never seem to pin down what evolution actually is or how it works. It's linear—*no, it's a bush*. It's gradual—*no, it takes leaps*. It's directionless—*no, not really, it's sort of purpose-driven*.

We are told, evolution isn't a steady march toward progress, —except when it is. Yet, despite this ever-shifting framework, Lents insists that Behe is the one who fails to understand evolution. But don't take Lents' word for it—one must read Behe's Darwin Devolves and decide for themselves whether Behe's argument holds up against the critique.[399]

In Figure 34.2, we further see how evolutionary explanations are often framed by what evolution is not not rather than by what it is. Anthropologist Zach Cofran points out explains and explains a common "misconception." He explains that "humans didn't evolve from any animals alive today."

> In 2017, actor-comedian Tim Allen famously tweeted a question that revealed just how little he understands about evolution. It seems he's not alone. His tweet got almost 50,000 "likes" and 13,000 retweets. It's safe to assume a lot of people reacting to Allen's post also wanted to know the answer to the question that he posed as a statement: "If we evolved from apes why are there still apes."
>
> The short answer is that "we didn't evolve from any of the any animals that are alive today," says Zach Cofran, an anthropologist at Vassar College. That is to say, humans didn't evolve from the gorillas we see at the zoo or the chimpanzees we snap pictures of on a safari. "It's a common misconception that apes are a step away from becoming human or something like a step along the way," says Cofran. But, he adds, that's not the case.

Figure 8.2 Excerpt from a Discover Magazine article discussing common misconceptions about human evolution.[400]

Evolution is ("not what most people think," "not from modern apes," or "not from current species") a moving target resistant to affirmations and scrutiny.

While misunderstandings about evolution seem to be the most widely understood aspect of speciation by natural selection, evolutionary biologists confidently reconstruct entire lineages from isolated bone fragments. Lents' critique of a march toward progress, however, aligns with Stephen Jay Gould's rejection of the March of Progress iconography in his book *Wonderful Life*, where he described it as a "personally embarrassing illustration," a misconception about evolution.[401] Gould goes further, asserting the damning statement: "My books are *dedicated to debunking* this picture of evolution."[402]

15 A personally embarrassing illustration of our allegiance to the iconography of the march of progress. My books are dedicated to debunking this picture of evolution, but I have no control over jacket designs for foreign translations. Four translations of my books have used the "march of human progress" as a jacket illustration. This is from the Dutch translation of *Ever Since Darwin*.

Figure 8.3 Image excerpted from *A Wonderful Life: The Burgess Shale and the Nature of History* by Stephen Jay Gould (W. W. Norton & Company, 1989). Used here solely for critical and educational purposes to examine how similar concepts have been misapplied in later contexts, including as evidence in the Dover trial. The use of this image is not a reflection of Gould's intentions, and many of the views critiqued here are explicitly opposed by Gould in his original work. Readers are encouraged to consult Gould's book for his full analysis and arguments.[403]

If the March of Progress is scientifically flawed, it raises a broader concern: whether the NCSE, Scott, Lebo, and even the courts have upheld a misunderstanding of 'good science' in their efforts to discredit the Dover school board. The destruction of a pseudoscientific mural—criticized by mainstream scientists, including one who has devoted entire books to debunking it—was nevertheless used by the school's science department, and endorsed by the NCSE, as evidence in the first federal trial aimed at labeling intelligent design as pseudoscience.

The Prefect

Scott explains to Swamidass and Lents, "[In] 2003 the biology textbooks came up for approval." The initial tension about the science curriculum arose because, "The teachers wanted to stick with Miller and Levine, which is a good solid biology textbook. These guys wrote a good book, and all their lesson plans were built around it," according to Scott.[404]

The school board resisted the teachers' recommendations, pushing instead for the inclusion of materials promoting ID.[405] This set off what Scott described as a "hostage situation," with the board tying approval of the preferred textbook to the teachers' willingness to consider ID materials.[406] "The school board said, 'Nope, we're not going to let you get the book you want unless you consider teaching some creationism,'" Scott recounts.[407]

She claims that teachers, despite their initial reluctance to openly defy the board, reviewed *Of Pandas and People* and delivered a firm rejection. In Scott's, words:

> They reviewed *Pandas* and said, 'No, we really don't think this is appropriate for our students. We think the science is really bad, and also it is not appropriate pedagogically—it's really a crappy book for high school kids.[408]

The board had the teachers review a videotape that presented the claims of ID. It is unclear whether watching the video was imposed or merely suggested as part of an effort to appeal to the teachers. These actions, however, seem to have been an attempt to engage staff in a hopeful discussion about ID, rather than to outright impose their perspective. This may reflect the board's genuine belief that they were advancing a valid scientific argument through these materials. It does not seem likely that they would ask teachers to review the video without believing it presented compelling evidence.

Additionally, according to Scott's accounts, the board made concessions more than two years before mandating the disclaimer. These actions could be interpreted as a professional effort and a willingness to accommodate established standards, with the disclaimer and the ID-related materials ultimately relegated to optional resources in the library—perhaps as a way to preserve some voice in the debate. Realistically, most students are unlikely to seek out supplementary library materials unless required for assignments or driven by personal interest. While the disclaimer was part of the curriculum debate, placing the ID materials in the library was entirely appropriate. It allowed access without imposing the content in the classroom. Nevertheless, it was this final attempt to be heard that shifted the focus of offense.

One might suspect that there were legal reasons for a coordinated shift in focus from teachers to students and parents. There might have even been an initial anticipation to pursue legal action much earlier, based on the burning of the sacred *March of Progress* mural in 2002, given its symbolic association with evolution. As Stephen Jay Gould noted:

> The march of progress is the canonical representation of evolution—the one picture immediately grasped and viscerally understood by all.[409]

However, if a lawsuit were pursued and the board's consistent concessions were examined, it would appear that they never definitively imposed their agenda.

Their final requirement—that teachers read a disclaimer mentioning ID—could be interpreted as an attempt to compel public employees to promote a religiously motivated viewpoint. Yet legal standing in such cases often hinges on demonstrating direct harm or coercion. Advocacy groups are likely to pursue only cases with a high probability of success, given the legal and reputational stakes. In this case, the actual burden on teachers was minimal, and the board's repeated concessions may have weakened the strength of any argument based solely on teacher objections.

If a few parents were found and encouraged to act—serving both as concerned parents and as unwitting proxies in a broader war—they could provide stronger legal standing. A disclaimer like the one issued by the Dover district would be interpreted as directly affecting students, who were its primary audience. As a "captive audience" in public schools, students could be seen as particularly vulnerable to religious or ideological influence.[410]

Therefore, if a lawsuit's focus were to shift to parents and students, it would align the case more closely with legal precedents concerning the separation of church and state in education, such as *Edwards v. Aguillard* (1987), which struck down the teaching of creationism in public schools.[411] Such a shift would be necessary to build a more compelling case against a school board's policy.

Notably, in the case of the Dover district, the school board was elected by its community, presumably to reflect the community's values and concerns. While the 11 parents involved in the lawsuit are often presented as representative of a consensus within the district, the larger context is frequently overlooked. Dover High School had roughly 1,000 students at the time, and the Dover Area School District served about 3,200 students overall.[412] The lawsuit, therefore, did not reflect the views of the majority of parents or families in the district.

Given the NCSE's early involvement and support from external organizations like the ACLU, the lawsuit appears to have been significantly shaped by outside parties, resembling astroturfing rather than a purely grassroots effort by Dover residents. The trial and the surrounding dramatized media coverage framed the conflict as a major battle between parents and a religiously zealous school board, inadvertently attacking the very community that had elected them. However, the participation of just 11 plaintiffs suggests that community engagement or outrage was far less widespread than the narrative implied.

Despite its limited local participation, the lawsuit became symbolic of a larger national debate over science and religion in public education. Since then, Scott has gone on victory-like tours, boasting about how the trial quelled what she refers to as "flare-ups." Scott's interview with DJ Grothe, for example, offers several additional insightful nuances. She acknowledges that the Pennsylvania Science Standards required the teaching of evolution, leaving the board "stuck with teaching evolution, so to speak, from their standpoint."[413]

This comment veers away from the common narrative that portrays the school board as solely motivated by religious ideology in science education or focused on eliminating the concept of speciation by natural selection. Apparently, it was understood from the outset that whichever textbook the board chose, it had to include evolution. This meant, even the school board members understood that they had no real voice or agency in the issue—about which textbook to use—beyond wishful posturing. Though critics—from the NCSE to the ACLU, their expert witnesses, and even the judge overseeing the case—relied heavily on consensus, this was one consensus that was overlooked.

The NCSE and the disgruntled teachers were fully aware of the implications of the opening statement of the disclaimer, a part that is often left out when presented to the public:

> The Pennsylvania Academic Standards *require* students to learn about Darwin's Theory of Evolution and eventually to take a standardized test of which evolution is a part.[414]

Teachers, thoroughly versed in standardized test requirements, would have understood that a textbook including evolution was never truly at risk of removal. The framing of the board appears to be projection; a more accurate interpretation is that they were baited—possibly by combative educators over a period of three years. While everyone involved had philosophical stakes, the school board's actions reflect a complex effort and professional caution to incorporate their perspective into an already established curriculum within a contentious environment.

Scott's following statement to Grothe better contextualizes the Dover conflict that was widely presented during the trial and its aftermath:

> The situation arose in Dover because the Pennsylvania Science Standards say, '*thou shalt learn evolution*,' and because the textbooks include evolution, and here they were having to adopt a textbook

that met the state standards, and so they were stuck with teaching evolution, so to speak, from their standpoint.[415]

This statement adds important context to the Dover narrative, revealing an intent to enforce a doctrinal perspective over the small-town largely Christian school district. Scott's characterization of Pennsylvania's science standards as *"thou shalt learn evolution"*—a clearly antagonistic Biblical allusion—exposes Scott's doctrinal perspective to teaching evolution. This phrasing, whether intentional or not, acknowledges that the board's actions were, at least in part, a reaction to what they perceived as a mandated adherence to Darwin's law.

Scott recounts to Swamidass and Lents:

> Finally, finally, finally—the last straw, as it were... while still holding the textbooks hostage, [the board] required the teachers to read an anti-evolution statement, which also promoted intelligent design, to the classes before starting their unit on evolution.[416]

And with this, the teachers submitted their formal memo of opposition to the superintendent on November 19, 2004, voicing their resistance to the mandated disclaimer issued on October 18, 2004. Shortly thereafter, on December 14, was the shift where a group of parents, represented by the ACLU and other legal organizations, filed a lawsuit challenging the school board's policy.

Finally, a Trial

As the lawsuit advanced to trial, both sides brought their expert witnesses to support their claims. During the proceedings, Kenneth R. Miller was called to testify against the validity of ID. He introduced the Type III Secretory System (TTSS) as a potential evolutionary precursor to the bacterial flagellum to refute Behe's claim of irreducible complexity. This argument, however, relied on a hypothetical scenario rather than empirical evidence, thereby shifting the focus of Behe's challenge. Miller's argument reflects a reasoning similar to the "God of the gaps" critique often leveled against proponents of intelligent design: 'The biological systems are too complex; therefore, a designer must have done it.' In Miller's case, the reasoning becomes: 'Though irreducibly complex, there's a simpler system; therefore, natural selection must have done it.'

The introduction of the TTSS as a precursor to the flagellum does not address Behe's challenge. In reality, Miller's argument inadvertently strengthens Behe's. If the TTSS is also irreducibly complex, the same problem persists: neither Behe's example nor Miller's makeshift alternative provides a demonstrated evolutionary pathway showing how either system could arise incrementally through natural selection. This is like asserting, "Here's a bicycle; therefore, a motorcycle is not irreducibly complex, so the motorcycle must have evolved from the bike," without explaining how one system incrementally transforms into the other while remaining functional at every stage.

Miller's reliance on co-option itself—the idea that components of one system can be repurposed to serve another—draws a parallel with principles seen in engineering, such as standardization and repurposing of parts. In engineering, examples abound of how components designed for one purpose can be adapted for another. For instance, bolts, bearings, and standardized fasteners can be used across vastly different machines due to deliberate human design for practicality. Similarly, modular systems in manufacturing are purposefully created to enable repurposing and upgrading. No real-world examples exist of stepwise co-option producing such intricate, interdependent functionality in irreducibly complex systems like the flagellum motor. Miller's evidence fits better within an ID framework, where modularity and repurposing arise from foresight rather than random mutations and selection pressures.

Jeffrey Koperski, a professor of philosophy at Saginaw Valley State University, critiques the *Kitzmiller v. Dover* trial in his paper, "Two Bad Ways to Attack Intelligent Design and Two Good Ones." The paper focuses on the primary strategies used to dismiss ID. Koperski identifies two ineffective criticisms: the ad hominem focus on the religious motivations of ID proponents and the rigid application of methodological naturalism as a boundary for defining science. He argues:

> One's motivations for presenting an argument have no bearing whatsoever on the validity of that argument. Evaluating a conclusion by questioning one's motivation is an ad hominem attack.[417]

Koperski also critiques methodological naturalism as a "shaping principle" rather than an immutable rule, noting, "It is undeniable that shaping principles have been suspended and changed throughout the history of science."[418] He argues that invoking methodological naturalism to exclude ID reveals a historically uninformed perspective. By relying on such tactics, the trial avoided addressing the actual scientific claims of ID, undermining its fairness.

However, Koperski himself appears to assume the premise he critiques by labeling ID as "radical" and unnecessary compared to less disruptive alternatives to Neo-Darwinism, such as evolutionary convergence. He writes:

> If anyone [of these alternatives] is capable of resolving the problems posed by complex structures and macroevolution, ID is a more radical solution than is needed.[419]

This characterization presumes that methodological naturalism remains a necessary boundary, even as Koperski acknowledges the uninformed historical context of such application. Ignoring the fact that modern materialism cannot consistently meet its own standard, many founders of modern science—such as Newton, Kepler, and Boyle—would themselves not meet the current criteria of methodological naturalism, as their work often relied on theological or metaphysical assumptions. Yet much of what they contributed remains foundational to science today.

Furthermore, the modern perspective overlooks the possibility that the rigid application of methodological naturalism is precisely what prevents ID from being fairly evaluated alongside other scientific theories. If methodological naturalism defines the boundaries of science, then dark matter presents a methodological conflict: it is inferred solely from unexplained astrophysical anomalies—typically attributed to gravity—yet still categorized as 'matter,' despite remaining undetectable and untestable.

The court relied heavily on methodological naturalism to disqualify Intelligent Design, with Judge Jones stating, ID failed to meet *the ground rules of science*.[420] This legal framework, combined with the use of ad hominem arguments, effectively dismissed ID without addressing its substance. Koperski's own observation that "placing the black hat on one's opponent is no substitute for an argument" highlights the failure of the trial in addressing ID's claims.[421]

Judge Jones permitted ad hominem attacks based on the plaintiffs' witness's definition of science. By adopting the plaintiffs' definition of science as "testable, natural explanations" (3:101-03 (Miller); 14:62 (Alters)) in his written decision, the judge formalized this definition as the court's position. This means the plaintiffs' definition not only frames science in a way that excludes ID, but also allows them to control what counts as a legitimate explanation—effectively deciding what "testable and or natural" must mean within the legal and scientific context of the case. This ensured that ID was excluded not based on its merits but on a framework designed by its critics and codified into law through the ruling.

This stance was compounded by extensive circular reasoning. The judge stated:

> For a view that has been unable to gain a foothold within the scientific establishment... ID's failure to meet the ground rules of science is sufficient for the Court to conclude that it is not science.

This opinion cited exclusion as evidence of ID's inadequacy, while the fact that ID was excluded was used to justify its exclusion. In other words: rather than recognizing that ID's exclusion suggests institutional bias against it, its exclusion was instead treated as proof that it is illegitimate science. Such reasoning conflates systemic exclusion with evidence of inadequacy, ignoring how institutional biases prevent ID from receiving fair evaluation.

Even while Koperski critiques ID proponents for not offering incremental contributions to science, he does not fully acknowledge the systemic barriers they face. Expecting ID to gain a foothold within the scientific establishment is about as realistic as expecting Richard Dawkins' books to gain a foothold in the Vatican Apostolic Library.

Such incidents illustrate how the current, institutionalized Materialism functions as a gatekeeping orthodoxy, ensuring that perspectives outside methodological naturalism are excluded rather than debated. Koperski himself critiques this, noting, "It borders on academic incompetence to pretend that science has strict boundaries and then gerrymander those boundaries to keep out the riffraff."[422] Yet, he does not connect this directly to the broader suppression of ID within scientific discourse.

Finally, while Koperski rightly critiques the use of ad hominem arguments during the trial, it is important to emphasize that the responsibility for adequately addressing these attacks lay with the defense attorneys, not ID proponents like Behe. Behe, a biochemist, was left to fend off rhetorical traps, a task far beyond his role or expertise. The defense attorneys, trained and paid to guide the courtroom discussion, failed to redirect the trial's focus to the scientific merits of ID. This failure by the defense team, rather than any inherent weakness in ID's arguments, contributed significantly to the trial's dismissal of ID.

Ultimately, the plaintiffs' reliance on speculative evolutionary mechanisms to counter Behe's argument for irreducible complexity exposed a key weakness in their case under sworn testimony. The lack of a demonstrated pathway functioned as a tacit concession. Even Eugenie Scott has acknowledged that certain biological features, like the bacterial flagellum, appear irreducibly complex. Even Eugenie Scott has acknowledged that certain biological features, like the bacterial flagellum, appear irreducibly complex. However, she makes a special pleading:

> It's not that it's impossible to think of something that at some level is irreducibly complex ... but the problem with intelligent design is that they want to argue that there's a whole class of phenomena in nature that we just take off the table for science to explain.

This characterization is misleading. Behe, for example, does not argue that all phenomena resist scientific explanation; rather, he focuses on specific biological structures, such as the flagellar motor, which he contends defy gradual evolutionary pathways. By framing ID as opposed to science altogether, Scott dodges the central question: whether the bacterial flagellum can be explained through current evolutionary models. If even one example exists that gradualism cannot explain, it should stand on its own as a valid counterpoint.

Like Miller, Scott has also forwarded the rebuttal that "not yet having explained something doesn't make something unexplainable," suggesting that science will eventually resolve these questions.[423] This deflection reframes the debate as a failure to appreciate science's long-term process, dismissing ID's skepticism as "ignorance." However, this posture avoids the biochemical evidence and theoretical challenges that ID raises. Instead, it places unjustified faith in evolution's eventual vindication—just as Darwin and Huxley did in the 19th century.

To illustrate the flaws in this reasoning, consider the following analogy. Imagine being a person kidnapped and flown to a house in the middle of a desert, far from food or water. Locked in a windowless room, they are given a loaf of bread and a cup of water, with strict instructions not to consume more than a few slices and sips. A week later, when the captor returns, the bread and water are gone:

> "What happened to the food and water?" the captor demands, pacing the room. "There's no way anyone else could have taken it. The door was bolted from the outside," he pauses, staring intently. "It's just you in this room."
>
> The captive shrugs and replies, "I don't know what happened to it."
>
> "What do you mean you don't know?" the captor counters, growing increasingly agitated. "No one else was here but you! There is no possible way this could have happened without your involvement."
>
> The captive giggles softly, shaking their head. "Just because we don't know right now what happened to the food and water doesn't mean it's unexplainable or that we won't understand what happened to it in the future. You see, there have been many phenomena we didn't know how they worked until we discovered more through further research. That's how science works!"

This response avoids the obvious. Materialists routinely acknowledge the appearance of design, yet reframe skepticism about explanatory gaps as a misunderstanding of science's iterative process.

Yes, there was a time when we didn't understand what caused a rainbow or when people doubted that human flight would ever be possible, but these challenges are fundamentally different. The assertion that there are irreducibly complex structures with no feasible pathway to form in a step-by-step Darwinian process poses a unique challenge. While earlier gaps in understanding were resolved within the framework of established natural laws, irreducible complexity confronts the fundamental issue of whether Darwinian mechanisms themselves operate within those laws or contradict them. This issue is a fundamental challenge of the framework itself, and these types of responses to the obvious are textbook examples of gaslighting.

It also shifts the burden of proof onto ID proponents, suggesting that skepticism about the sufficiency of evolutionary mechanisms is inherently unjustified. By framing evolutionary theory as widely accepted, it implies that any apparent contradictions or gaps must result from the skeptic's misunderstanding or error. Again, this reliance on the certainty of future evidence is no different from Huxley's and Darwin's approach nearly 200 years ago—they openly acknowledged fundamental weaknesses in the theory but remained confident that future discoveries would resolve them. Yet, more severe discrepancies have surfaced.

One of the most striking statements Scott has made was in the DJ Grothe interview. When Grothe pointed out that even within science, there are disagreements about evolution, asking whether that made the Dover disclaimer valid. She responded:

> No. The disclaimer is not valid because although within evolutionary biology, we argue about the details. We argue about the mechanisms of evolution and what the pattern of the branching tree of life is or what pattern it takes. We don't argue about whether living things descended with modification from [a common] ancestors, which is what biological evolution is all about. ... This Dover School Board wanted the students to doubt whether

> evolution had taken place. ... *We argue about the how. We don't argue about the whether.*[424]

Scott's response is remarkable precisely because it exposes the underlying hypocrisy. A self-professed skeptic who champions rational inquiry and evidence openly embraces a position grounded in faith-like certainty. By stating scientists debate the "how" but never the "whether," Scott effectively declares evolution itself beyond skepticism, even while admitting fundamental problems remain unresolved. In other words, it simply has to be true, despite any lingering doubts or scientific inconsistencies. Many prominent evolutionists such as Stephen Jay Gould, Richard Dawkins, Ken Miller, and Jerry Coyne have all, in various ways, employed this form of circular reasoning. When this belief system is institutionalized all the way to the Supreme Court, debate is no longer a real concept.

Scott's subsequent comparison to gravitational theory further illustrates this intransigence. Scott states:

> There are arguments about gravitational theory, but nobody doubts that masses attract each other and that, the Newtonian gravitation works.[425]

Her analogy relies on a false equivalence. She is correct; no one questions if gravity is real. But that rhetoric is no different from claiming a Creator must be real, simply because gravity is undeniable. What is debated is whether there is evidence that all life could have evolved from a microbial ancestor known as LUCA. Gravity is directly observable and measurable, while speciation by natural selection involves mechanisms that are inferred and remain unknown for speciation.

Forrest's Account

Although the Dover school board cited materials aligned with intelligent design, there was no formal connection between the board and the Discovery Institute. However, Barbara Forrest, a philosopher, played a central role in the *Kitzmiller v. Dover* trial by framing intelligent design as a repackaged form of creationism, a characterization that more traditionally fits the school board's actions than the Discovery Institute's stated goals. Her testimony drew connections between the DI's broader strategy and the Dover policy, arguing that both reflected a wider creationist movement aiming to undermine evolutionary theory in public schools.

Relying heavily on the Discovery Institute's "Wedge Document," Forrest argued that its agenda was ideologically driven, aiming to advance intelligent design and promote a theistic worldview. She traced linguistic shifts in the textbook *Of Pandas and People*, where "creationism" was systematically replaced with "intelligent design," illustrating her claim that ID was a strategic rebranding effort.[426] Forrest linked the Dover School Board's actions to the DI's broader goals, portraying the case as part of the institute's ambitions.

However, her role as an expert witness posed challenges under the *Daubert v. Merrell Dow Pharmaceuticals* standard, which requires expert testimony to follow a reliable methodology.[427] The court acknowledged that Forrest's interdisciplinary focus on history and ideology, rather than empirical science, complicated her fit within these criteria. During cross-examination, defense attorney Robert Muise argued that her analysis selectively emphasized religious affiliations while neglecting scientific aspects.[428] Notably, she admitted having no evidence that Dover School Board members were aware of the Wedge Document, raising questions about the direct relevance of her broader analysis to the board's specific actions.[429]

In a January 2021 video, Forrest introduced nuances that complicated her courtroom narrative.[430] She noted the DI's reluctance to engage with the Dover case, now acknowledging the DI actively discouraged the school board's policy, viewing the lawsuit as a liability they could not control.[431] This contrasts with her trial framing, which suggested a closer alignment between the board's actions and the DI's influence. Her more recent portrayal lines up with statements from the DI and even Eugenie Scott, who similarly noted the DI's apprehension about the Dover, trial.

In the video, Forrest reveals how she was recruited as a witness for the plaintiffs. She recalled contacting the plaintiffs' attorneys to offer her expertise, noting that, to her surprise, her book, *Creationism's Trojan Horse*, was already being utilized as a resource.[432] This suggests a more advocacy-driven involvement than the impartial expert role she presented during the trial. Although her analysis remains mostly consistent, her active engagement calls into question the neutrality expected of expert witnesses.

Forrest's tone in the video further contrasts with her courtroom demeanor. She described the DI's strategies informally, referring to their efforts as "shopping around for a lawsuit," and cited anecdotal examples like the incomplete erasure of the word "creationism" in *Of Pandas and People*, which she called a "smoking gun."[433]

Although Forrest has demonstrated notable analytical skill and professionalism in her testimony and subsequent reflections, there is a notable smudge in the lens through which she views the Dover case. Forrest's analysis of ID is shaped by the premise that its proponents operate within a vacuum of singular motive—one rooted in religious ideology and bereft of scientific legitimacy. She had been narrowly focused on exposing ideological motives, seemingly unaware that proving ultimate ambitions does not inherently refute the scientific claims themselves. She assumed that revealing these ties automatically discredits ID's arguments, overlooking the important distinction between motive and merit.

Had Forrest applied her analytical acumen to the motives and actions of the plaintiffs' side, she would have found ample evidence that the NCSE and its expert witnesses operated within an even more overtly ideological framework. The NCSE's mission, though ostensibly to defend [evolutionary] science education, has long been steeped in its own form of dogmatism, driven by a radical Materialism that dismisses any concept hinting at design or purpose.

Her focus on one side of the ideological divide helped to create a narrative that portrays ID proponents as uniquely compromised by religious convictions, while ignoring the convictions shaping the plaintiffs' actions. Concluding that ID is invalid solely because of its religious motivations is like dismissing Newton's theory of gravity after discovering that he said:

> This most beautiful system of the sun, planets, and comets could only proceed from the counsel and dominion of an intelligent and

powerful Being. ... This Being governs all things, not as the soul of the world, but as Lord over all; and on account of his dominion he is wont, to be called Lord God παντοκρατωρ or Universal Ruler.[434]

Newton's advancements can be traced back to his religious perspective and motives. This does not diminish the validity of his theory. Similarly, assessing the truth of ID should depend on its scientific merit, not the religious beliefs or motivations of its proponents.

It was a 19th-century creationist friar and abbot who discovered the laws of inheritance.[435] Overlooked in favor of Darwin's compelling narrative, this contemporary monk provided what remains the most significant contribution to the field of biology, the true cornerstone.[436] Intriguingly, it is his discovery—not Darwin's—that serves as the true cornerstone of modern biology. Darwin's theory had to be rescued and reformulated in light of Mendel's work. Speciation by evolution as the cornerstone rests on assumptions and extrapolations that are far less empirically grounded than Mendel's laws.

During their time, most naturalist scientists subscribed to the idea of blending inheritance—the notion that parental traits mix in their offspring, much like paint colors combine. Darwin, too, relied on this assumption. His work was more focused on observing and documenting variation and its role in his theory of natural selection rather than probing into the mechanisms of inheritance. In *The Variation of Animals and Plants Under Domestication* (1868), Darwin proposed his "pangenesis" hypothesis, theorizing that "gemmules" carried information from all parts of the body and blended during reproduction.[437] For example, if one parent had a trait for tall height and the other for short height, blending inheritance implied the offspring would always exhibit an intermediate height, with all traits blended together.

Darwin's letters reveal his struggle to explain why inheritance didn't produce the blended traits he expected. In a letter to Wallace, he described an experiment where he crossed Painted Lady and Purple sweet peas, stating:

> I crossed the Painted Lady & Purple sweet-peas, which are very differently coloured vars, & got, even out of the same pod, both varieties perfect but none intermediate.[438]

Darwin expected the offspring to exhibit intermediate colors, reflecting a blending of parental traits, but instead, he observed that the distinct parental varieties reappeared unchanged.

Perplexed by this outcome, Darwin speculated that "something of this kind… must occur at first with your butterflies & the 3 forms of Lythrum,"[439] though he could not provide a clear explanation for these non-blending results. This contradiction undermined his reliance on blending inheritance as a mechanism, exposing the flaws of his assumptions and his inability to identify the underlying principles at work.

In another letter to Romanes, Darwin expanded on this difficulty, writing:

> The absence in numerous instances of intermediate or blending forms in the border country between two closely allied geographical races or close species seemed to me a greater difficulty, when I discussed the subject in the *Origin*.[440]

This reflection further shows that Darwin was troubled by such anomalies but lacked the tools or insights to resolve them. The problem with this idea is that blending inheritance leads to the dilution of variation over generations. This posed a major issue for Darwin's theory of natural selection, as variation is the raw material for selection to act upon, an issue that refutes his assumption of natural selection in itself. Without raw materials, evolution under his framework becomes unworkable.

This is yet another example of how Darwin never fully realized the mechanism of natural selection beyond proposing it as a concept of necessity. The actual science came from Mendel. It was Mendel's laws of inheritance that later forced Darwinists to retrofit his theory into a "Neo-" version, incorporating the discoveries of the creationist friar. That retrofit wasn't just an update; it was an appropriation.

Chapter 9

Master Strategist

You can't really be scientifically literate if you don't understand evolution.[1173]
—Eugenie C. Scott

Eugenie C. Scott, by far, has been the most impactful figure in the modern atheist movement—its Dowager Cixi. Her true title remains hidden, a reflection of her skill with words: calculated, evasive, and aimed at winning the long war, not each passing skirmish. She has often claimed to respect religion, emphasizing that the NCSE is focused on defending science education. Yet it is precisely through education that she has quietly worked to shape minds, ensuring that only one worldview passes through the gate.

It is remarkable, however, that the title of "science education" or "literacy" promoter has endured for so long, when it's clear her role over the years has primarily been that of an evolution evangelist—contributing little, if anything, to genuine scientific literacy. Her obsessive surveillance of Christian culture outside the classroom reveals that undermining Christian ideology is her most pressing interest.

In 2012, she was presented with the Dawkins Award by the Richard Dawkins Foundation. While acknowledging her resourcefulness as he named her the recipient of the award, Dawkins pointed out a duplicity between Scott's actions and her words. In a prepared statement, he suggests that Scott's public posturing toward religion is more strategic than sincere.

As he reads the prepared statement, Dawkins' demeanor, as if anticipated, shifts noticeably, from offering flowery praise to delivering a pointed rebuke, making it clear that pretending to respect religion is not the same as genuinely respecting it:

> My own subject of evolutionary biology is in the frontline trench, and Dr. Scott is the commanding officer, the *master strategist* on our side, and the *general in charge* of intelligence and strategic planning. She also serves as the field officer *in charge of tactics and battle order.*

> Yet, she accomplishes it all with a most unmilitary grace and charm… She respects religion in a way that I do not. I can imagine good tactical reasons for pretending to respect religion… but to pretend to respect religion is different from really respecting it, which is the one place I cannot go with Dr. Scott.[441]

Rather than the usual confident and dismissive Dawkins, this statement sounds like someone who is feeling the pressure of an effective opposition. His defiant tone reveals frustration, perhaps a slight admission that the battle is not going as smoothly as he once thought.

He described Scott as a "master strategist," skilled at navigating the contentious debates over evolution and religion. His remarks suggest that her respectful tone toward religious belief is a calculated effort to disarm critics and win over more accommodating religious audiences willing to accept evolution, a strategy similar to Lyell's.

While Scott claims to encourage people to consider evolution regardless of their philosophical or religious beliefs, her tireless focus on monitoring Christian communities and organizations suggests she views them as a clear and persistent threat to her worldview. Since her 2014 retirement, she has continued this pattern, devoting her time to surveilling those same groups. She insists that "they," who reject speciation by evolution, are dogmatic—yet her work in Christian persecution never seems finished. Though she claims evolution and Christianity can coexist, Scott's broader efforts clearly target the core tenets of Protestant Christianity, particularly its affirmation of Special Creation.[442] For her, there is no conflict, so long as the Christian abandons a literal interpretation of Genesis.

Such a rejection, however, is incompatible with Christianity's foundational beliefs. The early followers, who were first called "Christians" at Antioch, held to a literal understanding of Genesis, believing it to be the direct account of God's creative acts.[443] Paul, a devout Biblical creationist, affirmed a literal Adam and the special creation of the world, writing: "For since the creation of the world God's invisible qualities… have been clearly seen, being understood from what has been made" (Romans 1:20). Paul grounded his theology in the reality of divine creation. In the same spirit,

Peter declared, "We did not follow cunningly devised fables" (2 Peter 1:16), rejecting the idea that the foundational claims of Christianity were inventions or allegories.[444] Unlike today, these beliefs were not debated among followers. Moses' narrative and the acts Jesus were essential to their faith.[445]

If there are those who follow some but not all of the words of Jesus, that is one thing, but to frame Christians who do believe His words as somehow illogical or incompatible with modern science means Scott sees evolution as compatible with a version of Christianity found outside the Christian Bible.[446] Special Creation, which holds that God created life directly and purposefully as described in Genesis, was integral to the Biblical authors' worldview.[447] Figures like Moses, David, and Isaiah affirmed this literal account as historical truth and built their teachings upon it. Jesus referenced Genesis as literal history, using it to affirm foundational doctrines about marriage, sin, redemption, and his return for those who believed.[448]

According to the Bible the belief in a literal Genesis, particularly the existence of a historical Adam, is inseparably tied to the theological foundation of Christ's death, resurrection, and the hope of redemption for believers.[449] Thus, to reject a literal Genesis is to sever this connection, thereby undermining the Christian framework that gives meaning to Jesus' sacrifice and the hope of eternal life.[450] If these beliefs were merely metaphorical, the very concept of faith would lose its meaning.

Despite this, in a March 2024 presentation titled, "Here Come the Creationists...Again," Scott opens her it with a provocative question: "Isn't creationism something that we, thankfully, don't have to worry about anymore?"[451] She then displays a Google Ngram graph, explaining that it tracked the frequency of keywords in books from 1970 to 2019. It notes that 1970 was when creationism gained prominence. Scott explains the distinct peaks and valleys of interest in Creationism, with a noticeable decline in recent years.[452]

Scott attributes these peaks to pivotal moments in legal history: the first major peak follows the 1980s court cases *McLean v. Arkansas* and *Edwards v. Aguillard*, which challenged the teaching of creationism in schools.[453] A second peak appears after the landmark 2005 *Kitzmiller v. Dover* trial, which addressed intelligent design. These trends, Scott suggests, indicate a waning interest in Creationism as a topic of public and academic discussion—at least up to 2019.[454]

In the second slide of her presentation, Scott shifts focus to Google Trends data tracking public interest in "creationism" from 2004 to 2023.[455] Unlike the previous slide, which focused on mentions of Creationism in books, these data reflect real-time internet searches, offering insight into how the public engages with the topic over time. Again, in this slide, Scott points out distinct peaks in interest, linking them to major cultural and political events.[456]

The first peak occurs in 2005, coinciding with the *Kitzmiller v. Dover* trial. This is followed by a spike in 2008, which she attributes to public speculation about Sarah Palin's stance on Creationism during her vice-presidential campaign.[457] The final major spike appears in 2014, which she says corresponds to the widely publicized debate between Bill Nye and Ken Ham on the topic of Creationism and science.[458]

What stands out in Scott's analysis is the casual manner in which she presents, and the crowd receives, what seems to be cultural cyber-stalking, along with the conclusions she draws from it, which both she and her audience find amusing. By analyzing public interest in Biblical creationism at a societal level, she reveals a focus on eroding Creationist beliefs in general. Scott's gleeful anticipation to see Biblical faith dissolve speaks volumes about the Dover trial, particularly because it was a trial litigated based on the motives of one side—a case where the separation of Church and State effectively drew a separation that positioned the State against the Church.

Next in her slide, Scott shifts from public discourse to privately owned Christian spaces, displaying creationist museums across the United States. Like a real-life villain, she declares, "What we really want is Creationism to flatline, don't we?[459] "Flatline" is a medical term meaning death or clinical extinction. When used about a cultural or religious belief, it pathologizes that belief, treating it as something sick that needs to die. That's dehumanizing, even if said in jest. She continues, "This is looking really good," but quickly tempers her optimism with a warning against complacency.[460] She states:

"Even if we're not seeing much public discussion of Creationism in the news, it definitely has not gone away in the United States."[461] Were this directed at any other religious or cultural group, it would be denounced as bigotry. In this case, it amounts to Christianophobia. It is a targeted hostility toward Christian belief, framed as intellectuality.

Moving along, she presents a detailed and condescending critique of these privately-owned Christian spaces. She points to a Wikipedia list of 13 creationist museums, noting their geographic spread "from New York to California."[462]

Figure 9.1 The entrance to the Glendive Dinosaur and Fossil Museum in Montana. This location features exhibits like the Tyrannosaurus rex skull "Stan," which was referenced in Scott's presentation, though not the same image as used there. **Image source:** Wikimedia Commons

Scott starts with the Glendive Dinosaur and Fossil Museum in Montana, owned by the non-profit organization Advancing Creation Truth. She emphasizes to her audience that the museum adheres to a traditional young Earth creationist perspective. Snidely, she states: "Everything was created at one time in essentially its present-day form." She continues, "so humans and dinosaurs [were created] together," before following up with a mocking tone, "and the Earth is about 10,000 years old, rather than billions of years old."[463] Imagine the public reaction if a prominent science advocate called for Native creation accounts to "flatline." Why is this rhetoric tolerated in the name of science literacy when aimed at Christian traditions?

Figure 9.2 A fossil of a Tyrannosaurus rex skull nicknamed "Stan," on display at the Glendive Dinosaur and Fossil Museum in Montana. This is the same fossil referenced in Scott's presentation, though not the same image used. **Image source:** Wikimedia Commons

Scott acknowledges the museum's notable achievements, stating, "This is not some storefront; it has the second-largest collection of dinosaur fossils in Montana." However, she immediately undercuts this acknowledgment with a sarcastic quip, "Life is short," when explaining why she hasn't visited.[464] This reveals her lack of sincerity, as she scrutinizes these Christian institutions.

Figure 9.3 The Ark Encounter, a full-scale replica of Noah's Ark, located in Williamstown, Kentucky. **Image source:** Cimerondagert, Wikimedia Commons.

Scott then shifts her attention to Answers in Genesis (AiG), the organization behind the largest creationist museum in the country located in Northern Kentucky. She describes its 60,000-square-foot facility, which opened in 2007, and the Ark Encounter, a life-sized replica of Noah's Ark spanning 510 feet. While admitting that the ark is "astonishing in many respects," she casts doubt on its reported attendance figures, calling the claim of one million visitors per year "exaggerated."[465]

While displaying images of these institutions, Scott emphasizes AIG's financial power, pointing out its 2002 purchase of the former Toyota headquarters in Northern Kentucky for $31 million. She displays this former Toyota plant, noting that it is a massive 205,000-square-foot building now serving as offices and a planned Christian school, further portraying AIG as a formidable player in promoting creationist beliefs.

Here, Scott's actions become even more concerning when contrasted with her public claim that her only concern is keeping Creationism out of public schools. Her actions reveal otherwise. Even when Christians invest in creating their own private schools—entirely separate from the public education system—Scott continues to monitor and critique their efforts.

AIG explains their private aspiration:

> About two years ago, the Lord enabled Answers in Genesis to acquire the building Toyota used as its national headquarters... This is one of those 'once in a lifetime' type situations. We have already renovated the left third of the building for our Answers Academy Christian school.[466]

Scott's tracking of this project, like her monitoring of their museums, exposes the hypocrisy of her claims. These private institutions are not imposing their beliefs on public schools or the wider population; they are spaces Christians have built for their families and communities. Yet Scott treats them with the same level of scrutiny and disdain, exposing that her true goal is not to "defend science education" but to dissolve the cultural foundations of Christian faith wherever they arise.

Figure 9.4 The exterior of the ICR Discovery Center for Science and Earth History in Dallas, Texas, a facility dedicated to promoting young-earth creationism and exploring scientific evidence through a Biblical lens. **Image source:** Wikimedia Commons.

Scott concludes her investigative briefing with the newest addition to the network of creationist museums, the Institute for Creation Research (ICR) Museum in Dallas, Texas, which opened in 2019. She notes that the 30,000-square-foot facility, while smaller than AIG's Creation Museum, "was built entirely with cash" drawing attention to the financial resources behind its construction.[467] While Scott suggests amazement by the professionalism of these spaces, her tone remains critical, as she bemoans their growth and influence with a mix of sarcasm and skepticism.

Scott's methodical presentation of images—from wide shots of museum buildings to detailed exhibits inside—feels nothing like a promotion of science literacy. Instead, it more like an Orwellian "Two Minutes of Hate," where the audience willingly engages with a presentation that antagonizes the perceived principal enemies of evolution, voicing their contempt and laughing at each snide remark. While she claims to respect religion and argues that Christianity and evolution can coexist, Dawkins' assessment of her duplicity appears accurate.

At times, Scott's tone suggests envy. Her focus on the financial success and large-scale operations of creationist institutions, such as the Ark Encounter or the Answers in Genesis Museum, reveals a frustration that these organizations have achieved significant reach through their messaging. Her repeated emphasis on their multimillion-dollar budgets, extensive facilities, and donor support expose a deeper resentment, one that cuts to the heart of her cause.

While these Christian organizations thrive in advancing Biblical teachings that challenge the evolutionary perspective, the NCSE has languished with a conversely stagnant budget of approximately $1.5 million annually for decades.[468] Recent financial disclosures reveal consecutive losses—$84,368 in 2022 and $167,948 in 2023—demonstrating its inability to secure the same cultural or financial momentum it seeks.[469] Rather than critiquing creationist success, the NCSE might better focus on recovering from its financial deluge by proving to donors the scientific value of promoting the so-called cornerstone of biology.

After Scott's exhaustive investigative report cataloging Christian institutions, she reveals a level of anxiety about the persistence of creationism. She laments the Supreme Court's overturning of the Lemon Test, calling it a decision that "bodes ill for evolution education."[470] The Supreme Court effectively overruled the *Lemon* test in its 2022 decision in *Kennedy v. Bremerton School District*.[471] The *Lemon* test originated from the 1971 case *Lemon v. Kurtzman* and was used to evaluate whether government actions violated the Establishment Clause of the First Amendment.[472] This test had three prongs: government action must have a secular purpose, not advance or inhibit religion, and avoid excessive entanglement with religion. In *Kennedy v. Bremerton*, the Court moved away from the Lemon test and adopted a historical approach. The majority opinion, written by Justice Neil Gorsuch, stated that the evaluation of Establishment Clause cases should focus on the nation's historical practices and traditions rather than the criteria outlined in the Lemon Test.

Although this decision was not specifically about creationism, it has significant implications for how courts may handle religion-related cases, including debates over the inclusion of creationism in public schools. Scott's concern is palpable as she admits, "The courts do not protect us against bad science in schools; they can only protect us against the advocacy of religion."[473] This frustration reveals how much she and others relied on the Lemon Test's ability to institutionalize ad hominem attacks against Christian beliefs under the guise of legal precedent. Now, the mere thought of having to consider perspectives rooted in Christianity within education seems enough to make Scott break out in hives. If the goal were truly to defend science, why not simply present the overwhelming evidence supporting evolution?

This duplicity brings to mind another interesting point from the interview with Swamidass and Lents. While recounting the events leading up to the Kitzmiller v. Dover lawsuit, Scott appears to preemptively redirect a question before it can be fully asked. When she praised the teachers for refusing to comply and noted how some teachers and community members ultimately decided to sue, stating, "We began assembling a team," Swamidass attempted to interject with a question.[474] Scott initially appeared receptive, tilting her head and resting her chin on her hand. He began, "I have a question about this, so um, you know there are… a lot of people are still…," Scott suddenly lifted her chin from resting on her hand and interrupted: "Excuse me, before you do, because we're going to get off and this happens a lot."[475]

At the moment Swamidass began with, "a lot of people are still," it appeared to shake Scott, as if he were about to ask a difficult question regarding the NCSE's involvement. She immediately diverted the conversation with a seemingly positive remark about the opposition: "The Discovery Institute did not want this."[476] This deflection created a veneer of neutrality by implying that even ID's most prominent advocates were reluctant about the Dover case. Scott then quickly pivoted, asserting, "There were other people who did want a trial," pointing instead to the Thomas More Institute, which she described as "much more enthusiastic about getting a test case."[477]

This sequence appears strategic. By first framing the DI as cautious, she distanced them and herself from the trial, subtly positioning the NCSE as a neutral party. She then redirected focus to the Thomas More Institute, casting them as the true zealots eager for legal confrontation. Notably, this detour had no logical tie to an unfinished thought—it served only to deflect a likely probing question. Her redirection allowed her to avoid scrutiny while reinforcing a narrative of defense-side overreach.

This move allowed her to preemptively respond to potential scrutiny, neutralizing it before it could be raised with suspicion. Once Scott had completed this reframing, she returned to Swamidass and said, "Now, what were you going to ask?" The interplay between projecting impartiality and steering the discussion shows her tactical effort to maintain conversational control and manage perception. Ironically, Scott had already neutralized herself minutes earlier stating that neither the DI, the NCSE, nor the plaintiffs wanted a trial. Her "important point" that halted Swamidass turned out to be a redundancy.

Scott allowed Swamidass to ask his question. He didn't raise a skeptical one about the NCSE's initial involvement in the Dover case, but he ultimately raised a thoughtful concern:

> Why teach evolution ... when their parents don't agree with that and it's clearly controversial? Why not just leave that out and ... focus on all these other things that aren't controversial?[478]

This question set the stage for Nathan Lents to interject. Lents began by justifying the teaching of evolution, stating:

> [Evolution] really organizes everything we know about biology ... there is a lot of information in biology, and so you have to wrap it

around something to make it interesting... and that framework is evolution.

Lents also argued, "You just can't leave it out."[479]

Scott supported Lents' response and pivoted to a story about a teacher in the Southeast. She described how the teacher told her class about the solar system, but "a couple of the kids got up and walked out because their father ... had said if that teacher ever starts talking about how the sun is the center of the universe, you just get up and walk out because ... the Bible says that the Earth is the center of the universe."[480] According to Scott, the teacher later reassured the students, saying, "You don't have to believe that the sun is the center of the universe; you just have to learn it to pass the tests."[481]

Scott's use of the phrase "center of the universe" is revealing. The Bible does not teach that the Earth is the center of the universe—a point Scott, who presents herself as an expert on creationist beliefs, should know. Worse, she appears to confuse basic astronomy herself, conflating the solar system with the universe in a story meant to mock others for scientific ignorance. This wasn't a slip of language; it was a recycled caricature—an exaggerated anecdote designed for effect, not accuracy. This reflected the kind of exaggeration she often relies on, where mocking the subject matters more than getting the facts right.

Even more telling is that neither Swamidass nor Lents corrected her, despite the scientific and educational weight of the discussion. Instead of engaging Swamidass's legitimate question about teaching evolution to dissenting Christian students, Scott pivoted to a deflective story that painted Christian parents as irrational. The anecdote didn't clarify anything—it reinforced a tired stereotype and revealed her deeper aim: not to educate, but to marginalize.

Even more telling is that neither Swamidass nor Lents corrected the inaccuracy. This is especially glaring given that just minutes earlier, Lents had taken time to critique Behe for using the word "devolve," accusing him of misunderstanding evolution's nature as non-directional. Yet when Scott conflated basic astronomical concepts to caricature Christian students, if aware, he said nothing.

The Ruling

In his ruling on December 20, 2005, Judge John E. Jones III officially declared that intelligent design is not science. He wrote:

> We conclude that the religious nature of ID would be readily apparent to an objective observer, adult or child. ... A significant aspect of the IDM [intelligent design movement] is that despite Defendants' protestations to the contrary, it describes ID as a religious argument.[482]

Judge Jones rejected the argument based on who said it, not on what was actually argued. He applied a philosophical litmus test to ID: if it overlaps with religious thought or carries theistic implications, it's disqualified from being considered science.

By that same standard, the religious nature of evolutionism would be readily apparent to an objective observer, adult or child. A significant aspect of evolutionism is that, despite its defenders' projections, it functions as a religious movement, marked by dogma, gatekeeping, and a cultish intolerance of dissent. The trial presented a consistent pattern of conflating dissent from Darwinian evolution with an attack on science itself.

Scott's role in orchestrating the plaintiffs' strategy underscores this bias. Scott's own words and actions reveal a vision of a sanitized public sphere where religious thought is relegated to irrelevance, replaced by a version of Christianity stripped of its traditional underpinnings and recast to fit her preferred narrative. If scientific claims are to be judged on empirical merit, arguments like Behe's should be addressed directly, not dismissed based on projected motives or worldviews.

It is peculiar that the textbook at the center of the Dover school board dispute was authored by Kenneth R. Miller. This is the same Kenneth R. Miller whom Scott selected as an expert witness, who received the NCSE's Darwin Award, and who now serves as the current president of its board of directors. This well-connected Darwinian organization, effectively a special interest group, wielded significant influence.

Judge Jones' decision ultimately conflicts with the pluralistic ideals the Establishment Clause is meant to uphold. He also made the following statement in his written decision:

> To be sure, Darwin's theory of evolution is imperfect. However, the fact that a scientific theory cannot yet render an explanation on every point should not be used as a pretext to thrust an untestable alternative hypothesis grounded in religion into the science classroom or to misrepresent well-established scientific propositions.[483]

Judge Jones acknowledges that evolution has flaws, conceding that some aspects remain untestable or unresolved, yet equates evolution with science itself, presenting it as the only acceptable explanation. That's a contradiction. If evolution's contradictions are acceptable, then mere unknowns can't be used to disqualify other views.

The case for ID, however, is only getting stronger. The bacterial flagellum, dismissed in the Dover trial as only a creationist talking point, is just the tip of the iceberg. The flagellum and the blood clotting cascade may have drawn the most attention, but they are only two among countless examples that expose the limits of Darwinian mechanisms. Behind these two systems lie a vast constellation of similarly irreducible systems, from the top to the bottom, within living organisms. We are dealing with irreducible systems nested within other irreducible systems, with even more beneath them.

Behe remains firmly focused on the molecular level, refusing to let the discussion drift toward larger biological structures. This is not because the argument for irreducible complexity fails at higher levels, but because Darwinists are cornered at the molecular scale, where their explanations break down.

Consider the human eye, which Darwin found perplexing even at a superficial level. The vascular arrangement itself is irreducibly complex. The retina's photoreceptors require a constant supply of oxygen from the choroid, a dense network of blood vessels lying just behind them.[484] If the choroid were absent or improperly developed, photoreceptors would die almost immediately, rendering vision impossible.[485] Simultaneously, the cornea and lens must remain completely free of blood vessels to preserve the eye's transparency.[486] These regions rely on nutrients diffusing from surrounding tissues, but this delicate balance only works within the context of a fully formed ocular system.[487] A partial or intermediate system, whether lacking the choroid or with blood vessels invading the cornea, would result in blindness, offering no evolutionary advantage.[488]

Within the lungs are many examples of irreducible complexity also. Oxygen delivery to the bloodstream depends on alveoli—microscopic air sacs with walls thin enough for gas exchange—and a surrounding capillary network.[489] These capillaries must be precisely positioned to pick up oxygen and release carbon dioxide.[490] Blood pressure must also be finely tuned; too high, and the alveoli rupture; too low, and oxygen transfer fails. If any of these components is missing or nonfunctional, the system collapses entirely.[491] There is no functional halfway point where a partially formed lung could sustain life.

Then there is the blood-brain barrier (BBB), a system that protects the brain by selectively controlling what substances can pass from the bloodstream.[492] Its effectiveness depends on tightly joined endothelial cells, astrocytes providing structural and regulatory support, and transporters that deliver nutrients like glucose while keeping toxins out.[493] Remove any one of these parts, and the barrier fails—either allowing harmful substances to flood the brain or depriving it of essential nutrients.[494]

The BBB works as a complete unit or not at all.[495] Behe's irreducible complexity principle emphasizes the molecular action point where components must work together simultaneously to produce function.[496] The BBB fits this description perfectly, making it a strong example of irreducible complexity at the molecular level.

Each of these systems are undeniable challenges to the Darwinian framework. By focusing on the religious motivations of ID proponents rather than addressing the empirical evidence they presented, the Dover court avoided confronting these challenges. That avoidance will eventually come back to haunt this decision. The irreducible complexity of these systems will not go away, and the dismissal of their implications will only grow more untenable as our understanding of biological complexity deepens.

The mobbing of ID finds a historical parallel in the infamous *100 Authors Against Einstein* campaign.[497] Many critics, including Philipp Lenard, dismissed relativity as "Jewish physics," a view fueled by a Nazi campaign against "Jewish science."[498] [499] Einstein famously responded, "If I were wrong, one would have been enough," astutely pointing to the principle that science is decided by evidence, not by the number of voices in opposition.[500] Similarly, the Dover ruling effectively disqualified ID by branding it with the stigma of "Creationist science."

Chapter 10

The in-Crowd

It is absolutely safe to say that if you meet somebody who claims not to believe in evolution, that person is ignorant, stupid or insane (or wicked, but I'd rather not consider that).[501] —Richard Dawkins

The NCSE's "Friend of Darwin" award is an annual ceremony honoring individuals who have played key roles in advancing evolutionism as a dominant narrative.[502] It reinforces a kind of groupthink, rewarding those who align themselves with the prevailing narrative. By honoring "friends" of Darwin, these awards subtly suggest that allegiance bolsters the validity of evolution.

But why does Darwin's theory require "friends" at all? Theories such as Newtonian mechanics, Boyle's laws, Schrödinger's equations, and Feynman's quantum theories, while contentious in their time, were not accompanied by symbolic affirmations or awards for loyalty. Their strength lay solely in their evidence and ability to withstand scrutiny. In contrast, the NCSE's "Friend of Darwin" awards subtly frame the evolution debate in dogmatic terms, as though public affirmation and consensus are more vital than scientific explanations. The need for such awards reveals a fundamental weakness: an implicit acknowledgment that the cultural battle for evolution is more significant than the scientific one.

One might wonder, why not simply call it the "Darwin Award?" By cultivating a sense of belonging to a collective in support of Darwin, the awards perpetuate a reliance on consensus-driven validation—implying, "We are all on Darwin's side." Notably, past recipients of the "Friend of Darwin" awards include individuals directly involved in the landmark Dover trial such as Kenneth Miller, Robert Pennock, Brian Alters, and Barbara Forrest—expert witnesses who were arranged by the NCSE to testify in favor of evolution.[503] Tammy Kitzmiller, the lead plaintiff, also received the award, along with attorneys Eric Rothschild, Witold "Vic" Walczak, and Richard B. Katskee—all of whom represented the plaintiffs in the trial.[504] Even the parent plaintiffs, Aralene "Barrie" D. Callahan, Frederick B. Callahan, Bryan Rehm, Christy Rehm, Julie Smith, Cynthia Sneath, and Steven Stough, received this accolade.[505] The ceremony appears less like a celebration of science-education achievements and more like a ritual canonizing its recipients as Darwinian saints.

Interestingly, the NCSE also honored Richard E. Lenski, an evolutionary biologist renowned for his Long-Term Evolution Experiment (LTEE) *E. coli* experiment, which was designed to demonstrate evolution over tens of thousands of generations.[506] Lenski's study has gone on for more than 35 years and over 75,000 generations of *E. coli*, equivalent to approximately 1.9 to 2.25 million years in human evolutionary time.[507] Yet, despite this extensive timeframe, the experiment has shown only microevolutionary changes and adaptations, with no evidence of speciation by natural, or any, selection mechanism. Lenski's LTEE reveals more than just the absence of a proposed mechanism; it suggests that the leap from a common microbial ancestor to all life does not occur, even under ideal conditions for evolution.

Darwin has friends in literature and broadcasting beyond Laurie Lebo, author of *The Devil in Dover*. Her narrative wasn't the only one that sought to immortalize the Dover trial as a cultural clash between the enlightened and the ignorant. Edward Humes' *Monkey Girl: Evolution, Education, Religion, and the Battle for America's Soul* and PBS's NOVA docudrama *Judgment Day: Intelligent Design on Trial* also entered the fray, aligning themselves with the Darwinian in-crowd of modern science.[508] This anthology forms a collection of biased narratives designed to reinforce groupthink and signal alignment with the dominant side, portraying the plaintiffs and their allies as champions of modernity, rationality, and progress while framing ID proponents as backward, disingenuous, or sinister.

Kenneth R. Miller also authored a 2008 book that discusses the trial—*Only a Theory: Evolution and the Battle for America's Soul*.[509] Miller's stance, however, is forthright, unapologetically defending evolutionary theory. To his readers, his position is clear and unambiguous. The others presented their opinions as neutral while implicitly aligning with one side of the debate.

Edward Humes

Humes' *Monkey Girl* presents an uncritical bias toward the NCSE, the ACLU, and the plaintiffs, portraying them as heroic defenders of science. He obscures this bias while pretending neutrality, turning his narrative into propaganda. By withholding his position, many readers may assume he is simply reporting facts rather than presenting an argument. He sanitizes the roles of these organizations and plaintiffs, casting their involvement as purely reactive and principled. He builds up disgruntled town members who opposed the school board's actions as brave champions standing against an oppressive board and a divided, hostile community.

The title *Monkey Girl* is emblematic bias. Though the title suggests that a student has been ridiculed with taunts of being called *Monkey Girl*, Humes does not make it clear if any student was actually called this. Nevertheless, he uses this title to prime readers to view the plaintiffs as victims before even opening the book. This frames the narrative emotionally, reinforcing a sympathetic portrayal of the plaintiffs and their cause.

Interestingly, two years before the Dover trial, Scott stated in a 2003 article that a student in Oklahoma had been called "Monkey Girl" for wanting to learn about evolution.[510] While the claim is difficult to verify, I found no evidence supporting it. Given Scott's long history of defending evolution, one must wonder: Could this have been a taunt she faced at some point, perhaps influencing her later views? If so, I wonder if this personal experience shape how she interpreted skepticism of evolution, such as in the Dover events, and, by extension, influence the narratives presented by authors writing on it.

There are a few instances where Humes mentions students being called "Monkey Girl," but in these sparse accounts, the usage is generalized. One such instance appears in the next-to-last paragraph of his book, where he states:

> The taunts of "monkey girl" have subsided, and evolution, as far as Dover's classrooms are concerned, has returned to the back

burner, where everyone seems to want it. In some ways, the children have been the most sensible players in this entire drama.⁵¹¹

This phrasing suggests that "Monkey Girl" was a persistent taunt, something heard repeatedly until it eventually subsided. But that raises the question: Was one particular (monkey) girl called this throughout the local conflict? Were multiple girls targeted? If boys were also mocked, why weren't they called "Monkey Boys?" Or did "Monkey Girl" somehow encompass everyone? The specificity of the phrase makes its supposed widespread use seem unlikely.

Despite the heated discussions in Dover over human origins, there's no clear evidence that Monkey Girl was ever a significant taunt in this conflict. Instead, the way Humes presents it—generalized, yet oddly singular—makes it seem more like a repurposed narrative rather than a factual account of what happened in Dover.

Another vague account is in his prologue where he creatively describes the monkey taunts:

> Children have been ridiculed in the schoolyard for being open to the concept of evolution, taunted and mocked for being related to monkeys.⁵¹²

The term "schoolyard" feels out of place in a high school context, as it is now more commonly associated with elementary or possibly middle school. Combined with the vagueness of the statement, it further undermines the credibility of the claim. The phrasing— "Children have been ridiculed in the schoolyard for being open to the concept of evolution, taunted and mocked for being related to monkeys"—lacks specifics and seems more like an embellished detail than a factual account. There are no details about who was involved, when or where this occurred, or how widespread such behavior might have been.

Humes also states:

> Buckingham's classic quip was already filtering down to the school yards, perfect for recess torture sessions: *Which side of your family has the monkey in it?*⁵¹³

Here, Humes uses "recess," a term traditionally associated with elementary school, making its use in a high school setting seem anachronistic. If high schoolers were engaging in taunts, one would expect terms like 'hallways,' 'lunchroom,' or 'locker rooms' rather than "recess" on the "school yard."

Further, "Which side of your family has the monkey in it?" is oddly specific and does not sound like something a high schooler would say. Even more suspicious is this taunt's resemblance to Bishop Wilberforce's famously alleged jab at Thomas Huxley in the 1860 Oxford debate. The idea that Dover students independently revived this phrase is highly unlikely.

Humes writes about another instance in which the Rehm family alleges they were taunted by a man performing a "monkey dance" at the end of their driveway, an incident described as a key factor in their decision to officially join the lawsuit as plaintiffs. Humes recounts the incident as described by the Rehm family:

> They had pulled out of their driveway, kids loaded in the van, and there on the sidewalk was a crazy old man hopping up and down and scratching under his armpits. He was doing the monkey dance. Bryan and Christy didn't know whether to laugh or ignore him or be afraid.
>
> They talked to almost everyone they loved and cared about: Christy's parents, who lived in Dover, their pastor, their friends, their employer. Their friends and family said: Go for it. And so they became two of eleven plaintiffs prepared to go to court to take on the Dover school board and, by extension, the proponents of intelligent design.[514]

In the town of 20,000 residents, however, Humes was not able to gather any more detail about who this "crazy old man" neighbor was. This absence is notable, given the alleged incident's significance as a tipping point for the Rehms family joining the lawsuit. Humes provides other very specific details about the aftermath, noting that: "They talked to almost everyone they loved and cared about: Christy's parents, who lived in Dover, their pastor, their friends, their employer." All of these individuals reportedly encouraged them to act, saying: "Go for it."

This narrative conflicts with Lebo's account in *The Devil in Dover*, which attributes the Rehms' involvement to a direct approach by ACLU attorney Paula Knudsen after a school board meeting.[515] Humes presents a completely different catalyst—a bizarre, emotionally fraught encounter with an anonymous neighbor. The two stories are disconnected in tone, timing, and context. They cannot both be accurate.

The only instance where Humes suggests the term "Monkey Girl" was specifically used toward a student is in reference to Tammy Kitzmiller's daughter and possibly others who opted out of being told about the intelligent design book in the library. However, it is framed cautiously, leaving room for interpretation.

As a Pulitzer Prize winner, it's likely no accident that Humes avoids explicitly committing to the claim that Kitzmiller's daughter was directly called this slur. This careful framing is a deliberate choice to evoke emotional resonance without fully substantiating the incident, ensuring the narrative remains impactful while avoiding scrutiny over factual accuracy.

He writes:

> A few students—some of those who opted out—were angry that they had to be singled out. "This stuff belongs in church, not school," one said. "It's stupid." Many people in the community wondered what all the fuss was about. If confusion was the main result of the statement, were constitutional questions really at stake here?[516]
>
> Tammy Kitzmiller thought so. It was her daughter who had to trudge out into the hallway with that first group of opt-outs. It was her daughter who had to contend with the taunt, "Hey, Monkey Girl!" And it was Tammy who had to see the look on her daughter's face when she came home, feeling at once proud and forlorn, because just about the worst thing for a fourteen-year-old is to be deemed different from everyone else.[517]

The passage is ambiguous and not an explicit statement that Tammy Kitzmiller's daughter was actually called "Monkey Girl." The phrasing— "It was her daughter who had to contend with the taunt, 'Hey, Monkey Girl!'"— leaves room for interpretation. While it suggests that the taunt occurred, it does not clearly attribute it to a specific person, time, or incident. Instead, it is left to be interpreted, possibly as a reflection of Tammy's perception or fear of ridicule her daughter might face for being singled out as an "opt-out." Thus, it is not clear how Humes arrived at the title *Monkey Girl* for his book.

The students who defied hearing that 'evolution is not a fact,' including Tammy Kitzmiller's daughter, are described as being vocal and deliberate in their actions, criticizing the disclaimer and expressing strong opinions like, "This stuff belongs in church, not school," and "It's stupid!" The opt-out students are framed as taking the proactive step of leaving the room in protest of hearing that evolution is just theory, yet the claim of ridicule ("Hey, Monkey Girl!") portrays Tammy Kitzmiller's daughter as a victim.

Humes' narrative does not read like an objective account—it reads like a scripted novel, where dialogue too conveniently reinforces his themes. The Monkey Girls are not given agency or voice beyond being framed as victims. Their opposition, the supposed taunters, are also vague, without specific personalities, interactions, or direct quotes. It's always "they were taunted" or "they had to endure," but we never know who or hear the actual words of their supposed bullies.

This portrayal makes it less clear why other students would target them with this taunt in this setting. It's curious that an otherwise quiet high school would have students brave enough to exacerbate a volatile situation by bullying these already angry students in front of teachers facilitating the opt-out. It seems unlikely that this would have occurred without some intervention, especially during a time described as having a heightened sense of guardedness.

Even if names weren't provided, one would expect some framing, background, or at least an implication of certain individuals known for such behavior. If bullying had been a real issue in this context, it's reasonable to think that someone—perhaps a student connected to the school board members—would have been identified or at least suggested as being involved. It's unlikely, however, that most students would have been as vested or involved in the issue as the adults.

It's possible that Humes felt bound to implicate children, despite providing little to no basis for his title. If the title was chosen early in the writing process, Humes may have had to reinforce the theme by weaving in references to bullying, even if they were vague or unsubstantiated. Without this framing, however, the book's emotional appeal of casting the plaintiffs as victims of a hostile environment would have been weaker.

Unlike Humes, in The Devil in Dover, Lebo names a specific student, Alix Rehm, and ties her to the school board side of the conflict. She recounts a debate between Rehm and Victoria Bonsell, then inserts the detail that Rehm was called "Monkey Girl."[518] But she never explains when, where, how, or by whom the insult was made. The timing and placement suggest a deliberate attempt to link the taunt to that debate, inviting the reader to associate Bonsell, or the school board's supporters more broadly, with the insult. Lebo frames the exchange as a clash between science and religion but provides no substance beyond the implication that rejecting the "ape-to-man" view of evolution is evidence of ignorance. This further reveals the her (and authors like her) assumptions. By constantly invoking the *March of Progress* imagery as if it represents real science, she presents a shallow grasp of the actual debate.

Humes reinforces this type of framing in his prologue, beginning with Casey Brown, a former Dover school board member who quit after losing the vote on the disclaimer. Humes portrays her resignation as a principled stand against injustice, quoting her disbelief at the outcome:

> As she comes to court to testify about her long tenure on and rancorous departure from the Dover school board, she can still scarcely believe it has come to this: a community divided, families divided, friends divided.[519]

Humes amplifies this emotional portrayal by detailing alleged community discord, adding dramatic claims:

> A Dover High School student's senior project, a sixteen-foot mural depicting the ascent of man from lower forms, which had been donated to the school and displayed in a science classroom, was taken down and burned—not by vandals, but by a school district official, with the tacit, if not *gleeful* approval of school board

members. Casey, meanwhile, having expressed her opposition to introducing religious ideas into public school science classes, has received hate mail and crank calls and angry stares in the street.[520]

Humes frames Casey Brown's resignation as emblematic of a broader societal injustice, but in reality, her departure was the result of a legitimate and necessary vote by an elected school board. Losing the vote was exactly what the democratic process required, reflecting the will of the community as expressed through their representatives. No injustice occurred—only the resolution of a disagreement through a fair process. Brown's resignation shows her refusal to accept the board's decision with dignity when it did not align with her views, contradicting the oppression Humes implies.

It is not uncommon in politics, however, for people to perceive losing in a democrat process as an injustice. Humes narrative sanitizes Brown's inability to accept the outcome of a vote and obscures the role of external organizations like the NCSE and ACLU, whose involvement sought to override the local board's decision. Instead of respecting the town's autonomy, these groups aimed to impose their priorities under the guise of defending science education.

Further, Humes' depiction of the timeline leading to the Dover lawsuit is riddled with contradictions. He narrates as though the ACLU's involvement began reactively, triggered by a single phone call from Steven Stough, a middle school science teacher who contacted them on the day of the school board's press release. Stough, described as a Republican and long-time Dover resident working in another district, is also portrayed as a principled yet unyielding defender of science. Humes quotes him as saying, "It didn't matter if the board had adopted a one-minute statement or a weeklong class: it was wrong." According to Humes, Stough, upon reading the press release, saw it as "an assault on science and an attempt to foist a religious idea onto impressionable young people."[521]

Humes casts Stough as a grassroots activist, yet this portrayal downplays the anticipatory nature of his concerns. Stough's daughter, then in eighth grade, would not encounter the policy until the following year, raising questions about the immediacy of his outrage. Humes says Stough, following news about the vote, called the ACLU and stated, "His daughter's school district might be violating *her* rights… I'm looking for somewhere to turn."522 While this framing suggests Stough acted spontaneously, it ignores whether the rapid response was influenced by prior contact with the NCSE, which Eugenie Scott has acknowledged had been working with Dover citizens for years. It is still unknown who were these citizens the NCSE were in contact with for two to three years preceding the lawsuit.

Immediately after Stough's call, according to Humes, Tammy Kitzmiller joined the effort, as if another domino had fallen into place. Humes describes her as a "naturally shy person" who "had also been stewing about the school board's actions," making her decision seem less like a spontaneous stand and more like the next inevitable step in a coordinated response. He writes, "Soon she, too, called the ACLU. A short time later, Kitzmiller found herself slipping quietly into a law office to discuss her options."523

Creatively, Humes pens Kitzmiller as a reluctant hero, outraged by what she saw as an intrusion into her family's private role in discussing matters of faith and science. "How dare they!" she reportedly exclaimed. This depiction frames her involvement as reactive and organic, yet Humes' timeline contradicts this. Humes admits:

> The next morning, with front-page stories on the board's action… and the ACLU among others already talking about lawsuits.524

This admission suggests that the ACLU had already begun organizing its legal strategy, before Kitzmiller became a prospective plaintiff. The description of her "slipping quietly into a law office to discuss her options" seems more about aligning her involvement with a predetermined course of action. There was apparently little to discuss beyond how the ACLU would proceed with the option of suing.

Humes' storytelling crescendos with Bryan and Christy Rehm, "Sunday school teachers and regular churchgoers" cast as reluctant plaintiffs who, despite fearing public backlash, join the lawsuit.525 Humes frames the plaintiffs as righteous Christians on the side of the in-crowd while devoting much effort to framing other Christians as ignorant.

Humes acknowledges how the ACLU carefully curated their public image, writing:

> Biographical materials provided by the ACLU made certain that press accounts dutifully reported the Rehms' volunteer work as Sunday school teachers and Bryan's status as an Eagle Scout—inoculation against the charges of atheism that, sooner or later, were bound to arise in the 'spin' war that would be fought during the yearlong wait from lawsuit to trial.[526]

Achieving the status of Eagle Scout is quite commendable because it is the highest rank attainable within the Boy Scouts of America program. As such, Eagle Scouts are the most likely to uphold the core values of the Boy Scouts of America.[527] Nevertheless, this reveals the deliberate staging by the ACLU to frame the plaintiffs as morally upstanding, faith-driven individuals. Rather than letting the facts of the case speak for themselves, the ACLU actively participated in a "spin war" to preempt criticism and reinforce their narrative.

This framing, however, is ironic given the ACLU's previous legal battles against the Boy Scouts of America, where it sought to dismantle the organization's religiously grounded membership policies. The Boy Scouts of America, founded in 1910, has always been a religious organization, not a secular one.[528] This is evident in the Scout Oath on which it was founded, which states:

> On my honor, I will do my best to do my duty to God and my country and to obey the Scout Law; to help other people at all times; to keep myself physically strong, mentally awake, and morally straight.[529]

The Scout Oath reflects a clear commitment to faith, reverence for, and allegiance to God as a central tenet. Despite this, the ACLU sought to force the Boy Scouts to relinquish their religious values in *Boy Scouts of America v. Dale* (2000), where they pushed the Supreme Court to require the Scouts to accept members whose values conflicted with their religious principles.[530] The ACLU ultimately lost, with the Court affirming the Boy Scouts' First Amendment right to freedom of association. Thus, in one instance, they demonized the Boy Scouts for adhering to their religious foundation, and in another, they leveraged the cultural and moral authority of Eagle Scouts to strengthen their case in the Dover trial.

Instead of interrogating this calculated strategy, Humes treats it as a morally necessary part of the plaintiffs' campaign. This framing further reveals the inundation of bias inherent in Humes' narrative. It becomes clear that this was a carefully choreographed proxy war, with the plaintiffs positioned as pawns in a broader ideological battle.

Humes introduces Mr. Rehm, a physics teacher, by stating that his field "did not spare him from the controversy," even though physics is unrelated to the debate over biological evolution.[531] According to Humes, Rehm began "cutting back" on certain classroom activities, citing a "chilling effect" caused by the board's stance on evolution.[532] Humes quotes Rehm describing this as "pressure-induced self-censorship" and notes that the teacher had "never used or thought about [the term chilling effect] before."[533]

Rehm claimed he abandoned a classroom essay assignment and discussion titled "What Is Science?"[534] because he feared provoking the board into adopting anti-science policies. Rehm's forsaken science activity, as Humes recounts, was designed to teach students the distinctions between hypotheses, theories, and "junk science" and the significance of peer review in validating scientific claims.[535] As he emphasizes Rehm's decision to eliminate this assignment, Humes attempts to position him as a casualty of the board's supposed hostility toward science, yet this framing is quite fallacious. It hinges on the assumption that unrelated classroom discussions about scientific methods were at risk, a claim that stretches the credibility of Rehm's reaction and the narrative's logic.

It is quite unusual for high school physics classes to include a dedicated lesson titled "What Is Science?" or to delve deeply into general discussions about scientific methods and philosophy, such as the distinctions between hypotheses, theories, and "junk science." "Junk science" isn't typically a topic for any science class. Other topics, such as "What is science," are often addressed in introductory courses like earth science, life science, or general science. Physics classes in high school usually focus on the principles of motion, forces, energy, waves, and electricity, with an emphasis on problem-solving and mathematical applications.

If it is indeed Rehm's account of abandoning an assignment titled *What is Science*, it casts doubt on the narrative, regardless of whether the account is true or false. If the activity was genuinely part of Rehm's teaching, it reflects a peculiar deviation from standard physics curricula. Yet, the low likelihood suggests that the anecdote was likely staged or exaggerated to bolster the narrative of a "chilling effect" caused by the board's actions.

In his portrayal of the NCSE and ACLU, Humes demonstrates an obsequiousness to this philosophical in-crowd. He repeats the claim that the ACLU turned to the NCSE because it served as "one-stop shopping" for biologists, philosophers, and other experts—a phrase taken directly from the NCSE's own self-promotions, such as what's stated explicitly in its 2004 Understanding Evolution website press release. It's telling that the ACLU justified its reliance on the NCSE using the NCSE's own canned PR language.[536] The uncritical recycling of insider language makes the entire story feel less like narrative choreography—or perhaps it never occurs to Humes to question their preexisting involvement in possibly coaching plaintiffs, each other or the likelihood that a coalition with the NCSE "just happened" to form after the disclaimer.[537] This cannot be considered neutral or investigative reporting.

Humes also adopts terms like "flare-ups," a term originated from and profusely used by Scott and the NCSE's web material to describe local disputes over evolution, as if skepticism were symptoms of a chronic disease. Humes irresponsibly frames these conflicts as a Christian "holy war" against science:

> Holy wars, however, are notoriously unresponsive to legal niceties... conflicts between the forces of science and faith have continued unabated, mostly at low intensity... though sometimes there have been flare-ups that led to lawsuits and national media attention before they faded again.[538]

Though Humes uses Scott's term "flare-up," his narrative amplifies the dramatic conflict beyond what is typical of Scott, particularly with his phrasing that "Holy wars" are "unresponsive to legal niceties."

Scott prefers to appear passive, positioning herself as reacting rather than attacking. She frames these conflicts with defensive terminology, such as "evolution wars," to suggest that she is merely responding to aggression against truth rather than advancing her own ideological battle. She presents her opponents as challenges but ensures they never seem like genuine threats to her authority or Darwin's theory. She has repeatedly emphasized that over ninety percent of the work the NCSE has done for decades occurred "behind the scenes," stating:

> Perhaps NCSE's most important role during the early decades was advising parents, teachers, and other citizens trying to oppose policies that compromised the integrity of science education in their local schools. Most of the help was behind the scenes. Probably the first major 'flare-up' (as they are known in-house) was the controversy over a creationism policy in Vista, California. But the longest-lasting flare-up, from 1998 to 2005, was the Kansas 'evolution wars,' during which NCSE worked closely with Kansas Citizens for Science—a descendent of a Committee of Correspondence—to reverse a series of creationist-friendly revisions to the state science standards.[539]

This acknowledgment of covert operations highlights the NCSE's strategic influence in shaping the public narrative "behind the scenes" while allowing allies to take the lead publicly. By framing disputes as "flare-ups" and "evolution wars," Scott's language reinforces a sense of urgency and conflict while positioning the NCSE as the discreet yet pivotal player in a long-standing cultural and educational battle.

Throughout the book, Humes portrays intelligent design as a rejection of modernity and evolution as the "bulwark of modern biology and medical research," suggesting that any challenge to it endangers scientific progress.[540] He frames irreducible complexity as a weak and politically motivated tactic from the start, asserting that science is "a brutal arena where ideas are picked apart, attacked, and tested to see if they hold up," and that survival depends on "vibrant, meaningful, replicable research."[541] Yet this standard exposes the double expectation applied to ID. Evolutionary theory itself has never demonstrated, in a step-by-step, testable way, how systems like the bacterial flagellum or blood clotting cascade arose—yet it is treated as foundational. ID, on the other hand, is dismissed for failing to produce "hard laboratory research," even though its central critique is precisely that Darwinism has avoided this burden.

While painting ID as opposed to modernity, Humes may not be aware of other legitimate critiques presented by ID advocates, such as the debate over 'junk DNA.' Evolutionary biologists had long assumed that much of non-coding DNA was functionless. However, later discoveries revealed significant functions for these previously dismissed sequences—validating a key prediction of ID and simultaneously refuting a central assumption of speciation by natural selection.

Instead of addressing legitimate critiques, Humes reinforces the narrative of progress versus dogma. For instance, he writes:

> The nearly unanimous opinion of the scientific community is that evolution is the bulwark of modern biology and medical research... and that America's next generation of scientists will fall hopelessly behind... if evolutionary theory is watered down or banished from our schools.[542]

Yet nowhere does he provide an example of how the belief that all life diversified from a common ancestor has directly advanced medical research—or how questioning this belief would somehow cripple the next generation of scientists. No other hard science makes similar claims. There is no fear of "watered-down" gravity, chemistry, or quantum theory. Only evolution is treated as so fragile that disagreement is portrayed as sabotage. And the term "watered down science" is yet another example of Humes relying on Scott's idiolect to craft his narrative.[543] This framing ignores the scientific process of critique and revision that ID advocates contribute. It also makes it the more curious how he arrived at the title for his book.

Humes' uncritical framing of skepticism toward evolutionary theory as ignorance, whether tied to the *March of Progress* imagery or broader assumptions, is mirrored in the outdated views of prominent evolutionists he never questions. For example, the idea of junk DNA. In his widely praised book *Why Evolution Is True*, Jerry Coyne presents examples meant to affirm evolutionary theory, yet several of his claims, particularly regarding noncoding DNA, have since been refuted by modern research.[544]

Coyne's reliance on the notion of a "graveyard" of outdated or non-functional genes stands out as a flawed yet principal argument.[545] Coyne's assertions about pseudogenes, which he describes as evolutionary artifacts or "dead genes," reveal a level of overconfidence that modern findings have significantly undermined.[546] These erroneous conclusions are reinforced by authors like Humes, who craft a narrative celebrating the evolutionary establishment as the arbiter of modernity. Coyne's writes his central claim:

> Virtually every species harbors dead genes, many of them still active in its relatives. This implies that those genes were also active in a common ancestor and were killed off in some descendants but not in others... Our genome—and that of other species—are truly well-populated graveyards of dead genes.[547]

Contrary to Coyne's conclusions, many so-called "dead pseudogenes" have been resurrected from this theoretical graveyard and revealed to serve critical functional purposes in gene regulation and other cellular processes. For example, the PTENP1 *pseudogene* produces RNA that regulates the tumor suppressor gene PTEN.[548] Rather than being a "dead gene," PTENP1 helps control critical cellular processes by acting as a decoy for microRNAs.[549] As a study in *Nature* demonstrates, this activity has significant implications for cancer biology and gene regulation.[550]

Similarly, a review in *Cancers* (2023) highlights the involvement of *pseudogenes* in tumor progression, with some functioning as oncogenes or tumor suppressors.[551] The authors of the *Cancers* review emphasize the functional significance of pseudogenes, writing:

> ...increasing evidence points [to] the important role of pseudogenes in diverse cellular functions, and dysregulation of pseudogenes [is] often associated with various human diseases including cancer. Like other types of lncRNAs, pseudogenes can

also function as master regulators for gene expression and thus, they can play a critical role in various aspects of tumorigenesis[552]

These findings contradict Coyne's characterization of pseudogenes as nonfunctional, revealing instead that they are active participants in cellular networks.

The ENCODE project further complicates Coyne's argument. By demonstrating that much of the genome previously dismissed as "junk" is transcribed into RNA, ENCODE suggests that so-called pseudogenes may have broader roles than previously assumed.[553] While their exact functions remain under investigation, these findings challenge the assumption that pseudogenes are evolutionary leftovers with no purpose.

Coyne also uses the GULO pseudogene (ψGLO), related to vitamin C synthesis, as an example of evolutionary loss. He frames it as evidence of shared ancestry, asserting that:

> The most famous human pseudogene is GLO, so called because in other species it produces an enzyme called L-gulono-lactone oxidase. This enzyme is used in making vitamin C (ascorbic acid) from the simple sugar glucose... The reason why primates and these few other mammals don't make their own vitamin C is because they don't need to. Yet DNA sequencing tells us that primates still carry most of the genetic information needed to make the vitamin.[554]

While Coyne presents ψGLO as a "dead gene," he does not consider the possibility that it better reflects functional loss due to disuse rather than random accumulation. Unlike the original framing of junk DNA as purposeless debris, GULO's inactivation suggests a more specific process of genetic entropy where a previously functional gene became unnecessary in certain species due to dietary changes.

Coyne's discussion of embryonic hair (*lanugo*) further demonstrates his reliance on outdated assumptions. He claims that *lanugo* is a vestigial remnant of primate ancestry, writing:

> We are famously known as 'naked apes' because, unlike other primates, we don't have a thick coat of hair. But in fact, for one brief period we do—as embryos. Around six months after conception, we become completely covered with a fine, downy coat

of hair called lanugo... Now, there's no need for a human embryo to have a transitory coat of hair. After all, it's a cozy 98.6 degrees Fahrenheit in the womb. Lanugo can be explained only as a remnant of our primate ancestry.[555]

Lanugo, a fine hair covering the fetus during gestation, is often mischaracterized as a vestigial or functionless trait. However, research reveals that it serves a series of critical purposes during development. As described in *StatPearls*:

> Lanugo plays an essential role in binding the vernix caseosa to the skin of fetuses. Vernix caseosa is the viscous white covering on newborns that protects their skin, prevents water loss, plays an important role in thermoregulation, and contributes to innate immunity. It protects the fetus from damaging substances found in amniotic fluid, most notably urea and electrolytes.... It is shed at about 33 to 36 weeks gestation, when it becomes incorporated into the amniotic fluid, eventually contributing to the composition of the meconium.[556]

This refutes the claim that lanugo is a meaningless evolutionary remnant. Coyne's certainty in dismissing traits like lanugo as vestigial reflects a broader issue with overconfidence in Darwinian predictions that lack empirical substantiation. His assertions typify a pattern in Darwinian thinking that declares bad design while assuming such declarations require little scientific evidence to support them, because, after all, speciation by natural selection is certainly a fact.

Humes fails to see how many prominent figures, like Coyne, exemplify the dangers of conflating speciation by evolution with infallible science.

But remember, as we are frequently reminded, the scientific consensus is quite strong. Kenneth R. Miller has also championed the notion of "junk DNA" and pseudogenes as critical evidence against ID, asserting that their existence aligns with evolutionary theory while challenging the premise of a purposeful designer. Like Coyne, Miller has argued that features like pseudogenes represent evolutionary remnants, "mistakes" that a designer would not include.

In his 1994 article "Life's Grand Design," published in the *Technology Review*, Miller opens with a bold statement that encapsulates his central argument:

> Though some insist that life as we know it sprang from a Grand Designer's Original blueprints, Biology offers new evidence that organisms were cobbled together layer upon layer by a timeless tinkerer called evolution.[557]

Following this opening statement, Miller proceeds to argue that ID fails to account for the imperfections and redundancies found in the genome. He states:

> Intelligent design cannot explain the presence of a nonfunctional pseudogene, unless it is willing to allow that the designer made serious errors, wasting millions of bases of DNA on *a blueprint full of junk and scribbles. Evolution, however, can explain them easily*. Pseudogenes are nothing more than chance experiments in gene duplication that have failed, and they persist in the genome as evolutionary remnants of the past history of the b-globin genes.[558] [559]

Miller adheres more closely to the traditional evolutionary narrative of junk DNA as the accumulation of nonfunctional sequences through blind processes rather than focusing primarily on the loss of function in previously active genes. Miller expands this argument to dismiss the genome as a whole, describing it as a "hodgepodge" of "borrowed, copied, mutated, and discarded sequences," which he claims reflects "millions of years of trial and error" rather than deliberate design. Yet, as with Coyne's assertions, this view has been significantly refuted by subsequent research. Had Humes taken the time to explore the arguments of intelligent design instead of dismissing them with a handwave in an attempt to align with and appease the in-crowd, he might have avoided presenting skepticism of Darwinian evolution as ignorant or regressive.

PBS/NOVA

Another narrative following the Dover trial was PBS's docudrama *Judgment Day: Intelligent Design on Trial*, produced by PBS/NOVA and Vulcan Productions.[560] The program followed the same disinformation narrative, condescendingly framing the Dover board and ID as regressive and unscientific, while aligning with the in-crowd. The docudrama also emphasizes that Dover, Pennsylvania, was a town evenly divided over the issue of ID versus evolution. From the beginning, the narrator states: "like much of the United States, Dover has become a town divided."[561]

This suggests a balanced conflict, with equally weighted cultural backgrounds and competing perspectives. However, the docudrama contradicts its split down the middle narrative as it shifts between two conflicting portrayals of Dover. When expedient, it depicts the town as dominated by Christian creationists imposing their views, while at other times, it frames these traditionalists as fringe thinkers destined to be overpowered. By portraying the town as evenly divided, the trial appears to resolve a national-level conflict mirrored in Dover's microcosm. But this glosses over important details about the demographics and motivations of each side. It, too, ignores, for example, how national organizations like the ACLU and NCSE were involved in shaping the case, providing resources that gave one side, though outnumbered, disproportionate representation.

At the same time, it ignores the fact that the ID policy reflected the community's legitimate cultural priorities as expressed through their elected officials—not a radical imposition. This same pattern is evident in all the accounts—Humes, Lebo, Miller, the national press, and others—each presented as neutral, yet all systematically mute the voices of those who elected the board and legitimized its decision.

One of the more revealing moments in the PBS docudrama is its subtle yet deliberate narrative strategy to contrast the plaintiffs' arguments with what it portrays as the scientific ignorance of the Dover school board members. The segment highlights the courtroom testimony of Kevin Padian, a paleontologist and evolutionary biologist who served as an expert witness for the plaintiffs. The docudrama frames a presentation of "transitional fossils" as definitive evidence supporting evolution and refuting ID. From the narrator's perspective, the scene is triumphant:

> With each fossil, Padian refuted *Of Pandas and People's* claim that different life forms appear suddenly, by showing how fossils of

extinct organisms bridge the gaps between species, resulting in a picture of gradual evolution, just as Darwin proposed.⁵⁶²

Calling this a picture of "gradual evolution, just as Darwin proposed" ignores what must be demonstrated. Darwin proposed a slow, continuous process driven by natural selection and slight modifications. Padian's isolated fossil snapshots assumed to fit into that process are ad hoc evidence not triumphant presentations. These specimens are placed into a theoretical gradient that cannot be independently verified, only assumed to exist. Notably, the docudrama makes no mention of key contradictions in the fossil record, such as the Cambrian Explosion and other sudden appearances of life, what Stephen Jay Gould called "the trade secret of paleontology," a secret perhaps unknown to the PBS/NOVA producers, or simply unnecessary to their narrative.

Following this embellished framing, Padian himself reflects on the impact of his testimony with an air of satisfaction:

> The reporters in the courtroom were just amazed that we knew all this stuff. And how come they hadn't learned about this stuff before? And the reason is it's not in textbooks because the creationists fight so hard to keep it out. That's been a big influence.

This sense of intellectual triumph is continued by Eric Rothschild, the plaintiffs' attorney, who recalls how even Judge Jones was captivated by the testimony:

> The court took a break. And I remember the judge saying something like ... 'biology class adjourned,' you know, 'for lunch.' And he was, you know, smiling. And it was clear that we had the judge interested in science.⁵⁶³

The narrator pivots abruptly from celebrating the supposed explanatory power of evolution to asking a cleverly reversed question that feigns neutrality:

> Lawyers for the parents may have impressed the judge and reporters. But many in Dover wondered, 'Why is evolution taught as fact if it's just a theory?'⁵⁶⁴

Then, Bonsell's remarks are positioned immediately after the plaintiffs are portrayed as having convincingly impressed everyone—from the media to the judge—with overwhelming evidence in support of evolution. The camera cuts to Bonsell, the school board chairman, who responds:

> Maybe Darwinism is the prevalent theory out there today, but it is a theory. It isn't a law of science. It isn't, you know, a fact. It is a theory.[565]

The editing splices in Bonsell's comments as if to provide a counterpoint, but instead uses his words to highlight what the filmmakers framed as ignorance. This setup ensures Bonsell's statement stands in contrast to the narrative of scientific triumph, portraying him as the voice of outdated thinking opposing what is presented as irrefutable common knowledge. This type of gaslighting seems to never grow old.

It's interesting, however, that these scientific experts accused ID proponents of bypassing scientific norms by attempting to introduce ID into the curriculum without broader acceptance by the scientific community, while simultaneously bringing local school board members to trial and asking the court to declare that ID is not science. Rather than confronting the more formidable ID proponents directly within academia, they relied on a judge's opinion to determine what qualifies as science. This judicial ruling, combined with their consensus, now serves as a kind of deed of trust, claiming rightful ownership over scientific thought.

The docudrama portrayed Behe in a manner that continued the mockery. The antagonistic framing reduces an esteemed biochemist to a caricature rather than addressing his arguments thoroughly. One example of this antagonistic tone is the description of Behe's testimony when he is confronted with a stack of scientific literature that allegedly refutes his claims of irreducible complexity. The narrator states:

> Michael Behe was asked to look at a stack of scientific papers... he acknowledged he had not read most of them, yet he insisted they were irrelevant.[566]

This scene dramatizes the courtroom exchange. As if merely stacking a mountain of unidentified books with unverified arguments in front of Behe refutes his argument. The camera cuts to Nick Matzke, who boasts, "Behe was almost dwarfed by the stack of scientific literature." This is followed by a shot of the actor portraying Behe, looking disoriented and responding in a strained voice: "Mr. Rothschild, would you like your books back? They're heavy."

Yet this "stacking" tactic misrepresents Behe's core argument. He never denied that superficial evolutionary explanations exist; rather, he argued that at the molecular level, no form of Darwinism adequately explains irreducibly complex systems like the bacterial flagellum. His challenge was whether these explanations provide a feasible, testable mechanism for how such structures could arise through random mutation and natural selection. The dramatization, however, paints Behe as someone unwilling to consider evidence, while it fails to provide the audience with any specifics about the content of the literature stacked up before him. The choice to dramatize and dwell on this moment as a spectacle diminishes the seriousness of this docudrama.

This antagonistic portrayal contrasts sharply with how the docudrama treats proponents of evolution like Kenneth R. Miller. His speculative arguments are presented as authoritative and unassailable, with his explanations supported by confident narration, while Behe's arguments are ridiculed or dismissed, often accompanied by a skeptical tone from the narrator.

Further, plaintiffs like Tammy Kitzmiller are presented as relatable, vulnerable figures. Figures such as William Buckingham, are reduced to stereotypes of ignorance or extremism. Kitzmiller is depicted as the emotional and moral center of the case. In a dramatized scene, the docudrama depicts her walking to her mailbox, accompanied by ominous western-style guitar strums that evoke the tension of an impending duel. The narrator notes:

> While the battle in federal court heated up, the atmosphere in Dover had gone from divisive to dangerous. Tammy Kitzmiller, the lead plaintiff in the case, who had a daughter in ninth grade biology

class at Dover High School, had been receiving hate mail since the start of the trial.

The scene transitions from her walk to the mailbox to her sitting at her kitchen table, where she removes a letter from an envelope and begins reading aloud. Her tone turns somber as she comments:

> One letter was pretty disturbing. I think this was the one with the passage that...the last sentence especially:
>
> *Madeline Murray was found murdered for taking prayer and Bible reading out of schools, so watch out for a bullet.*
>
> This was a letter that I made sure my lawyers got a copy of, and it was forwarded to the FBI. [567]

The one "pretty disturbing" letter they chose to dramatize was a threat citing the murder of "Madeline Murray." However, no such person was murdered for removing prayer from schools. This seems like a badly staged reference to Madalyn Murray O'Hair, the well-known atheist activist who was murdered in 1995—but not for her role in the school prayer controversy.[568]

O'Hair was involved in one of the key cases that led to the removal of school-sponsored Bible readings, but she did not single-handedly "remove prayer." Her lawsuit, *Murray v. Curlett* (1963), was consolidated with *Abington School District v. Schempp*, leading to the 8-1 Supreme Court ruling that struck down mandatory Bible reading and prayer in public schools.[569] However, *Engel v. Vitale* (1962) had already prohibited state-sponsored prayer a year earlier.[570]

Notably, Kitzmiller's letter's claim is not only historically false but completely absurd—O'Hair was kidnapped and murdered by a former employee, David Roland Waters, in a crime motivated by money, not ideology.[571] Waters, a former atheist, had worked for American Atheists, the organization O'Hair founded, before being fired for embezzlement. The fact that O'Hair was murdered by another atheist further questions the letter's credibility. If anything, it exposes its author as deeply misinformed or deliberately misleading.

PBS had covered O'Hair multiple times in the past—interviewing her on PBS Late Night, its first nationally broadcast talk and viewer phone-in television program, and publishing several articles about her after her murder. O'Hair was a prominent figure in church-state debates, and her grisly death was widely reported. Any competent researcher or producer working on a documentary involving science, religion, and public education would have been familiar with her name and case.

Most notably, the PBS docudrama refers to Madalyn Murray in the dramatized letter, deliberately omitting "O'Hair" from her full name. This omission alone is suspicious, but the official PBS/NOVA transcript goes further by misspelling it as "Madeline" instead of "Madalyn," mistakes not made in any of its other coverage on her. The misname is familiar enough, however, to ring a bell, triggering an emotional association. With knowing these details, it is the plausible that the letter itself was fabricated or deliberately staged for dramatic effect. Given PBS's prior interviews and coverage of O'Hair, they were clearly aware of the real circumstances of her death. The name alteration appears designed to exploit public familiarity while distancing the program from any accountability for perpetuating a bogus threat.

This reminds me of an experience from my late teens when some friends had a damages dispute that ended up on Judge Joe Brown's TV court.[572] According to the plaintiff, my friend and the cousin of the defendant, the show asked him for receipts. When he said he had none, they simply made receipts for him to use as props. That's what the letter presented in the docudrama reminds me of, something contrived yet useful for framing a dramatic narrative.

Nevertheless, this scene casts Kitzmiller as a vulnerable yet brave individual standing up against an oppressive environment that even threatens her life. The deliberate choice of guitar strums and the slow, deliberate pacing of the dramatization reinforce her role as a damsel in distress. It frames Kitzmiller as a victim of a broader societal struggle, which implicitly elevates her moral standing.

Another creative moment in the docudrama involved the Rehm family, framed inside a church, singing hymns alongside their children. For this spiritual scene, the production team had to secure permission from the church, arrange the props, and direct the family to perform hymns to create a sense of moral and religious authenticity. This choice is used to counter accusations that the trial was anti-religious, painting the plaintiffs as "rational Christians" who stood on the right side of both faith and science.

The PBS documentary subtly frames the narrative to condition viewers into believing that:

- A Christian who conforms to evolutionary theory and rejects a literal Genesis is to be praised as a "model Christian"—rational, enlightened, and acceptable in secular discourse.
- A Christian who affirms a literal Genesis, supports intelligent design, or questions evolution is to be dismissed as an "insufferable Christian"—anti-science, ignorant, or even a problem to be corrected.

This selective framing ignores the fact that many ID proponents, such as Michael Behe, were practicing Christians or other individuals of faith who saw no conflict between their beliefs and their scientific critiques of Darwinian evolution. At the time, Behe did not reject evolution entirely—he accepted common descent but argued that natural selection alone was insufficient to explain irreducibly complex biological structures. Yet the docudrama refuses to acknowledge this nuance, offering no positive framing of Behe or any other Christians who support ID. Instead, the design argument itself is treated as irreconcilable, regardless of one's broader theological or scientific beliefs.

The PBS special even positively highlights Lauri Lebo's personal connection to Christianity, with the narrator stating:

> But her interest in the issue was not just professional, it was also personal. Lauri's father had been the owner of a local radio station, but the oldies format wasn't paying the bills, and the electric company was about to put him off the air.[573]

Narration cuts to Lebo, and she states:

> The next day a gentleman came in who belonged to a local church…wanted to lease programming on the radio station and offered to pay a decent sum of money. And overnight the radio

station became [a] Christian radio station. My father became born again.[574]

Thus, the docudrama goes out of its way to portray plaintiffs and their in-crowd affiliates as either fundamentally Christian or having Christian ties. In contrast, it avoids addressing the secular or overtly anti-religious motivations of figures like Eugenie C. Scott and organizations like the ACLU, among others.

In truth, the 'Wizard of Oz' behind the consensus-of-science curtain was the NCSE's Eugenie C. Scott. Her and her organization acted as the chief architect, educating disgruntled teachers, board members, plaintiffs, the ACLU, Lauri Lebo, Edward Humes, local newspapers, PBS, and by extension, Judge Jones on what intelligent design is and why it should not be considered science. Each of these players relied explicitly or implicitly on the NCSE's framing to build their case and shape public perception. Eugenie Scott has repeatedly and explicitly stated that the NCSE was the mastermind behind educating concerned citizens who contacted her organization to oppose ID. She has also acknowledged that many of these citizens had little to no understanding of why ID was not considered science.

Scott's organization provided the attorneys and witnesses for the case. Eric Rothschild and Vic Walczak, two of the lead attorneys for the plaintiffs, relied heavily on NCSE guidance. Walczak even admitted that he knew little about science before becoming involved in the case.[575] Despite his lack of scientific expertise, he played a critical role in crafting the legal strategy, which was built entirely on NCSE arguments against ID.

Similarly, Judge Jones openly admitted in interviews that he had no background in science before presiding over the case, at one point even referring to the courtroom as Miller's biology class. This reveals the extent to which Jones deferred entirely to the NCSE's definition of science and its arguments against ID, rather than independently evaluating the claims at issue. In a way, Scott and the NCSE even supplied the court's opinion. Consider this: an organization founded on promoting speciation by evolution acted as the state's authority in determining whether ID should be considered science. The very group ideologically opposed to ID was given the power to define science, ensuring that the ruling aligned with their preexisting position.

PBS/NOVA mentions that the Discovery Institute declined their invitation to participate in the docudrama, stating:

> We asked proponents of intelligent design, including the Discovery Institute, to participate in the documentary. They declined our invitation to be interviewed under NOVA's normal journalistic conditions.[576]

This framing suggests that the DI refused to engage in a fair dialogue, subtly implying weakness or evasion. However, PBS/NOVA failed to disclose the DI stated reasons for declining, which casts their absence in a very different light.

The DI seems to have had legitimate concerns about misrepresentation, citing PBS's past productions—particularly the *Evolution* series—as evidence of editorial bias. To address this, the DI says it requested to independently record their interviews as a safeguard, ensuring they could verify the accuracy of how their statements were presented in the docudrama. According to the DI:

> We asked for the right to videotape our interviews so we would have a full record of what we actually said. PBS refused.[577]

This request, based in concerns over potential selective editing, was allegedly dismissed by the producers of PBS/NOVA. Notably, from the final product of the docudrama *Judgment Day: Intelligent Design on Trial*, it is clear that the DI's caution was well-founded. Yet PBS/NOVA presents the DI's refusal without context, leaving the impression that their absence reflected an unwillingness to defend their views rather than an effort to ensure fair representation. By omitting the DI's rationale, PBS's online disclaimer about why the DI didn't participate misleads viewers.

The Discovery Institute

In some discussions of origins, there remains a lingering ambivalence in how certain figures at the Discovery Institute rhetorically position themselves. At times, their posture resembles a kind of intellectual

Stockholm syndrome. Certain members and associates seem psychologically or socially tethered to the same academic establishment they claim to critique. It's as if they still feel the need to earn credibility from institutions and traditions whose core assumptions they supposedly reject.

They distance themselves from Biblical creationists—sometimes with unnecessary condescension—as if doing so secures their place within the intellectual in-crowd. There's a tendency to tread carefully—publicly critiquing methodological naturalism while constrained by an unspoken expectation to stay within its guidelines for academic respectability. In this way, the DI is diminished as a revolutionary force and more like a group seeking to preserve a seat at the decrepit table of an intellectual elite that has already defined the terms of acceptable discourse. This tendency is sometimes evident in their affirmations of mainstream cosmology, particularly their description of the "Big Bang"—a theory that, stripped of euphemism, is a claim of instant creation rebranding as "inflation."[578]

It is clear from the vast array of supernatural theories relied upon by proponents of radical Materialism that the rules of the game are rigged, leaving no reason for the Discovery Institute or associates to adhere to these arbitrary constraints or to distance themselves from Biblical creationists due to a stigma that is merely projected by materialists. After all, the rhetorical framing of special creation pales in comparison to the notion of a cosmic, self-replicating organ that takes nothing and produces indefatigable special creations.

The notion that nothing must accumulate or grow into functioning cosmic and biological systems through unrealized processes—rather than being created at once—does not resolve the issue; it only makes it more absurd. It deepens the problem rather than explaining it. Given the premises of radical Materialism, Biblical creationists have no reason to set aside their faith or relinquish their motives and Christian values just to conform to the rules of an ideology that refuses to acknowledge its own contradictions.

Biblical creationists should never be discouraged from resisting religious-viewpoint discrimination, especially when legal or academic institutions selectively apply standards to silence certain perspectives while protecting others. If radical materialist worldviews are allowed to shape scientific and educational discourse, then Biblical creationists have just as much right to challenge these narratives without being dismissed as the ones religiously motivated.

The way the Dover school board, for example, handled their local situation and their form of resistance should not be ridiculed or sold out for the approval of those who sued them to uphold a self-refuting theory. The issue is not when or how the challenge was made, but that the state compelled the school district—against its will—to teach what may well be a scientific folk tale as legitimate science education. Objectively speaking, despite ridicule and stigmatization, traditional creationists have been the most consistent in their positions and predictions—especially when compared to the shifting strategies of materialists and even some mainstream ID advocates.

Consider the DI's Casey Luskin, a scientist and an attorney, for example. He has presented a contradictory defense of the Dover school board's actions that reflects a deeper, fundamental divide between the DI and Biblical creationists. These traditional creationists openly embrace their faith as the foundation for their views on life's origins, while the Discovery Institute strives to frame ID as a purely scientific theory, divorced from religious underpinnings.

In doing so, they hold themselves to an impossible standard—one that neither materialists nor Biblical creationists adhere to, as each clearly chooses their philosophical line. Despite the semantic games, by definition, Materialism cannot be strictly scientific, as it begins with a metaphysical assumption that excludes anything beyond naturalistic explanations, regardless of the evidence. It declares, 'We can't say anything about that, nor can we see your evidence about that.'

This contrast becomes especially apparent in how the DI continues to straddle the line between public scientific neutrality and private philosophical commitment. In a 2021 video on the Discovery Institute YouTube channel, Luskin begins by scolding the Dover school board, claiming they ignored the

DI's explicit warnings against mandating the teaching of ID in classrooms. He asserts:

> Discovery Institute explicitly said to Dover: 'Don't adopt a policy that requires the teaching of intelligent design.'[579]

Contrary to Luskin's adamant claim, as mentioned, the Dover school board did not require the teaching of ID. Their policy included a brief disclaimer stating that evolution is a theory, and it directed students to a library resource, *Of Pandas and People*, for those students interested. Luskin himself admits this when he subsequently states:

> The whole controversy and the most controversial part of the short four-paragraph statement was this paragraph right here. It said: 'Intelligent design is an explanation of the origin of life that differs from Darwin's view. The reference book *Of Pandas and People* is available for students who might be interested in gaining an understanding of what intelligent design actually involves.' It was this short, two-sentence statement that basically caused all of the controversy.[580]

This contradiction between accusing the board of mandating ID while simultaneously rationalizing their decision reveals a fundamental discrepancy in Luskin's argument and underscores the difference between how the DI and traditional creationists approach such debates.

He continues, explaining the DI's reasoning:

> It's important to understand why Discovery Institute takes this approach. It's not the case that somehow, we think that ID is unconstitutional or that it's not science and therefore shouldn't be taught. No, we think ID is science. *We think that ID should be considered constitutional to teach in public schools.* The reason why Discovery Institute opposes pushing ID into public schools—and this was our policy before Dover, this is our policy after Dover, and this has been our policy since Dover—the reason we oppose mandating ID is because *our priority with intelligent design is to see it grow and develop as a scientific theory.*[581]

On the one hand, the DI critiques methodological naturalism as an unfair limitation imposed by the scientific establishment to exclude ID from being considered a valid scientific theory. On the other hand, they advocate for ID to "grow and develop as a scientific theory" within the same framework that upholds methodological naturalism as its foundational principle.

Emphasizing ID's potential as an 'accepted' scientific theory perhaps reflects the DI's desire to be taken seriously by the academic in-crowd from which its fellows received their education and a sense of scientific value. The DI's approach betrays a certain naïveté. Its strategy assumes that if ID can be framed scientifically enough, it will eventually gain acceptance within the academic establishment. But this ignores much deeper ideological forces at play—ones that cannot be rationalized away because they are not based on scientific inquiry or reason.

The more we uncover the implausibility of the universe and diverse life arising by chance, the more materialists respond with increasingly speculative conclusions. Consider this: if every molecular interaction and biochemical reaction is counted as an individual process, a single human cell experiences millions of simultaneous interactions at any given moment. Cells contain billions of molecules. A simple cell contains an estimated 42 million protein molecules, along with vast numbers of RNA molecules, lipids, metabolites, and ions.[582] Water molecules, while smaller, are present in trillions per cell and undergo approximately 10^{27} hydrogen bond exchanges per second, further amplifying the sheer scale of molecular interactions occurring at any given moment, all engaged in constant, coordinated activity.[583] [584]

With approximately 10,000–15,000 distinct protein types per cell, over 100,000 across all cell types in the human body—many of which catalyze thousands of reactions per second—the biochemical complexity is staggering.[585] Human cells alone execute over 25,000 documented metabolic reactions, occurring across cytoplasmic and organelle compartments in perfect synchronization.[586] This level of organization defies the notion that life arose spontaneously in prebiotic conditions.

Despite this, materialists cling to the notion that the first microbial cell formed in an environment such as in deep-sea hydrothermal vents, where mineral-rich, hot water met cold ocean water, supposedly creating energy gradients sufficient to drive these complex chemical reactions.[587] From this single hypothetical organism, they conclude that an indefatigable process eventually resulted in the human body, while failing to address the origin of the very conditions necessary for this hypothetical process. To put this into perspective, the number of biochemical reactions occurring in the human body every second could exceed the number of stars in the observable universe. While the cosmos contains an estimated 10^{22}–10^{24} stars, the 37 trillion cells in the human body, each carrying out millions to billions of interactions per second, together likely surpass this count.[588]

Rather than acknowledge the overwhelming evidence for design, materialists create increasingly elaborate workarounds to sustain their framework. Forgive the redundancy here. Let's revisit some key concepts that testify to the intransigence of these thinkers. The inflationary multiverse was introduced to explain the homogeneity of the cosmic microwave background, yet it ultimately concedes what it was meant to avoid—that the universe appeared at once in a highly ordered state. Rather than acknowledging this as evidence of design, inflation is framed as a 'natural' process, even though it describes an event that, by all observable evidence, resembles an instantaneous, finely tuned beginning.

Likewise, the Many-Worlds Interpretation of quantum mechanics proposes that every possible outcome spawns a new universe—an ad hoc move that sidesteps the question of why quantum systems appear influenced by observation. In the case of abiogenesis, materialists also turn to speculative ideas like panspermia, suggesting life came from elsewhere. The Anthropic Principle is often cited as an alternative to design, but like inflationary theory, it amounts to a tautology: we observe a life-permitting universe because we're here to observe it.

Beyond biology, we are told that 95% of the universe is composed of invisible matter and energy—yet this claim rests on logic similar to that used by ID proponents, which is typically dismissed as unscientific. The term "invisible" is conveniently euphemized as "dark." As discussed in Chapter 21, quantum mechanics presents phenomena such as entanglement that defy classical materialism. Rather than entertain models based on information or observer-dependent realities, many physicists fall back on hidden variable theories like superdeterminism—a view that the universe is entirely deterministic, and that measurement outcomes are pre-correlated with the choices of what and how to measure.[589]

When faced with the hard problem of consciousness, materialists like Robert Sapolsky and Daniel Dennett declare phenomena such as consciousness and free will to be illusions, paradoxically denying the very faculties through which they reason. This stance dismisses subjective experience and undermines the basis for moral and personal responsibility. Others, struggling to explain why we perceive an ordered universe rather than randomness, propose the Boltzmann Brain hypothesis, suggesting we are disembodied, fleeting fluctuations in a meaningless cosmos—an absurd conclusion born out of strict adherence Materialism.[590]

Similarly, evolutionary biologists frequently construct just-so stories to explain the emergence of irreducibly complex systems in the absence of conclusive fossil or genetic evidence. Perhaps most telling is the rise of the Simulation Hypothesis, where materialists openly entertain the idea that the universe is designed—but by an advanced civilization rather than a Creator.

The increasing reliance on untestable, speculative theories reveals that the resistance to design is not rooted in science but in a cult-like ideology—one that operates as if driven by a compulsively insidious spirit. The DI's vision sounds appealing, but there will be no slow and steady rise of ID into mainstream science. It won't gradually earn a seat at the traditional table. Standard origins science is a situation that defies reasoning. No amount of empirical evidence will persuade those committed to a worldview chronically allergic to the idea of purpose, especially spiritual. Design will not gain acceptance by conforming to materialist expectations; it will only be recognized when the current paradigm collapses under its own contradictions.

For Biblical creationists, their statements about evolution are not only essential to a worldview that acknowledges the role of a Creator but also represent what they see as scientifically accurate interpretations. This conviction transcends strategy—it does not allow for distancing from what they see as true. They should not be demeaned for holding that both evolution is implausible and that Genesis accurately describes creation and history.

Luskin insists—almost pretentiously—that ID is a scientific theory, not a religious belief, stating:

> What we're doing is *substantively different* from Creationism. Creationism *always appeals to a* supernatural Creator, and what we wanted to do was to stay within the empirical domain and not get into this *religious stuff*.[591]

Avoiding the name of the designer does not change the fundamental nature of the argument—it only introduces ambiguity about who or what the designer is. From a Biblical creationist perspective, "always" acknowledging a supernatural Creator isn't just "religious stuff"—it's a fundamental truth about reality. For them, debating whether a universe could evolve from the absence of space and time to a world with weddings and college graduations is the real "religious stuff." They would likely argue that the distinction being drawn here, between empirical science and Biblical Creationism, is itself a product of methodological naturalism, which arbitrarily excludes the possibility of design from scientific consideration.

For traditional creationists, this concession is unacceptable. They see it as denying the truth of Romans 1:20 (NIV), which declares:

> For since the creation of the world, God's invisible qualities—his eternal power and divine nature—have been clearly seen, being understood from what has been made, so that people are without excuse.

Yet, materialists are free to hold to their own sweeping metaphysical claims under the guise of scientific neutrality. As written in the Book of Sagan, Chapter 1980:

> The cosmos is all that is, or ever was, or ever will be.

Unlike creationist claims, such pronouncements are rarely scrutinized as religious or ideological. Just as materialists do, Biblical creationists view separation from their religious foundations as unnecessary and even harmful, as it reinforces the false narrative that science and faith must remain separate.

The DI's approach, as defended by Luskin, also highlights a divide in how these two groups view the consequences of conforming to the secular establishment. Luskin laments that the Dover trial politicized ID and caused backlash against its proponents, resulting in religious persecution. He states:

> We speculated—correctly—that if ID got pushed into public schools, it would take the debate out of the scientific realm and push it into the political realm. Unfortunately, that's exactly what happened in the wake of the Dover case.[592]

He further argues that the board's actions "increased discrimination against pro-ID scientists." Luskin adamantly expressed concern about the repercussions of the Dover trial, stating:

> It's actually going to result in more and more discrimination and *persecution* against pro-ID scientists at the universities. It's going to make it harder for them to make their case for ID to the scientific community. ... We saw an intense spike in the level of persecution of pro-ID scientists and faculty in the post-Dover era.[593]

This framing portrays the DI as foresighted and strategic, while casting the Dover board as reckless for not heeding their advice. While Luskin views this as a strategic failure, traditional creationists would argue that enduring such challenges is part of standing for truth. As Jesus taught in Matthew 5:10 (ESV):

> Blessed are those who are persecuted for righteousness' sake, for theirs is the kingdom of heaven.

They view the willingness to face opposition for the sake of proclaiming God's truth as a central tenet of their mission, consistent with Biblical teachings like 2 Timothy 3:12 (ESV):

> Indeed, all who desire to live a godly life in Christ Jesus will be persecuted.

For Biblical creationists, avoiding persecution by separating faith from science is not an option, as doing so compromises the integrity of their testimony about their Creator. By criticizing the board's disclaimer as problematic while still affirming its message, Luskin muddies the waters, making it unclear whether the DI supports challenging evolution in classrooms or simply finds the board's method inconvenient.

This ambiguity highlights the difference between the DI's cautious, secular strategy and the unapologetic stance of Biblical creationists, who refuse to hide their faith under the guise of neutrality. As Jesus said in Matthew 5:14-15 (ESV):

> You are the light of the world. A city set on a hill cannot be hidden. Nor do people light a lamp and put it under a basket, but on a stand, and it gives light to all in the house.

The difference between the Discovery Institute and organizations like Answers in Genesis is significant—not just on issues like the age of the Earth, but also in certain aspects of their worldview. For Biblical creationists, any effort to separate faith from discussions of life's origins is tantamount to hiding that light under a basket.

Unlike public institutions, which conform to the dominant paradigm's definition of secular neutrality, the Discovery Institute is not bound by such constraints and has the liberty to reject them. However, rather than exercising this freedom, it operates within the same framework by avoiding explicitly religious claims or naming a designer—an approach that traditional creationists reject as incompatible with their faith. Those who dismiss the Discovery Institute's approach as a mere ploy fail to recognize the genuine philosophical and theological divide at play, only reinforcing the distinction and proving that the two cannot be conflated.

What is most striking about Luskin's argument is his assertion that the judge should have stopped at the first prong of the Lemon Test, which examines whether a government action has a secular purpose. Luskin states, "Once you find evidence of religious motives... you should stop," citing *Edwards v. Aguillard* (1987) as precedent. This interpretation aligns with how courts have applied Lemon, striking down policies based on religious intent alone. However, this approach is legally flawed because a secular purpose does not require the absence of religious motivation—a policy can still serve a legitimate secular function even if some supporters are religiously motivated.

Although *Edwards* did not establish the Lemon Test (which originated in *Lemon v. Kurtzman* (1971)), it expanded its application, making perceived religious intent a decisive factor in constitutionality. This shift meant that a policy could be invalidated not for what it did but for why legislators supported it. Luskin, as a lawyer, would be aware of this, making his acceptance of the ruling seem like a deeper bias rather than legal deference.

Judge Jones relied on this same flawed reasoning in *Kitzmiller v. Dover*, treating the board members' religious beliefs as proof that their policy lacked a secular purpose. Yet Lemon is supposed to evaluate the policy itself—not the personal motivations of those who support it. By accepting the court's reasoning, Luskin implicitly conceded to an expanded interpretation of Lemon rather than contesting whether the policy had a legitimate secular purpose apart from any religious motivations.

This is an odd argument for Luskin to make. Legal reasoning does not demand surrender at the first sign of religious influence—courts are supposed to interpret laws within the broader constitutional framework of neutrality. Yet Luskin's position effectively concedes that ID was being taught as religion, which contradicts the Discovery Institute's core claim that ID is a scientific theory. Though this is surely not his intent, it is unclear why he frames the board's actions as strategic malpractice. It may suggest that the Discovery Institute never intended to be an ally from the beginning and was uncomfortable with the resistance of traditional creationists in a fight they saw themselves as leading.

The distinction between *Edwards* and *Kitzmiller* is that Biblical creationism was not recognized as a scientific theory, whereas flaws in evolution are openly debated within scientific circles. The *Edwards* ruling rejected mandating Creationism because it was seen as advancing a religious doctrine rather than scientific inquiry. However, critiquing evolution serves a secular purpose and is not inherently religious, as debate over its weaknesses exists outside of religious contexts—public schools exclude it only because of legal and ideological barriers.

Thus, the court's reasoning in the Dover trial, taken to its logical conclusion, suggests that a school board would be barred from introducing any scientific ideas that align with religious perspectives. For example, if a school board were the first to introduce the idea that the universe had a beginning—a scientific position that also aligns with Biblical creationism—would that have been considered religious instruction or a primarily religious effort to be struck down? This does not seem to reflect the original intent of the Lemon Test. The mere fact that a scientific claim has religious implications does not mean its *primary effect* is religious. To interpret the law this way is to engage in *viewpoint discrimination*, where only perspectives that align with secular Materialism are permitted in public education.

The Constitution does not entitle courts to sanction or suppress religious perspectives. Dover's board did not attempt to mandate the teaching of Noah's flood or a young age of the Earth; rather, it questioned the sufficiency of Darwinian explanations. The disclaimer itself was non-religious, and while its implications may have supported religious belief, implication is not the same as primary purpose or effect. The law must be clarified in the higher court, not conceded through vague interpretations that allow it to be wielded as a tool for suppressing certain viewpoints.

It doesn't seem likely that a competent lawyer would have given such legal counsel or abandoned a viewpoint discrimination case simply because a lower court applied *Edwards* to a distinct situation like Dover. A serious legal challenge would have exposed how secular critiques of evolution remain permissible, while any skepticism aligned with religious perspectives is treated as unconstitutional.

Instead of contesting this form of viewpoint discrimination—one that disproportionately impacts those whom religious freedom laws are meant to protect—the Discovery Institute distanced itself from the case, reinforcing the precedent rather than challenging it. With stronger institutional support, the case could have been elevated to a higher court, where the misapplication of *Edwards* could have been properly challenged. Twenty years have passed, and the precedent set by Dover still stands, reinforcing the ideological cleansing of religious perspectives from public discourse. Had there been real resistance, the issue could have been clarified, even if it meant losing at the highest level. What was there to lose in standing firm—not just for academic freedom, but against a legal double standard that permits secular critiques of evolution while silencing any that align with religious beliefs?

By failing to show up and challenge this misapplication of the Lemon Test, the Discovery Institute stood by as the board was vilified for promoting ID. And then, to add insult to injury, there has been the repeated "We told you so" antagonizing from those who had insisted the board's actions would fail. This raises the question of whether its initial engagement was merely to reproach the board, only to later stand by, wagging their heads as it sank.

The court's decision ultimately elevated evolution beyond scientific critique, granting it a privileged, sacred status in public education. If ID was wrongly categorized as religious, then the Discovery Institute should have fought to correct that classification—regardless of the risk to its institutional credibility. If Luskin was right that the judge correctly ruled it as religious, then DI has fundamentally undermined its own claim that ID is science. It cannot be both ways. In Luskin's public video, he conceded far too much in his acceptance of the court's reasoning, failing to acknowledge that this case was not just about ID or its strategy—it was about (Christian) viewpoint discrimination.

Discrimination has never been overturned by passivity or compromise. It has always required bold resistance, often at great cost, even precious blood. History does not show that injustices resolve themselves. Progress comes from persistence in the face of persecution. The Dover trial should not have been the end of the debate, nor should it have "quelled flare-ups." It should have ignited a wave of new challenges that forced the courts to clarify their stance: Are they merely preventing state-sponsored religious indoctrination, or are they actively suppressing a worldview while elevating another?

The proper response to such a ruling was to force the courts to confront the consequences of their own logic. Materialists were never content to accept a competing view in scientific discourse; they pushed relentlessly until their worldview was enshrined in law, academia, and culture. That same level of persistence is required to challenge a legal system that now favors them not because their arguments are stronger, but because their opponents have been discouraged from fighting back. This was about whether a Christian perspective could exist within scientific discourse at all. It cannot be overstated that that fight should not have ended with Dover; it should have escalated.

Chapter 11

Dystopian Tale

> *But, among the things that science does know, evolution is about as certain as anything we know. And that, of course, as you know, is accepted by responsible educated churchmen, as well as scientists. ... Evolution has been observed. It's just that it hasn't been observed while it's happening. ... Once you understand how Darwinism works, then you could easily see that that's a far better, far more parsimonious, far more scientific explanation than intelligent design.*[594]
> —Richard Dawkings

The Dover trial was ostensibly about science education. Its dynamics revealed a struggle over control, narrative, and the boundaries of permissible thought. Let's take a closer look at the details of how surrounding elements of this trial evoke striking parallels with Orwell's *1984*, a dystopian tale of an authoritarian regime that manipulates truth, suppresses dissent, and enforces ideological conformity. Orwell's Party in *1984* sought to maintain dominance by controlling information and thought; similarly, the trial's focus on enforcing radical Materialism and silencing dissenting perspectives reflects the conflict between authority and intellectual freedom. But first, let's take a detour and look at Ultron.

Ultron

The ideology driving the Dover trial was like something out of a Marvel comic. Similar to Ultron in *Avengers: Age of Ultron*, those opposing Creationism sought to portray their materialist vision of human origins as the only acceptable narrative.[595] Ultron's philosophy of evolution also revolves around enforcing a singular perspective on human progress. Ultron's belief in *forced evolution* parallels the mindset of radical materialists who view spiritual perspectives, such as creationism, as outdated obstacles.[596]

His famous line, "How is humanity saved if it's not allowed to evolve?"[597] embodies an ideology that prioritizes deterministic progress while dismissing alternative viewpoints as impediments. Similarly, such figures aim to eradicate dissenting beliefs through cultural and educational dominance.

Ultron dismisses humanity's emotional and spiritual essence, seeing it as a flaw in the evolutionary process. He positions himself as the catalyst for progress. His disdain for the Avengers, whom he mocks as "unbearably naive," underscores his belief that opposition is futile and merely delays the inevitable. This reflects the attitude of those who view spiritual beliefs as temporary resistance to a perceived march of intellectual progress—a march they believe will inevitably extinguish spirituality.[598] What this ideology overlooks is that spirituality is an integral aspect of humanity, as demonstrated by the tendency to ascribe creative qualities to nature itself.

Mr. O'Brien

In *1984*, Orwell captures the Party's totalitarian grasp over truth and reality through the protagonist Winston Smith's internal reflections. Winston observes the Party's inevitable demand for absolute belief:

> In the end the Party would announce that two and two made five, and you would have to believe it. It was inevitable that they should make that claim sooner or later: the logic of their position demanded it. Not merely the validity of experience, but the very existence of external reality, was tacitly denied by their philosophy. The heresy of heresies was common sense... The Party told you to reject the evidence of your eyes and ears. It was their final, most essential command.[599]

Here, Winston identifies the Party's ultimate strategy—not just denying objective truth but forcing individuals to internalize and believe falsehoods. By targeting "the heresy of heresies," common sense, the Party ensures that nothing outside its narrative can exist. This passage foreshadows the lengths to which the Party will go in breaking Winston, illustrating the terrifying consequences of authoritarian control over reality.

The Party manipulates reality by erasing objective facts and enforcing collective acceptance of its narrative. Winston is coerced into believing the Party's claim that "two and two makes five." Through this mantra, reality becomes whatever the Party decrees, irrespective of evidence or logic, and dissent is eradicated by the force of authority rather than debate.

A pivotal moment occurs when Winston, subjected to torture and psychological manipulation in Room 101, faces the authority of the "Ministry of Love." The Ministry of Love, through Room 101 and its other methods, is the embodiment of the Party's psychological dominance, demonstrating how it enforces obedience not just through physical torture but by eroding personal loyalties, breaking down individuality, and instilling unconditional loyalty to Big Brother.[600] Here, Mr. O'Brien is a high-ranking member of the Inner Party and plays a central role in Winston's "re-education."[601] Mr. O'Brien holds up four fingers and asks Winston what he sees, and Winston states: "two and two are four."[602] This simple declaration of truth is seen as defiance against the Party's absolute control over reality.

Though Winston simply said what he saw, O'Brien inflicts pain anyway—because what he saw was not an acceptable answer. "'How can I help it?' … [Winston] blubbered. 'How can I help seeing what is in front of my eyes? Two and two are four.'"[603] In response, O'Brien, who is administering the "curing," calmly retorts, sometimes two and two "are five." "Sometimes they are three. Sometimes they are all of them at once."[604]

O'Brien's statement reveals the Party's authoritarian philosophy: understanding is not necessary, and truth is not an objective. While the Party uses this flexible truth, the goal is not to persuade or force Winston into compliance but to obliterate his ability to distinguish reality from illusion.

O'Brien's question— "And why do you imagine that we bring people to this place?"—is a notable moment that exposes the Party's deeper motives. Winston initially assumes the purpose is to force a confession or to punish dissenters, but O'Brien forcefully rejects these answers. Instead, he declares, "To cure you! To make you sane!" By portraying himself as Winston's "protector," O'Brien deepens the psychological manipulation, framing surrender to the Party's redefinition of truth as a form of salvation.

The Party does not just seek obedience—it demands total psychological submission. The Party is not content with persuasion, punishing rebels or extracting false confessions; it must reshape their very thoughts until they no longer require coercion. As O'Brien chillingly states, "We do not merely destroy our enemies, we change them."[605] By the end, Winston internalizes their propaganda and "loves Big Brother," reflecting the terrifying power of totalitarian control to redefine truth and reshape an individual's beliefs.[606]

Similarly, in the Dover trial, the plaintiffs dismissed Behe's observations on irreducible complexity and invoked scientific consensus as the ultimate authority on legitimacy. Just as O'Brien redefined truth to suit the Party's narrative, experts like Kenneth R. Miller framed co-option as the definitive explanation for irreducible complexity, while figures such as the NCSE's Eugenie C. Scott, in public statements, pointed to the rejection of ID by "every major scientific organization" as irrefutable evidence.

On the stand, Behe was subjected to an attempted reeducation, where authority was used to silence skepticism. This appeal to consensus over fair debate echoed O'Brien's philosophy—which suggests that truth in science is not determined by evidence but by institutional decree. This is why the NCSE and others assertively refer the public to Judge Jones' ruling rather than to scientific evidence. Yet they are quick to insist, "There's so much evidence—just look, and you'll see." Padian introduced a handful of fossils as evidence of a gradience while concealing paleontology's inconvenient trade secret: the gradience is missing.

Positing a few vague transitional forms does not support speciation by natural selection, nor does it reflect the fossil record's pattern of abrupt appearances. In doing so, he effectively presented "two and two make five" as scientific proof.

This reliance on institutional agreement as a rhetorical weapon reflects Orwell's warning about the dangers of authority defining reality—particularly when conclusions are drawn from the authority itself rather than through evidence-based reasoning. Orwell's Party permitted the illusion of debate while ensuring that only its perspective could prevail. Similar to Winston, Behe was compelled to leave the trial with his evidence dismissed, despite the fact that what he observed was plainly before his eyes. And the narratives that followed parallels Orwell's Party, which manipulates history and records to ensure its narrative is the only one remembered.

Another striking similarity lies in the redefinition of concepts to maintain control. The Party redefines terms like "freedom" to mean "slavery," embedding submission into the language itself. In Dover, the plaintiffs redefined science to adhere strictly to methodological naturalism, disqualifying ID by definition because of the non-naturalistic implications. The defense argued that teaching ID alongside evolution would foster critical thinking by exposing students to competing ideas. The court outright rejected the idea that critical thinking was a necessary part of the science curriculum.

Their argument centered on the belief that evolutionary theory is "true for now," despite any contradictions, and therefore, challenging it or allowing space for alternative perspectives, such as ID, was unnecessary. Eugenie Scott echoed this in the interview with Grothe:

> We're not talking about what should everybody know about and what is the best way to, develop critical thinkers... We're talking about what do you teach in high school science class.[607]

Scott's statement paradoxically suggests that the science classroom—arguably the most fitting arena for fostering critical thinking—should abandon its core principle.

By narrowing the discussion to "what do you teach in high school science class," she effectively suggests that the role of science education is to indoctrinate students into the prevailing consensus. This logic is eerily Orwellian, similar to the Party's doublethink. To teach science without critical thinking undermines its foundation, reducing it to dogma rather than investigation and skepticism.

The trial's reliance on philosophical definitions and rhetorical strategies turned it from a defense of science into an endorsement of a specific worldview, erasing the distinction between epistemological fairness and ideological control. The Dover trial reflects a recurring tension in history: the seesaw of consensus between authority and dissent. This dynamic has shaped civilizations, revolutions, and cultural paradigms, from ancient Rome to the scientific battles of the modern age.

In Rome, Jesus of Nazareth was crucified by a consensus driven by the intertwined authority of Roman politics and some Jewish religious leaders. Yet, in an ironic twist, the faith of the man they sought to silence eventually overturned the Roman consensus, becoming its dominant religion. This exemplifies how dissent, even when suppressed and met with persecution, can eventually grow into a new authority. The Catholic Church similarly wielded immense power in the Middle Ages, enforcing religious orthodoxy and suppressing dissent through mechanisms like the Inquisition. Yet, as alternate perspectives emerged, the consensus shifted, exposing the Catholic Church's inability to suppress dissent permanently when free thought proved incompatible with suppression.

The Victorian era saw another dramatic seesaw, this time within science. The X Club fervently promoted Darwin's theory of evolution, positioning themselves as defenders of naturalism against a religiously infused scientific consensus. Ironically, while they fought against the influence of religious authorities, the X Club's exclusionary tactics mirrored the very suppression they opposed, showing how dissent can adopt authoritarian methods when it gains power.

Even in the Enlightenment and Reformation, the seesaw persisted. Martin Luther's dissent against the Catholic Church's dominance sparked the Reformation, shifting the religious consensus of Europe. Likewise, Enlightenment thinkers like Voltaire and Locke challenged monarchical and religious authorities, replacing them with ideals of reason, liberty, and individual rights—new forms of consensus that reshaped the modern world.[608]

The *Kitzmiller v. Dover* trial is but another chapter in this historical narrative. Just as Rome, the Catholic Church, and the X Club revealed the interplay between authority and dissent, the trial highlights how these forces continue to shape societal consensus. History shows, however, that when voices are suppressed for long periods, if they carry truth, they will ultimately be heard—shifting the consensus once more.

CHAPTER 12

Radical Metaphysics

This crazy-sounding belief of mine—that our physical world not only is described by mathematics, but that it is mathematics—makes us self-aware parts of a giant mathematical object. As I describe in the book, this ultimately demotes familiar notions such as randomness, complexity and even change to the status of illusions...[609] —Max Tegmark

Ma'at

Mathematics is the foundation of physics, serving as its language and essential framework for understanding the laws of nature. In recent years, there has been growing discussion about the inherently mathematical essence of the universe, including theories such as the Mathematical Universe Hypothesis (MUH) proposed by Max Tegmark, a professor at the Massachusetts Institute of Technology (MIT).[610] [611] Tegmark suggests that the universe itself is a mathematical structure, where math is inherently part of its fabric. He proposes that math isn't just something humans came up with to understand the world; it's a fundamental quality that *shapes* the universe itself.[612] [613]

Tegmark's idea that mathematics forms the very fabric of the universe hints at underlying engineering, much like Einstein's calculations initially hinted at the universe's expansion, though he missed recognizing its full implications. However, Tegmark's strict Materialism causes him to overlook this elegant, natural engineering, instead attributing the universe's exquisiteness to the concept of mathematics.[614] [615]

This speculation challenges the traditional separation between the abstract and physical reality, suggesting that math plays a physical role in shaping the cosmos. This perspective has sparked a mix of skepticism and fascination among scientists, stirring debates about how deeply intertwined mathematics and the physical world really are.[616] While mathematical models effectively describe the physical world, they can also obscure the true nature and significance of what they represent, leading to a perception of math as more tangible than the phenomena it describes.[617] In Tegmark's case, the descriptions have more significance than the things they describe. Imagine believing that embryology is the actual essence of a baby rather than just a way to understand its development.

Tegmark's hypothesis lacks empirical support, testability, and methodological rigor; thus, by definition, it is a pseudoscience. However, the mainstream scientific community often tolerates speculative ideas from their own. Max Tegmark considers his view that the universe is a structure of mathematics as non-negotiable.[618] In one discussion, he remarked:

> That's a fantastic question. Why is mathematics the way it is?... My guess is that this ultimate reality really had no choice but to be precisely like that... there is no way that pi could have not been between three and four because it just has to be that way.[619]

Tegmark's mindset is like having all the answers without fully understanding all the questions.[620] His statement is an example of circular reasoning. Saying, "There is no way that pi could have not been between three and four because it just has to be that way," is essentially asserting that pi is inherently fixed because it is inherently fixed.[621] He presupposes the conclusion (pi must be between three and four) as a premise in his argument without providing an external justification or explanation for why this must necessarily be true beyond it being an observed fact.[622]

As it fails to recognize the interconnectedness of the NatTech that governs the universe, this perspective overlooks a fundamental truth—the essence that shifts the universe from a series of random events and indifferent processes into a purposeful and unified whole. In Tegmark's context, mathematics takes on a role similar to the concept of Ma'at in ancient Egyptian philosophy. Similarly seen as both a symbol and agent of cosmic order, thinkers like Tegmark regard mathematics in much the same way Ma'at was viewed—as the active principle maintaining and enforcing that order.[623]

Tegmark sees mathematics as the intrinsic fabric of the universe, imbued with a pantheistic quality. For him, mathematics itself bridges the gap between the seen and the unseen, the known and the unknowable. As materialists align with these and other theories that are deeply rooted in speculative concepts, they stray even further from their empirical-evidence-only stance. Metaphysical considerations do not inherently conflict with logic; however, these thinkers must maintain consistency in their evaluations of what constitutes proper science.

Dr. Adrian Currie, a Senior Lecturer in Philosophy of Science and Epistemology at the University of Exeter, suggests that certain speculative hypotheses might be classified as egregious speculation. Due to their lack of epistemic support, untestability, and potential to lead to miscommunication, these hypotheses are more about reinforcing existing ideas than contributing new scientific knowledge.[624]

It's as if those in the materialist club are issued VIP passes for entertaining certain theories—like the multiverse, primordial soup, or the idea that gravity alone can create a universe.[625] These theories, deficient in empirical data, seemingly get unlimited passes in the "free lunch" program.[626] This illustrates how the pursuit of understanding the profound complexities of the universe can lead even militant materialist thinkers to embrace ideas that carry significant metaphysical implications.[627]

Tegmark has openly stated that his Mathematical Universe Hypothesis hinges on the premise that all aspects of the world can be described mathematically.[628] He posits that the falsification of his theory would occur if just one element of the universe defies mathematical description.[629]

A compelling example is life itself. It's the foundational element that transcends the bounds of mathematical description.

CHAPTER 13

Sensational Science

> *It's not a speculation that we do have a crisis in the foundations of physics. It's a fact that we haven't made progress with theory development for 50 years. People who work in the field will often try to tell you that, oh, we have learned this or that obscure mathematical fact, and it's all so very exciting and soon, soon there will be a breakthrough. And you will have no idea what they're talking about; you'll think it's just over your head, so better not ask. I want to strongly encourage you: please do ask. Ask them what it's good for. Ask them what we've learned from it. Ask them what we can do with it. Ask them why your taxes should pay for them producing papers. I think they owe you an answer.*[630] —Sabine Hossenfelder

In addition to biases within the scientific community, there is a significant extension of this issue: media bias and sensationalism. The media frequently amplifies materialist speculations, often exaggerating and promoting views that fall in line with a materialistic perspective of the universe. The media's selective promotion of theories and research supporting Materialism shapes public perception and amplifies a worldview that frames material conditions and processes as the foundation of reality. This portrayal skews public understanding, making materialist explanations appear more conclusive than they are, while sidelining competing viewpoints that could offer a more accurate understanding of the universe.

Like, Share, Conclude, and Leave a Comment

Driven by an insatiable appetite for ratings and revenue, media outlets frequently portray every discovery, even the seemingly mundane, as paradigm-shifting revelations, only to move on to the next story in which to invoke hyperbole.[631] This creates a sense of dramatic irony, as those who understand the complexities and uncertainties of scientific research often feel compelled, yet unable, to alert the public or media to the oversimplified narratives being presented. Media outlets often mislead the public by elevating tentative findings to the status of groundbreaking truths.

A clear example of mainstream media sensationalism is captured in a CNN segment where host Abby Phillip and her guest, astrophysicist Hakeem Oluseyi, discuss a new study suggesting that asteroid dust may have played a role in the extinction of dinosaurs.[632] Phillip introduces the topic, stating, "How exactly this [asteroid] doomed the dinosaurs remained unclear for a long time." She continues, revealing that "the fine dust from the pulverized asteroid may have played a bigger role than previously known, blocking out the sunlight and shutting down life nearly two years... leading to mass extinction."

Phillip asks Oluseyi to explain these findings further. He clarifies that researchers "found this fine dust" and notably adds, "and on the computational side, they had to actually create these models that show not only how the dust interacts with sunlight." This statement highlights the speculative nature of the study; these models are not direct evidence but tools to hypothesize scenarios based on certain assumptions. Furthermore, the phrase "on the computational side" is a misleading primer, suggesting a level of scientific precision and certainty that may not exist in the following statement. "What they found is this particular type of material could stay airborne for 15 years." Phillip reacts with a "Wow!" emphasizing the impressive nature of the claim.

The segment progresses with Oluseyi explaining, "And producing, basically, a chain reaction killing off plant life first, and that is what basically caused the dinosaurs to go extinct," to which Phillip agrees. This narrative, while intriguing, exemplifies a common issue in scientific reporting: presenting computational models and speculative assertions as if they were conclusive facts.

Computational models are invaluable in science; however, they fundamentally rely on the assumptions and variables input by researchers. These assumptions dictate the outcomes of simulations, which are not direct observations but can vary significantly depending on the input. The statement about the dust remaining airborne for 15 years and blocking sunlight is a model output based on such assumptions. It should not be misconstrued as direct observation or conclusive proof.

In the YouTube comment section of this segment, a comment by @GabGotti3, which received a high number of likes, stated, "We need more content like this on the news." Such comments reflect the appeal of sensationalized material to viewers, exposing the danger of media sensationalism in science reporting for an uncritical public.[633] This creates a feedback loop of bias. Positive engagement with this type of content, as indicated by the likes received on @GabGotti3's comment, can encourage media outlets to produce more of the same, potentially increasing public preference for such stories.

Each presentation of these studies perpetually labeled as definitive feeds into a cycle of fascination with speculative revelations. The audience, often quick to forget the last proclaimed 'breakthrough,' eagerly moves on to the drama of the latest findings, unaware of the elusive nature of these new 'truths.' This cycle of continuous discovery and forgetfulness keeps the public ever learning but never quite reaching a stable understanding.

Consider a different narrative, one often crafted around the unveiling of exoplanets. Each newly discovered planet outside the bounds of our solar system is heralded with headlines bursting with the enticing possibility of harboring life. Often, media coverage ramps up astronomical findings with worn-out speculations. They tend to focus on sparse requirements, like the presence of water or oxygen, without fully contemplating the complex conditions necessary for life.

A case in point is a Fox News segment titled "Scientists discover seven Earth-sized planets." At the top of this segment, hosted by Bret Baier, who announces the big news about NASA's discovery of "planets that could contain life," setting the tone for the ensuing discussion.[634] His correspondent, Kristin Fisher, is brought on to explore this significant revelation further.[635] The focus of the segment is predominantly on the potential of newly discovered planets to support life, driven by factors like the presence of water and their location in the habitable zone.

The excitement around the discovery of these planets is amplified to a level that misleads the public about the current state of our understanding. The narrative is primarily constructed around the assumption that similarities to Earth's physical characteristics inherently increase the probability of finding life. The phrases used by FOX News, like "this is huge news in the search for extraterrestrial life" and descriptions of planets sitting within a "habitable zone that could support alien life," set a tone of excitement and high expectation.[636]

These claims capture the public's attention but often distort the true significance of these discoveries. Moreover, describing these discoveries as "giant accelerated leaps forward" exaggerates the typically slow pace of scientific progress in fields like astrobiology and exoplanet research. This sensationalized portrayal tends to blend the existence of life-supporting conditions with the possibility of life itself emerging. Yet, the mere presence of life on Earth does not confirm abiogenesis as its origin. The belief that abiogenesis is the only conceivable explanation for the origin of life is held by those who mistakenly think Materialism is the sole source of truth, thus treating abiogenesis as an unassailable fact.

Furthermore, in the quest to discover extraterrestrial life, while scientists often search for planets that mirror the conditions of modern Earth, characterized by an oxygen-rich atmosphere and stable, life-sustaining environments, this seems at odds with the prevalent theories of abiogenesis, which suggest that life on Earth began in vastly different, inhospitable conditions filled with gases like methane and ammonia.

This discrepancy raises a compelling question: If life is believed to have originated under the harsh conditions of early Earth, characterized by an atmosphere rich in methane and ammonia—or, alternatively, scenarios of extreme heat or minimal water—why do scientists predominantly target planets that resemble our planet's current, more hospitable state, specifically seeking an Earth-like atmosphere and abundant water? Why aren't researchers also excitedly suggesting, 'Look, this new exoplanet might have methane, ammonia, or extreme conditions; there could be life there too?' On the contrary, the focus is invariably on water, a solvent that paradoxically represents one of the many dangers that would destroy emerging life.

Moreover, it's quite presumptuous to search for life on planets similar to our own when we have no definitive understanding of how life arose here on Earth. Despite its widely assumed plausibility, abiogenesis remains a superstition not a scientific fact. There remains no empirical evidence or even a feasible thought experiment that definitively explains how life could spontaneously arise from non-life.

Yet, based on these unsubstantiated premises, many conclude that finding extraterrestrial life is just a matter of locating the right planet that has the right amount of water. Moreover, the low public skepticism seems to stem from a deep-seated allure toward the mysteries of the cosmos, manipulated by media outlets for clicks and views.

The uncritical acceptance of the repeated showering of these simplistic and often sensational claims about extraterrestrial life reflects not just a misunderstanding of astrobiology but a broader issue of public credulity towards scientific reporting. Thus, individuals well-versed in the complexities and the astronomically low probabilities of life arising via abiogenesis are less likely to be misled by sensationalized reports. Yet, conversations that explore these complexities and probabilities are often kept out of the classroom, restricting wider understanding.

Similar to the embellished stories about exoplanets, media coverage of evolutionary biology often oversimplifies complex topics, resulting in widespread public misconceptions. For example, the discovery of a single fossilized specimen morphs into a sensationalized headline heralding it as a "missing link" in evolution. This kind of oversimplification even misses the basic points outlined in neo-Darwinian theory.

Carl Zimmer, a science writer and columnist for The New York Times, has a distinguished reputation for his engaging communication of complex scientific topics.[637] Zimmer has authored several popular books on science, contributed to magazines like National Geographic, and was a three-time winner of the American Association for the Advancement of Science's Journalism Award—an ideological sister organization to the NCSE.[638]

In his 2010 article "Evolution and the Media," however, Zimmer offers a detailed examination of the media's historical coverage of evolution.[639] He reflects on the evolution of science writing and the challenges of accurately reporting on complex scientific topics in an era saturated with information.[640] Zimmer discusses the downsides of the vast amount of content available on the internet, pointing out that much of it can be "misleading or poorly written," which poses challenges in discerning accurate and high-quality information about evolution.[641]

Zimmer also discusses how the media's portrayal of scientific findings, particularly in the field of evolution, often leads to misunderstandings and oversimplifications of complex concepts. He notes that while the media has the power to bring scientific discoveries to a broad audience, sensationalized and sometimes reductive coverage distorts the process and findings. A notable example Zimmer provides is the Darwinius affair of the early '80s, where a new fossil was unveiled with considerable fanfare and hyperbolic claims.[642]

The unveiling of the fossil Darwinius masillae, named in honor of Darwin but popularly known as Ida, marked a sensational moment in paleontology, drawing attention from high-profile figures, including New York City Mayor Michael Bloomberg.[643] [644] The event was not just a scientific announcement but also a well-orchestrated media spectacle, complete with a television documentary and a trade book release timed to coincide with the fossil's unveiling.[645] This strategic media approach significantly amplified the discovery's reach.

However, the extensive media coverage and hype led to misleading portrayals of Ida's significance in Darwin's evolutionary tree. The History Channel's involvement in a documentary production further amplified these claims, presenting Ida as a "missing link."[646] The scientific community did not fully support such claims, leading to debates and criticism regarding the portrayal of Ida's role in our understanding of human origins. This situation revealed a desire to capture public interest with groundbreaking paleontological discoveries, which in turn produced an early form of clickbait.

As in the case of Ida, where later scientific analysis reclassified the fossil's significance, Zimmer discusses the important role of experienced science writers in providing skeptical and informed coverage of such events. In this case, media sensationalism prematurely elevated findings before they had undergone proper scientific scrutiny and peer review.

In the context of Zimmer's critique of media sensationalism and its impact on the public's understanding of science, the role of social media platforms in science communication gains additional significance. The rise of platforms like YouTube, X, Facebook, and TikTok has significantly altered how scientific information is shared and consumed. These platforms are increasingly becoming primary sources of scientific information for the general public, a transition that moves away from traditional news outlets. All major networks, such as CNN, Fox, and ABC, have adapted to digital trends by uploading their content to platforms like YouTube, blending traditional and new media forms. However, despite their presence, these established networks are significantly outnumbered by a plethora of independent news sources, including science communicators and other content creators.

Content creators on YouTube and other social media platforms are driven by engagement metrics, just like traditional news sources compete for ratings. In this competitive environment, channel views and likes often take precedence over accuracy and reliability, leading to the rise of clickbait news. This includes the promotion of sensationalized or speculative science content, which users tend to choose based on what aligns with their pre-existing beliefs and curiosity rather than what's accurate and objective. There is a broad spectrum of misleading content, ranging from secret, forbidden knowledge claims to more subtle forms of disinformation.

Professors of Faith

This subtler dynamic can be seen in the interactions between various social media science communicators, such as Dave Farina, who goes by Professor Dave. Farina, through his YouTube channel "Professor Dave Explains," which is sailing towards 4 million subscribers, positions his platform as a comprehensive resource for self-education across a wide array of academic subjects.[647] His stated goal is to create content that is engaging, concise, and accessible to a diverse audience.[648]

In his welcome video, Professor Dave differentiates his channel from others by stating that his focus is on delivering substantial knowledge rather than just entertaining science-related content.[649] He expresses a desire to offer an educational experience that is informative and digestible, avoiding overly long lectures while still delivering critical understanding across various subjects like chemistry, physics, biology, and even fields outside of science like American history. The tone set by Professor Dave in his welcome message (and his book's description on Amazon) conveys a commitment to combat misinformation and pseudoscience.[650]

While Professor Dave's welcome message promises a commitment to factual content, he sometimes deviates from this script, especially when tackling speculative or philosophical topics. His audience, who are accustomed to his usual precision, might not notice the shift when he addresses existential questions. Here, his approach changes, marked by a zealotry contrasting sharply with his typical methodical presentation. This shift reveals a mix of personal conviction and enthusiasm, subtly influencing how he presents these more abstract subjects.

An example of this deviation in addressing existential questions is evident in the public dispute between Professor Dave and Dr. James Tour about the origin of life. Dr. Tour has categorically stated that scientists are still at a loss to explain how life originated or even to define what life essentially is.

Dr. Tour, a distinguished figure in the field of synthetic chemistry, is mainly known for his work in nanotechnology. He is a Professor of Chemistry, Materials Science, and NanoEngineering at Rice University.[651]

Professor Dave, frustrated with Tour's claims about the scientific ignorance surrounding abiogenesis, released a video intended to refute him.[652] Professor Dave titled the video "Elucidating the Agenda of James Tour: A Defense of Abiogenesis." Framed as a scientific rebuttal to Tour's arguments on abiogenesis, the video quickly veers off course. From the first minute of content and throughout the video, Professor Dave repeatedly ties Tour's scientific arguments to his Christian beliefs, despite promising to keep them separate.

Thus, Professor Dave glosses over much of Tour's arguments by steering the topic toward Tour's religious beliefs, distracting the focus from the central claims. This becomes particularly troubling as he cuts to a clip in which Tour speaks about his faith. Professor Dave primes his audience by stating that he needs to "properly contextualize" the discussion and then introduces a clip of Tour saying, "Not only am I a Christian, but I love Jesus tremendously." By opening with a presentation about Tour's faith as part of his scientific argument, Professor Dave employs a tactic that philosophers would not describe as "properly contextualizing" but rather as properly "poisoning the well."[653]

The fallacy of poisoning the well occurs when "adverse information about a target is preemptively presented to an audience, with the intention of discrediting or ridiculing everything that the target person is about to say" or all that follows, thus undermining the individual's credibility.[654] The audience is subtly encouraged to position themselves with the "us" (the correct worldview and reasoning) against "them" (the supposedly religion-clouded perspective).[655] Professor Dave's hostility towards Tour's faith borders on Christianophobia—not that Christians are usually allowed to call it that.[656] If Professor Dave or anyone else is qualified and genuinely intends to refute Tour's arguments, the focus should be on the scientific claims rather than Tour's expression of his love for Jesus.

Professor Dave seems to cater to an echo chamber, with many of his followers leaving flattering comments that extend the ad hominem attacks on Tour. He engaged with some of these comments, showing his approval by hearting or replying directly. For instance, a user named @ParaSpite, whose comment garnered over 600 likes, wrote: "You're so unreasonably generous in your assumption that he's merely incompetent, rather than outright dishonest." To this, Dave responded: "Don't worry, my response will be much more appropriately scathing."[657]

In various YouTube videos of his own, Dr. James Tour consistently challenges the notion that a prebiotic, indifferent Earth could spontaneously assemble life through random natural processes, a scenario that modern scientists cannot replicate even in high-tech, "pristine" laboratories.

Professor Dave finds Tour's questioning of abiogenesis absurd, expressing disbelief that Tour, an accomplished scientist, does not grasp the "basic principles." He addresses Tour's pointing out of our inability to assemble a single bacterium by declaring, "This is absolutely irrelevant. The instructions for assembly are coded in the DNA, and DNA predates all bacteria. The issue is to arrive at the bacterium genome, not to somehow be able to assemble a bacterium from its fully formed constituent parts, because nature doesn't do that either. *Nature assembled* some dramatically simpler precursor which was self-replicating and also self-improving due to natural selection."[658]

He continues to focus on the importance of DNA, arguing that "DNA is literally what contains the instructions to put the bacterium together." Aside from his use of "literally" for emphasis, to better understand why this statement is antiquated, I recommend reading *Dance to the Tune of Life: Biological Relativity*, by Denis Noble or *How Life Works* by Philip Ball. As Noble and Ball suggest, the genome in isolation cannot create or define an organism, as development also depends on interactions with the environment and other cellular processes.[659]

Extending this idea, one could compare these interactions to wave-like systems in physics, where uncertainty, entanglement, and wave collapse offer a metaphor for understanding biological phenomena like gene expression or protein folding.[660] For example, the probabilistic nature of gene regulation, influenced by molecular noise and external signals, parallels how quantum states resolve into specific outcomes only when observed.[661] These processes, analogous to quantum systems, are probabilistic and shaped by both internal cellular states and external environments.

Such insights challenge the reductionist view of DNA as a static "blueprint" and complicate abiogenesis theories. Rather than focusing narrowly on DNA or theoretical precursors, these theories must first account for the integrated interplay of molecular systems. Though thinkers like Noble emphasizes the self-organizing nature of this symphony, self-organization alone cannot fully explain the purposeful coordination and interdependency evident in these sophisticated systems.

Though Professor Dave claims that Dr. James Tour, a decorated professor of chemistry and nano-engineering, lacks a basic understanding of organic chemistry, his arguments reveal limitations in his understanding, reflecting an outdated view of the complexity of DNA's influence. He asserts that nature crafted a "dramatically" simpler self-replicating and self-improving precursor, contending that "every bacterial cell alive today is tremendously more complex than the first protocell that must have formed." Like others discussed in this book, he also makes the unusual claim that nature is both the creator and the created, bringing itself into existence and enhancing itself with systems that surpass the full comprehension of even our most intelligent minds. He concludes that Dr. Tour's caution in embracing current theories of abiogenesis "is not a valid argument... and also incredibly anti-intellectual."

As noted, Philip Ball explores the complexities of genetic and epigenetic factors, dedicating substantial discussion to the misconception that the genome alone determines an organism's development or function.[662] He argues that biological systems exhibit emergent properties that arise from interactions within and between cells, which are not dictated solely by DNA. Ball challenges the reductionist view held by Professor Dave, highlighting his overconfidence in antiquated, Dawkins-esque genetic interpretations and his reluctance to consider newer insights that question this perspective.

In his attempt to counter Dr. Tour's claims, Professor Dave poses a challenging question:

> We can't make planets and stars either; does that mean nature can't have made them spontaneously?

Although this analogy might seem persuasive to his audience, it is fundamentally flawed for reasons we've previously discussed. Similar to Scott equating denying evolution is like denying gravity, the logic in Professor Dave's question does not follow because it conflates two different kinds of processes and forms of evidence. His faith rests on the belief that abiogenesis is the only explanation tenable.

Mainstream theories on the origin of stars and planets, though steeped in supernormal speculation, at least offer a pathway through some established physical mechanisms, whereas the origin of life involves the emergence of biochemical information and molecular machinery that currently lack any natural explanation. Equating these distinct phenomena ignores the specific challenges posed by Dr. Tour's critique of abiogenesis, leaving his argument unaddressed.

And, once again, if I may reiterate, the presence of life on Earth does not inherently confirm its origin through abiogenesis. This assumption is a fundamental presupposition of radical Materialism. The notion that abiogenesis is the sole conceivable explanation for the origin of life typically arises from those who are entrenched in this worldview, thus treating abiogenesis as an unassailable fact.

He presents his materialist perspective as the only truth, using his beliefs to interpret the evidence rather than allowing the evidence to inform his views. He bases his conclusions on what are essentially superstitions rather than established facts. It's simply, 'we are here, thus, abiogenesis.' The inability to replicate cosmic phenomena in the laboratory does not diminish the substantial evidence suggesting that life arising through abiogenesis is highly improbable.

Despite Professor Dave's dogmatic claims, he continues to shape the narrative in a specific way. Over and over, he primes his audience to perceive Dr. Tour, calling him the C-word with an anti-science agenda, a portrayal that the video's title, "Elucidating the Agenda of James Tour," initially sets up. This title and Dave's commentary suggest that expressing skepticism about the theory of abiogenesis is tantamount to opposing science itself. This tactic, which has been effectively used for over a century, is a powerful rhetorical strategy to shape the perceptions of an uncritical public.

To be fair to Professor Dave, a considerable body of scientific literature explores various speculative scenarios on how abiogenesis might have been possible on a prebiotic Earth. However, one must be cautious not to interpret these speculations as certainties, a trap he has often fallen into.

Moreover, Dave often uses "matter-of-fact" and "must-have-occurred" statements, similar to those made by figures like Dawkins, who are confident about these yet-to-be-verified processes. The rant, seen in this video where Professor Dave claims that "Tour's religious beliefs influence his scientific perspective," would serve as an intriguing case study on science popularizers in the social media era. There's a wealth of material to examine in this video and its potential impact on Dave's audience of over three million followers, more than I can address here.

Given his educational background, Professor Dave certainly has an impressive grasp of the subject. However, he possibly projects his view of religion as ignorance onto Tour, underestimating the extensive expertise of this scientist. The problem seems to be that he does not grasp that Tour's argument isn't a matter of philosophy. This isn't one of those old-school debates with Dawkins or Hitchens about whether God exists. Tour presents facts grounded in the current state of knowledge in the field of chemistry, where he is a recognized expert.

Tour does not even claim that abiogenesis is impossible; he simply states the fact that no one knows how it could occur. While Dawkins has admitted, "we don't know" how life started, there are moments when Dave, much like Dawkins, confidently tells his audience how it must have occurred. He dismisses those like Tour who disagree, labeling them as "anti-intellectual" and "way out of his element."[663]

Though Dave has a bachelor's degree in chemistry, it's important to note that, despite his ridicule of Tour's comprehension of organic chemistry and his strong stance on these scientific issues, Professor Dave is not a professor of science or any field of education. This might also explain why he relies so heavily on extreme ad hominem attacks, such as labeling a scientist of Tour's caliber as anti-intellectual. This is an exceptionally flippant statement against Tour, the institutions that granted Tour's degrees, and his current employer—a disrespectful accusation that a pensive person would not recklessly hurl.

Interestingly, Professor Dave states, "Sensationalist reporting of science news is destroying public perception of science no matter which way it leans, but the blame is with the media outlets, not with the scientists."[664] Professor Dave's religious adherence to inconclusive theories such as abiogenesis misinforms many of his supporters to the complexities and uncertainties inherent in the scientific process. Respectfully, embracing such beliefs with zealous certitude does not turn them into reality, no matter the passion or number of supporters.

He seems to reflect the Dunning-Kruger effect, where overconfidence often stems from limited understanding, leading individuals to overestimate their grasp of the subject. Similar to the Biblical definition in Hebrews 11:1, which describes faith as "the assurance of things hoped for, the conviction of things not seen," Dave exhibits a kind of faith in scientific hypotheses about the origins of life.[665] Simply put, the Biblical definition of faith is "trusting in something you cannot explicitly prove." Professor Dave's belief in and evangelizing of abiogenesis mirrors the very religious convictions he critiques, embodying a staunch faith in scientific speculations as though they were unseen truths.

Additionally, even Ball points out that the general perspective is too optimistic about what we really know in this field. He shares a sentiment similar to Tour's, especially after the Human Genome Project. Ball notes, "Not only has this information brought us little closer to understanding life itself; it has in some ways shown us that we're even further from that understanding than we thought."[666] He goes on to say that the genome isn't just a simple "instruction book" but something far more complex, sometimes even staggeringly so.[667]

Ball states that the initial belief—that genome mapping would lead to simple solutions—was overly optimistic. He notes, "We thought we'd be done. The reality, of course, is we're not."[668] He adds that recent molecular and cell biology research has revealed a far more complex and astounding reality than the outdated mechanical metaphors once suggested.[669] He has also stated that "just about all the neat stories that researchers routinely tell about how living cells work are incomplete, flawed, or just totally mistaken."

Echoing Ball's observations, Noble also criticizes the oversimplified gene-centric view, such as Professor Dave's, commonly seen in popular discussions on biology. He argues that the complexities of life cannot be fully understood just by looking at genetic sequences. In light of these understandings presented by Ball and Noble, Professor Dave might be the one "way out of his element" when it comes to this topic.

Definitive assertions by figures like Professor Dave, who seem to overlook the vast complexities and uncertainties still dominating this field, do a disservice to the public. This is especially problematic given his potential influence over more than 3 million subscribers. Despite his attempts to refute Tour's claims, Tour's core argument remains valid: "We do not know how to build even a simple bacterium…"[670]

Furthermore, in How Life Works, Ball points out a critical aspect of biological systems that aligns with Tour's skepticism. Philip Ball cites Henry D. Potter and Kevin J. Mitchell, scholars who have contributed to discussions on "holistic integration":

> Potter and Mitchell add that agents must also show 'holistic integration': they are more than the sum of their parts. We can usefully take an organism apart and look at the components—but we can't truly understand what it does unless we put them back together again. As Potter and Mitchell say, there's a distinction to be drawn here with a machine that is, so to speak, just 'pushed around by its own component parts'.[671] [For further statements on this concept, see footnote referencing Potter and Mitchell's work.][672]

Moreover, Professor Dave's claim that "we have a lot of … [the process of abiogenesis] mapped out with multiple cogent possibilities for each step" is not even supported by materialist researchers in the field of the origin of life.[673] For example, a group of researchers who are recognized experts in this 'element,' emphasize the field's complexity and the lack of coherence on many aspects of abiogenesis in their 2020 paper, "The Future of Origin of Life Research: Bridging Decades-Old Divisions."[674] They call for a new interdisciplinary approach and collaboration due to the lack of progress over decades of research. This reveals the significant uncertainty, competing hypotheses, and ongoing debates that characterize the research of abiogenesis.

These researchers acknowledge the "diversity of theories" and the "lack of consensus on a single pathway," a stance that is at odds with the unwavering certainty often displayed by Professor Dave. Remarkably, while displaying pugnacious cockiness, he seems unaware of the need for caution in his words, overlooking the fact that his videos will circulate forever.[675]

The Search for a Baby Universe

This type of bias was also clear in media coverage before and after the James Webb Space Telescope's (JWST) observations. As more observations emerged, they revealed how reluctant materialists in science and media were to remain objective and acknowledge any personal biases in relation to their evolutionary perspective on the universe's history. The launch of the JWST was met with huge excitement, with the media celebrating the idea that the telescope would confirm existing cosmological models by looking back in time to see the universe as it was in its infancy.[676]

A year before the launch, a 2021 study by ScienceDaily.com, based on supercomputer simulations at Lund University titled "How Disorderly Young Galaxies Grow Up and Mature," suggested that galaxies evolve from chaotic to mature structures.[677] This excitement was later met with surprise and efforts to reconcile the evidence with these long-held hypotheses.

Maruša Bradač, an astronomer at the University of California, Davis, was among those enthusiastic about the JWST's potential. She shared her expectations in a December 2021 NPR article titled "This New Space Telescope Should Show Us What the Universe Looked Like as a Baby," stating the telescope could reshape our understanding of cosmic history.[678]

Bradač described the JWST as "a time machine," expressing her excitement by saying, "We're going to see the universe as it was a couple of hundred million years after the Big Bang."[679] She further noted the importance of having the opportunity of accurately understanding the universe's early stages to better understand its development, a perspective that anticipated validation of the standard cosmological model.[680]

Garth Illingworth, an astronomer at the University of California, Santa Cruz, echoed this excitement, revealing the broader implications of the JWST's mission. In the same article, he predicted, "But we will go back to the point where we really start to see the galaxies at a very early stage, so that we can trace the whole history, essentially, from then, 200 million years after the Big Bang, through to now."[681] He notes the significance of this mission in addressing existential questions. He asks, "How did we get here?[682] What is the history of our universe that brought us to the point where we can sit here and think about it?"[683] These questions reveal these scientists goal to interpret reality through a reductive approach, using the JWST to confirm their evolutionary narrative by revealing the universe's infancy and the early formation of galaxies. This oversimplification is evident in the subsequent headlines describing scientists "grappling" with their assumptions as they struggle to fully account for the contradictions observed in the JWST's findings.[684]

The debate concerning the inception and development of the universe often unfolds without much contention within mainstream science, or even among proponents of ID, such as those from the DI. These groups generally accept the standard cosmological model, focusing their debates primarily on the emergence and historical development of life on Earth. However, this discourse frequently marginalizes literal Biblical interpreters or creationists, despite their views being increasingly supported by recent findings from the JWST.

While ID proponents, many of whom are aligned with Christianity, often participate in discussions about the origins of life and the evolution of the universe, their shared focus on exploring evidence of design accommodates diverse views on topics such as a universe originating from a singularity or existing for billions of years, setting them apart from literalist groups who give no concessions to interpretations that deviate from a strict reading of Genesis.

These Biblical creationists, often dismissed as fringe and marginalized in scientific discussions, have seen their existential positions increasingly supported by new empirical observations—from scientific evidence showing the universe having an absolute beginning to the Earth experiencing a worldwide inundation at some point in the past, to the complex genetic code discovered by Watson and Crick, to now seeing a fully-formed universe at its dawn.[685]

Conversely, materialists continually contort their models to reconcile phenomena they label as problems, all while building on their ever-shifting foundations. Unfortunately for them, they're now forced to catalog the 'Mature Universe Problem,' filing it away as yet another piece that does not fit into their puzzle. The findings of the JWST expose the same flaw evident in Lyell's uniformitarianism: an overreliance on assumptions and a truculent refusal to consider opposing views.

It is worth noting that for much of the 20th century, mainstream geology and popular science education dismissed the idea of a global flood. The prevailing consensus, rooted in Lyellian uniformitarianism, held that Earth's landscapes were shaped by slow, gradual processes over millions of years. Any suggestion of a worldwide flood was often categorized as religious myth rather than a serious geological hypothesis.

However, in recent decades, large-scale flood events have gained recognition within mainstream geology. Some researchers have even reconsidered the role of catastrophic megafloods in shaping Earth's surface, acknowledging their impact as more significant than previously thought. Yet rather than recognizing a single, global flood, modern geology has instead classified numerous regional or continental-scale deluges, each occurring at different times in Earth's history. A few notable examples include:

> *The Missoula Floods* (North America, ~13,000–15,000 years ago) – Repeated glacial outburst floods that carved the Channeled Scablands.[686]

> *The Zanclean Flood* (~5.3 million years ago) – The refilling of the Mediterranean Basin when the Atlantic breached the Gibraltar Strait.[687]

The Black Sea Deluge Hypothesis (~7,500 years ago) – A proposed catastrophic flooding event that may have influenced ancient flood myths.[688]

The Bonneville Flood (~14,500 years ago) – A massive outburst flood from ancient Lake Bonneville in North America.[689]

The Burckle Crater Hypothesis (~6,000 years ago) – A controversial theory suggesting a comet impact triggered massive tsunamis.[690]

As mentioned in Chapter 18, while the standard explanation of how Earth acquired its water contains multiple contradictions, many modern catastrophic 'discoveries' add to the confusion within the mainstream narrative of Earth's hydration. While early uniformitarian geologists scoffed at the idea that cataclysmic flooding played a major role in shaping Earth's surface, modern research has now confirmed multiple such events. The key difference? These floods are accepted only as isolated, independent catastrophes rather than components of a singular, global event. What was once dismissed as myth, however, is now carefully embraced—rebranded under a different framework. The excuse often seems to be that science changes with new information, but this new information quietly and consistently aligns with the ancient Biblical text.

Another example of this is Dr. Jason Lisle, an astrophysicist who adheres to a literal interpretation of Biblical scripture, who accurately predicted in a January 21, 2022, article that the JWST would reveal fully-formed galaxies at vast distances—findings that present significant challenges to the timelines proposed by standard cosmological models.[691] Lisle stated, "Rather than galaxies just starting to form, I expect to see fully-formed (fully-designed) galaxies at unprecedented distances. This will force secular astronomers to adjust their estimates of when the earliest galaxies formed, pushing them much closer to the supposed big bang."[692]

He also predicted that JWST would find evidence contradicting the existence of Population III stars, which are theorized to contain no elements heavier than lithium: "Furthermore, I expect the signal of some heavy elements in these galaxies. That is, I don't expect to see evidence of genuine Population III stars – those with no heavy elements at all."[693]

Months after Lisle's predictions, as data from the JWST became available, astronomers observed mature galaxies in regions where only young, chaotic ones were expected. For example, a November 2022 report titled "NASA's Webb Draws Back Curtain on Universe's Early Galaxies" from NASA noted that galaxies like GLASS-z12 appeared merely 350 million years after the universe's inception, much earlier than traditionally assumed, confirming Lisle's prediction.[694] These observations challenge the expected timeline of galaxy formation and evolution, as well as the theoretical infancy stage of the universe.

As noted by Jonathan O'Callaghan, a respected science journalist known for his work in prominent publications such as *Scientific American*, *BBC*, and *Nature*, "candidate galaxies in the early universe are popping up in numbers that defy predictions, with dozens found so far. Explaining this excess may require substantial revisions to prevailing cosmological models, changes that could involve the first galaxies forming sooner, their stars shining brighter—or perhaps the nature of dark matter or dark energy being even more complex and mysterious than previously thought."[695]

Despite these findings, which fundamentally contradict existing models, O'Callaghan's words reveal the remarkable bias inherent in radical Materialism.[696] More interestingly, he fulfills Lisle's prediction that findings will force "secular astronomers to adjust their estimates of when the earliest galaxies formed, pushing them much closer to the supposed big bang."

Rather than questioning the foundational assumptions, as foreseen by Lisle, O'Callaghan suggests merely adjusting the data to fit within the existing framework. This response exemplifies a reluctance to reconsider core theories, showing an inherent bias that assumes the correctness of the prevailing models despite clear contradictions presented by the new evidence. Ironically, this attempt to fill in the gaps between what was theorized and what is observed is what most may stereotype religious groups, such as creationists. One can only imagine the inundation of celebratory headlines had these existential presuppositions been confirmed.

Further supporting Lisle's foresight, an April 26, 2024, article on Space.com, titled "James Webb Space Telescope discovers some early universe galaxies grew up surprisingly fast," reveals how conjecture is used for plastering over contradictions in the materialist narrative.[697] The article suggests that early universe galaxies developed more quickly than previously believed.[698] An international team led by researchers from Durham University in the U.K. claims to have found evidence of "star bars" in galaxies a few billion years post-Big Bang. These structures indicate a more mature phase of galaxy development than previously thought.[699] The article states, "This means we will have to adjust our views on early galaxy evolution."[700] Note, the first and only conclusion was to reconcile unexpected data with the standard assumptions, rather than questioning them.

If these findings accurately reflect the early cosmos, the unexpected complexities revealed by the JWST suggest a sense of primordial order in the way galaxies formed, raising questions about whether there are underlying laws or mechanisms guiding these structures. While this interpretation does not confirm any specific technological framework within nature, it is one of many pieces that fit my hypothesis of a universal technological framework. Although the red-shifting of light from distant galaxies is commonly interpreted as evidence of an expanding universe, it is important to note that these wavelengths are not definitive indicators of age spanning billions of years.

In a recent online video, Dr. Jason Lisle proposed alternative explanations for redshift, such as the Doppler model.[701] He suggested that the redshift observed in distant galaxies might result from their motion through static space rather than the expansion of space itself. According to Lisle, this model implies that galaxies are moving away from each other, causing the observed redshifts and challenging the standard cosmological models that rely on space expansion. Lisle's analysis of JWST data indicates that the expected magnification effect at certain redshifts is absent, aligning more closely with the Doppler model. As he pointed out, "According to the Doppler model, the angular sizes of distant galaxies are consistent with their redshifts being caused entirely by the Doppler effect and not the Robertson-Walker metric, which describes the expansion of space."[702] If space is not expanding, the Big Bang model, which relies on this premise, would be fundamentally refuted.

Lisa

This situation is reminiscent of a common human tendency to misinterpret signals based on personal bias. Imagine a scenario with a very attractive Lisa, who is known to be very polite. Tom, intensely infatuated with Lisa, mistakenly concludes that her politeness is a sign of romantic interest. In his mind, he crafts a scenario where Lisa is interested in him and only waiting for him to make the first move. Acting on this belief, Tom finally asks Lisa out. She politely declines but leaves the door open for a possible future encounter by saying, "Maybe some other time." Despite this gentle refusal, Tom interprets her words as a hopeful sign and continues to hold onto his belief that she might eventually agree.

Over the next two years, Tom persists, periodically asking Lisa out, convinced that the timing will eventually be right. Each time, Lisa continues to decline politely, leaving the possibility open without ever committing. Her responses remain vague and non-committal, such as "I'm just not in the right headspace right now" or "You don't want to go out with me; I've got a lot going on, but perhaps later in the future." Misinterpreting the cues, Tom's belief is reinforced each time. He remains convinced that Lisa's repeated use of "maybe" and "perhaps, some other time" indicates a delay or love game rather than a clear denial.

This naivete leads him to share optimistic updates with his friends and family, saying things like, "Lisa is interested, but she's just too busy right now," or "She's not in the right headspace, but she's definitely considering it." Over time, as he continues to enthusiastically relay these interpretations, his friends, lacking the full context, begin to believe that Lisa might truly be interested.

Tom's friends who hear only of Lisa through Tom's hopeful distortions remain unaware of her ambiguous deflections. They support Tom with favorable feedback. However, when Tom overhears his father, who has been observing this ongoing cycle, suggesting to a friend that Lisa might not actually be interested and that Tom could be misreading her politeness as a romantic interest, Tom reacts defensively. "No! I know she likes me. I have evidence that spans six years," he insists, unwilling to reconsider his interpretation despite the repeated pattern of gentle letdowns.

In the realm of origin of life research, this analogy fits well. For decades, scientific literature has been filled with "maybes" and "perhaps" without openly admitting the absence of a feasible explanation, often appealing to a future occasion. This scenario illustrates how disconfirmation bias and personal desires, coupled with varying degrees of information, can shape perceptions and lead to the spread of misinformation, fostering misguided beliefs unsupported by the broader context of available evidence. Just like Tom, many people are confronted with long-held hopes and perceptions that clash with reality, revealing a fundamental aspect of human nature to which no one is immune: our tendency to cling to familiar beliefs despite contradictory evidence.

Thus, this dynamic is not unique to Scott, O'Callaghan or Professor Dave; it is a universal phenomenon. Everyone has biases shaped by their personal experiences, education, culture, and belief systems, operating from a particular worldview.[703] A worldview shapes how each interprets and understands the world around them, including scientific theories and data.[704] When a tightly held worldview is challenged, particularly if it forms a core part of one's identity or understanding of the world, the experience can be disorienting or even traumatic. This disruption can lead to a psychological state where one experiences discomfort or distress in the face of conflicting beliefs or ideas.[705]

Despite the stronghold of materialist bias in the media, the decentralization of media platforms is inevitably providing a voice for alternate perspectives. Stephen C. Meyer, labeled a "pseudoscientific creationist" by contributors on his Wikipedia page, has been making his way onto platforms with large audiences. In July 2023, he appeared on episode 2008 of Joe Rogan's podcast, and in May 2024, he was a guest on the Piers

Morgan show. Rogan and Morgan afforded Meyer a grace and respect traditionally not given to ID proponents on major shows.[706]

CHAPTER 14

The Chocking Truth

> *Scientific understanding requires both facts and theories that can explain those facts in a coherent manner. Evolution, in this context, is both a fact and a theory. It is an incontrovertible fact that organisms have changed, or evolved, during the history of life on Earth. And biologists have identified and investigated mechanisms that can explain the major patterns of change.*[707] —
> Richard E. Lenski

Professionals across fields, from various scientists and researchers to NASA employees and educators, who dare to challenge radical Materialism often face a relentless storm of resistance from the scientific establishment.[708] This resistance acts as a *chock*, effectively wedging itself under the wheels of transformative progress, muting the voices of dissenters, thereby stalling scientific advancement.[709]

Joshua May, a professor in both Philosophy and Psychology, at the University of Alabama, Birmingham whose research investigates the impact of biases in scientific research, sheds light on the challenges faced by competing scientific perspectives. May elucidates the issue by stating, "Science has long been influenced by financial conflicts of interest, politics, and other biases... These biases have led to concerns about the generation of biased data and conclusions, influenced by non-epistemic values such as political ideology and personal gain."[710]

Robert T. Blackburn and Molly D. Hakel, in their 2006 study "An Examination of Sources of Peer Review Bias," discuss the challenges of objectively assessing the true quality of research and the potential biases that can obstruct the acceptance of novel theories.[711] Advocates of alternative perspectives who attempt to introduce competing theories and evidence often encounter an unyielding wall of resistance from the scientific establishment. This creates an environment in which young scientists hesitate to challenge prevailing views, fearing that doing so could derail their careers or block future opportunities.

As Carole Lee, associate professor of Philosophy at the University of Washington, and her colleagues explain in "Bias in Peer Review," systemic features of the peer review process tend to disadvantage novel or disruptive research. As noted by Lee and her colleagues, peer review can exhibit "content-based bias," defined as "partiality for or against a submission by virtue of the content (e.g., methods, theoretical orientation, results)."[712] One form of this is *confirmation bias*, described as "reviewer bias against manuscripts describing results inconsistent with the theoretical perspective of the reviewer."[713] The authors cite empirical research showing that "reviewers judged the methodological soundness, data presentation, scientific contribution, and publishability of a manuscript to be of higher quality when its data were consistent with the reviewer's theoretical orientation."[714]

A closely related concern is conservatism—"bias against groundbreaking and innovative research"—which, according to the authors, "threatens scientific progress by stifling the funding and public articulation of alternative and revolutionary scientific theories." Supporting this, they reference findings that "studies supporting unorthodox medical treatments were rated less highly even though the supporting data were equally strong." They also observe that uncertainty surrounding novel research "may make it more difficult for frontier research to appear excellent qua methodologically rigorous or solid."[715]

Bias can also be driven by the social status of authors. Lee and her colleagues discuss "prestige-based bias," a form of "social bias [that] challenges the thesis of impartiality by suggesting that reviewers do not evaluate submissions—their content and relationship to the literature—independently of the author's (perceived) identity."[716] The paper notes that "outsiders may find 'old-boy networks' that control journal and conference content." It references a study noting:

>They resubmitted published articles by prestigious individuals from prestigious institutions under fictitious names associated with less prestigious institutions. They found that resubmitted manuscripts were rejected 89% of the time (higher than the journal's 80% rejection rate) on the grounds that the studies contained "serious methodological flaws."[717]

This shows that peer review is influenced by overt prejudice and deeper structural and cognitive tendencies that influence how reviewers assess unfamiliar, unconventional, or low-status contributions.

Importantly, these forms of bias are often implicit. Drawing on cognitive psychology, Lee and her co-authors suggest that such patterns may reflect what could be described as disconfirmation bias—where reviewers scrutinize submissions they disagree with more harshly, seeking out flaws in claims they already believe to be false. That is, reviewers may look more vigorously for reasons to reject a paper than under normal pretenses. This ambiguity—whether bias is conscious or not—makes reform difficult, since "implicit biases... are not usually blocked by the conscious, deliberative processes by which egalitarian beliefs are formed and sustained," and may be "rationalized" using ostensibly neutral standards.[718] While Lee does not address specific fields like ID, her findings help explain why unconventional perspectives often face structural hurdles to impartial consideration.

Denis Noble, in an interview, discussed the bias and resistance he has faced from the scientific community when questioning established neo-evolutionary thought. Noble, who doesn't shy away from pointing out the complexities of biological systems, spoke about the challenges in advocating for a top-down, holistic systems perspective to biology amidst a field dominated by reductionist perspectives. The interview was conducted by Ard Louis, a professor of theoretical physics at the University of Oxford, and David Malone, a British filmmaker known for his science documentaries.[719]

The first question asked by Malone was, "Can you tell me what reductionism is?" Noble responds:

>I think reductionism is the idea that from the molecular level, you could reconstruct everything: that, in principle, at the molecular

level, everything is there that is needed in order to know how your body works, and that cannot be true. [720]

Noble argues that reductionists confuse the musical score of life for the music and the recipe for the dish.[721]

He posits the concept of integrative biology, which recognizes that functional properties emerge at higher levels of organization that cannot be predicted solely by examining molecular components.[722] For example, the rhythm of the heart, essential for life, results from interactions that scale from molecules to cells, tissues, and the full architecture of heart chambers and vessels—something not captured by examining isolated parts.[723]

He criticizes the overconfidence of those who believe that reductionism is the only valid scientific approach. He recounts an anecdote about Francis Crick, who, after discovering the structure of DNA, proclaimed that he had found "the secret of life."[724] Noble counters Crick by stating, "if I take the DNA out of a cell and I put it in a Petri dish with as many nutrients as you like, I can keep it for 10,000 years: it'll do absolutely nothing. It can't be the secret of life." [725] Noble notes that interactions between the cell and the organism give it functional significance.

Noble recounts an incident where a colleague expressed reluctance to support his arguments against reductionism, fearing it would inadvertently "bring God back in."[726] Noble argues that this fear stems from an unnecessary concern that acknowledging the functional organization and system-level causation in biology might validate religious views. He argues that science, however, should not fear spirituality, noting that it is essential for a comprehensive understanding of the human experience. He suggests that acknowledging spiritual aspects can enhance ones grasp of complex phenomena that purely materialistic approaches might overlook. According to Noble, spirituality is "to be able to give meaning to things" and the recognition of processes and relationships that transcend material explanations.[727]

Further, he makes a distinction between atheism and anti-theism. He notes that some atheists simply do not believe in God, whereas anti-theists actively oppose religious beliefs and often adhere strictly to reductionism as a counter to religious explanations. Noble says that this stance is as limiting as the religious dogma it claims to be above. The interviewer, Malone, who identifies as an atheist, also acknowledges this common fear within mainstream science. He likens it to the historical actions of "the Church," which rejected ideas perceived as threats to religious doctrine. In response to this 'inverse' fear, Noble argues that it stifles scientific progress, as scientists feel compelled to reject any notion that could be interpreted as supporting religious beliefs. Noble states:

> [Reductionism] is a house of cards built on some very bad concepts and some very poor science: poor because of the insistence that it is the only truth.[728]

In a different talk, Noble also points out the good ole boys' style politics. He explains that aligning with Darwin enhances the credibility and public acceptance of one's views:

> Darwin is up there as an icon, and if you can claim, as it were, that you're children of Charles Darwin, you're doing very well from the point of view of publicizing your point of view. And I think that's the explanation, but it needs to be emphasized very clearly indeed that Darwin would not have recognized Neo-Darwinism as his inheritance.[729]

Noble confronts reductionism head-on, yet his continued acceptance within mainstream science may stem from the fact that he challenges its foundational assumptions from within the naturalistic paradigm, rather than rejecting that paradigm outright.

The overall receptivity afforded to Noble, however, is starkly denied to scientists from camps such as ID, even though they present similar arguments against the sufficiency of blind mechanisms to create the sophisticated systems Noble discusses. Noble can at least sit at the table, but ID proponents cannot. However, should Noble ever outright renounce his confidence in Darwinism, he will likely experience a dramatic fall from grace. He would possibly be dismissed as having had a change of heart due to a debilitated mind in old age, similar to what happened to the former atheist philosopher Antony Flew.[730]

Behe, who now satirically refers to himself as a "(R)evolutionary biologist" on his website, exemplify the difficulties encountered by those presenting ideas that diverge markedly from reductionism.[731] Behe faces more than just obstacles to publishing in mainstream scientific journals—he is the target of a sustained rhetorical campaign aimed at discrediting his work.[732][733] Nevertheless, this kind of gaslighting cannot persist indefinitely and will likely lead more scientists to challenge Darwinian materialism—many of whom may already do so privately but remain silent out of fear.

Puzzling

Imagine you're an aspiring scientist, analogously a "puzzle assembler." You've inherited an old, incomplete puzzle from a revered family elder. Your family has always insisted that this puzzle, once completed, will showcase a stunning beach scene with a vivid sky. Eager to contribute to this legacy, you dive into the puzzle assembly. Each piece that seems to fit is met with a family celebration, amplifying your pressure to uphold the prevailing narrative about what the puzzle represents.

However, as you sift through the pieces, you notice something unsettling: there are far fewer 'sky' pieces than you'd expect for a beach scene. Eventually, you find a piece that doesn't fit perfectly, but it seems to fit ok into the sky area, and your announcement is met with family applause. This accolade adds another layer of complexity, further entrenching you in the established narrative while also increasing the internal struggle you're starting to feel.

You struggle with a growing awareness that the number of 'sky' pieces doesn't line up with the family's long-standing beliefs. Despite the public affirmations, privately, you grapple with an emerging realization that the puzzle may not depict the scene everyone has assumed. This growing dissonance between your observations and your family's preconceived beliefs creates a difficult quandary: do you dare to question the narrative or continue to force pieces to fit?

You're faced with a dilemma. You have to make a lasting decision. Do you voice your doubts and risk dismantling the family lore? Do you question the intellectual legacy you're supposed to inherit? Or do you conform, like most who are skeptical, celebrating each new 'fitting' piece while suppressing your growing uncertainties?

This analogy reflects a real dilemma faced by certain scientists, particularly those working in theoretical physics, cosmology, and evolutionary biology, where the prevailing paradigm discourages open questioning. They are torn between a commitment to objective inquiry and the very human fears of social ostracism, loss of funding, and professional stagnation. It's a question that often gets lost in public dialogues around scientific discoveries and critiques: How do new and established researchers navigate a landscape populated by powerful institutions and influential predecessors?

Unfortunately, many of the most established scientists actively enforce these pressures, inflicting the ostracism and professional stagnation, reinforcing ideological conformity within their fields. A rare, candid admission from an anonymous physicist—if genuine—captures this dilemma. In an email shared by Sabine Hossenfelder, a scientist confesses that much of the research in high-energy physics is, in his own words, "pretty useless stuff"—models that serve little purpose beyond sustaining an insular academic system.[734] The anonymous physicist states:

> We all do the same stuff and have some trade secrets. I am one of the authors of the so-called [....] model, pretty useless stuff, old refurbished [....] with a couple of new blows and whistles. But if people buy this [....] and it helps them get grants, who cares?[735]

This is a quiet truth that many in the field recognize but rarely admit. This physicist acknowledges that the system operates on economic and institutional inertia. Numerous researchers are not necessarily seeking truth, but ensuring that their work appears valuable enough to maintain funding and career stability.

The anonymous physicist cynically describes how funding is allocated, suggesting that those who approve research grants—whether university administrators or government agencies—often have little understanding of what they are actually funding. Instead, they prioritize projects that sound impressive or fashionable, helping to justify spending reports and attract students. The scientist states:

> For people who pay us, all we do is just noise. They have zero idea that elementary particles exist; they pay us from public funds (not from their own) and basically pay for "something cool", some new crazy hype, which they need either to include into their science spending reports or (in case of universities) to attract students.[736]

The statement about public funds "(not from their own)" reinforces this interpretation, implying that decision-makers are less discerning because they are not personally invested in the money being spent. This statement exposes the belief that as long as taxpayers remain unaware, it doesn't matter if the research is empty, misleading, or entirely speculative. The scientist frames this not as a failure, but as a necessary function of the system, a way to protect the academic elites from economic instability.

Worse still, this particular scientist makes no pretense of scientific integrity—his concern is not with knowledge or progress, but with ensuring that thousands of researchers like him remain employed. He admits:

> If you like, yes, what we created is a bubble, but it helps thousands of those guys and their families not to die from hunger.[737]

This astonishing admission reveals the true priority: self-preservation. It exposes an academic culture that has transformed into a self-sustaining jobs program, where livelihoods matter more than legitimacy. Every bubble, however, eventually bursts. The question is not if, but when.

CHAPTER 15

Celebrity Scientist

> *Examples of unintelligent design in nature are so numerous that an entire book could be written simply listing them. I will permit myself just one more example. The human respiratory and digestive tracts share a little plumbing at the pharynx. In the United States alone, this intelligent design feature lands tens of thousands of children in the emergency room each year. Some hundreds choke to death. Many others suffer irreparable brain injury. What compassionate purpose does this serve? Of course, we can imagine a compassionate purpose: perhaps the parents of these children needed to be taught a lesson; perhaps God has prepared a special reward in heaven for every child who chokes to death on a bottle cap.*[738] —Sam Harris

Over the years, celebrity scientists such as theoretical physicist Lawrence Krauss, evolutionary biologist Richard Dawkins, neuroscientist Sam Harris, and astrophysicist Neil deGrasse Tyson have, in various ways, taken up the role of Darwin's new bulldogs. Operating under the banner of science popularization, they have used their public platforms to promote militant atheism, often accompanied by antagonistic rhetoric.[739] They often dismiss religious texts with condescension toward the ancient authors, using ad hominem attacks like labeling them as "Bronze Age goat herders."[740] This tactic entertains an uncritical audience while undermining the ancient authors' ideas based solely on their background.

These modern scientists frequently overlook the contributions of scientists with traditional creationist worldviews, such as Georges Lemaître—a Belgian cosmologist and Catholic priest whose 1931 theory first presented in scientific form the idea of the universe having a beginning—or Sir Isaac Newton, the father of modern science.[741] [742] For example, although it is well-known that Sir Isaac Newton was profoundly religious, Richard Dawkins has attempted to clarify Newton's faith as more likely a product of societal pressures than genuine personal conviction. Richard Dawkins has suggested that if Sir Isaac Newton had lived during the 19th century, amidst the era of Darwin and the X Club, he might have been liberated from religious thought.[743]

Ironically, however, Newton's religious beliefs, notably similar to those of the ID community, were directly linked to his scientific inquiries and discoveries.[744] Yet, when today's scientists reach similar conclusions about intelligent design as did the father of modern science, they are dismissed as wacky pseudoscientists. These celebrity scientists selectively frame the history of science to fit a particular narrative.[745] Richard Dawkins, Sam Harris, Neil deGrasse Tyson, and Lawrence Krauss are better known for their vocal opposition to religion than for their scientific contributions. In turn, those with similar worldviews regard them as brilliant, as they devote considerable time to explaining how religion is supposedly warring against science.

Although they often speak as authorities on reality, addressing fundamental questions about existence, their assertions starkly contrast with the cautious approaches of researchers who study these topics in depth. These researchers, often away from the public eye, grapple with the complexities and significant challenges that continue to question the plausibility of such a continuum.

The reality is that celebrity scientists like Richard Dawkins are more aptly described as authors, public speakers, or social media personalities rather than practicing scientists. Over the last 50 years, Dawkins has primarily dedicated his career to writing, averaging a book every 2 to 3 years since 1976, with around 20 books in total. A schedule like that leaves little time for science. Considering that writing books was his day job and the primary social medium for communicating his ideas to the public, it may be more fitting to describe him as a "science influencer."

His prominence has come more from shaping public discourse than from active scientific research. Unfortunately, much of the public isn't interested in the hard truths found in scientific literature or in understanding the actual state of knowledge on big questions. Instead, they gravitate toward these figures whose confident proclamations entertain while reinforcing the beliefs systems of their listeners.

We can find further analysis of this dichotomy in Dr. Declan Fahy's work. In his book, *The New Celebrity Scientists: Out of the Lab and Into the Limelight*, Fahy examines how some scientists transition from research to becoming figures of public celebrity.[746] Fahy, an expert in the public communication of science, offers a critical examination of the evolving role of scientists in today's society.[747]

Fahy's book's title says it all, implying that these scientists have moved from traditional research roles within the laboratory to the forefront of popular culture and media. Fahy argues that for these celebrity scientists, public fame has eclipsed their academic and scientific contributions, warranting a critical examination of their true utility and impact on the field of science.[748] Indeed, steering followers away from a God they claim does not exist does nothing to advance scientific understanding.

Moreover, Fahy associates this transition to public visibility with an overarching narrative of scientism.[749] He suggests that these individuals exchange their lab coats for broader philosophical and ideological roles. The implication here is that while these individuals gain widespread popularity, their standing and credibility within the traditional, peer-reviewed academic community might not be as prominent.

Fahy's analysis is particularly pertinent in discussing the influence of celebrity scientists on public understanding of complex topics like ID. Their prominence often aligns with the narrative of radical Materialism, shaping public discourse in a way that does not capture the ongoing investigations in the world of science. Nevertheless, these high-profile scientists are often the first to inform the public about the latest developments and understanding of science. The dramatic irony must be intense for researchers actively engaged in their fields, as they watch speculative ideas being conveyed to the public with such confidence.

By quickly labeling perspectives like ID as purely religious or pseudoscientific, these figures thereby guide the public towards a skewed interpretation of these ideas to be at war against science and the advancement of humanity. This guise, aimed more at upholding scientism while discouraging open discourse, enables them to disseminate a narrative that is readily absorbed by the general public, who are often not familiar with the complexities of these arguments.

Such rhetorical tactics operate on multiple subtle layers. Those who support competing theories face rhetorical sophistry and projection, accused by critics of the same biases and shortcomings they themselves exhibit—such as reliance on outdated speculative concepts.[750] The dichotomy between these celebrity scientists' rhetorical approaches is also sharply different from those they often attack in the ID community, such as Behe and Meyer, who tend to engage in a more rationally informed debate, essentially free of ad hominem attacks and straw man arguments.

An article by Lawrence M. Krauss primes the reader with the provocative, propaganda-laden title "When Worldviews Collide: Science and Religion Face Off Again." This follows the familiar pattern of attacking religions rather than tackling the scientific arguments themselves.[751] Krauss relies on a friend's informal survey of over 10 million scientific articles, comparing the frequency of evolution-related pieces to the scarce presence of ID in scholarly journals.[752] He uses this to measure ID's scientific validity, but this gaslighting ignores the real challenges new or controversial ideas face in gaining recognition within academic circles.

In an embellishing, Lauri Lebo-esque manner, Krauss' narrative opens with a historical analogy, drawing parallels between the Taliban's destruction of the Buddha statues at Bamiyan and the resistance to evolutionary theory in the United States.[753] This comparison introduces a false equivalence, equating a physical act of cultural destruction with an intellectual debate.[754] The two situations are fundamentally different in their motivations and consequences. Central to Krauss' argument is the sanctity of the scientific method. He claims that opposition to evolution is not merely a disagreement over a theory but an attack on—wait, you guessed it— "science itself," implying that critics of evolution are, by extension, anti-science and irrational.[755]

In the context of examining the influence of personal beliefs on scientific discourse, it is insightful to refer to the work of Edwards and Smith.[756] Their study, "A Disconfirmation Bias in the Evaluation of Arguments," is a critical reference point. It demonstrates how individuals, including scientists, exhibit a propensity to intensely scrutinize and potentially undervalue arguments that conflict with their pre-existing beliefs, whereas they more readily accept those that align.[757]

Their research reveals that this tendency poses a significant challenge to the objective evaluation of scientific theories. Conversely, arguments that align with one's beliefs are scrutinized less and often accepted at face value. This suggests that the scientific community's less frequent discussion of ID in literature points to an influence of a prevailing bias against it rather than a straightforward assessment of its scientific merits.[758]

Further, Krauss' narrative seems to imply that religious individuals are generally opposed to understanding his "proper" worldview, seeing reality through the lens of the cosmic evolutionary continuum. He attributes the persistence of religious worldviews to "ineffective science teaching" in public schools.[759] Thus, he dismisses skepticism of Darwin's theories as "a huge waste of time."[760] Apart from conflating ID's arguments with religious fanaticism, he fails to acknowledge the historical and contemporary contributions of religious individuals to various scientific fields.

Apart from his poisoning the well with attacks on religion, his climatic focal point is the informal survey of over 10 million scientific articles used to measure legitimacy of ID by its prevalence in scientific literature.[761] The search results of over 10 million articles in major scientific journals, spanning a period of twelve years, form the corpus of his analysis.[762] This large-scale analysis is designed to provide a broad and comprehensive overview of the scientific discourse surrounding these topics. The methodology focuses on comparing search results for the frequency of the keywords "evolution" and "Intelligent Design" in scientific publications.[763]

The search term "evolution" yielded approximately 115,000 articles, predominantly related to biological evolution.[764] Krauss boasts, "searching for the key word evolution pulled up 115,000 articles." He interprets this high number as a marker of validity, assuming that widespread acceptance equates to established scientific credibility. By now, I assume my readers see the glaring, almost comical, but not really, problem with the logic of this redundant argument.

In contrast, he gloats:

> Searching for Intelligent Design yielded 88 articles. All but 11 of those were in engineering journals, where, of course, we hope there is discussion of intelligent design. Of the 11, eight were critical of the scientific basis for ID theory, and the remaining three turned out to be articles in conference proceedings, not peer-reviewed research journals.[765]

By his own admission, it's a shame that not one result for ID yielded a peer-reviewed paper on the theory. As people often say in situations this absurd, "you can't make this up!"

Despite the fallacious argument, it's refreshing that ID consistently shows up as valuable within engineering. Krauss, who has cited these findings repeatedly, seems to overlook this aspect, adding a comical layer of intrigue to his flawed reasoning. His conclusions, for example, reveal how data interpretation can shift dramatically based on the assumptions and biases of the interpreter.

In the case of figures like Krauss, Dawkins, deGrasse Tyson, Harris, Scott, and YouTubers like Professor Dave, their firm opposition to religious influence in science appears more as a response to perceived threats to their conclusions about reality than to science itself. Their criticisms frequently arise from the mere existence of such beliefs, which inherently challenges their reality. There's a palpable sense of agitation among them, rooted in the conviction that their worldview is the unassailable "correct" one, yet not universally accepted or reconciled by others. This is particularly evident in their reactions within discussions around mysteries like the origin of the universe, the emergence of DNA, and the diversity of life, where the presence of religious interpretations, regardless of their explicit mention, creates cognitive dissonance for these materialists.[766]

Focused on Science

Contrary to claims like Krauss' assertion that "to oppose evolution is to be opposed to science itself," scientific thought encompasses a far more diverse range of perspectives.[767] Scientists come from a variety of backgrounds and hold a range of personal beliefs. Many understand that science operates in a realm distinct from personal belief systems and ideologies.

Researchers in numerous scientific disciplines typically focus on immediate objectives. For instance, researchers in fields such as epidemiology, genetics, and pharmacology are primarily engaged in combating diseases, unraveling the complexities of genetic disorders, and innovating new medicinal treatments. Similarly, ecology's primary aim often involves assessing how environmental changes impact different species. In DNA research and genetic therapy, scientists usually focus on developing effective treatments and a more comprehensive understanding of the underlying genetic mechanisms.

In these contexts, the broader theoretical discussions about macroevolution or the origins of life are not the central focus. Instead, the emphasis is on tangible, immediate scientific goals that have direct applications and implications. However, research findings are often retrofitted into the broader context of evolutionary theory, regardless of whether they directly support its assumptions. For example, the discovery of a new aspect of animal behavior, a unique biochemical pathway, or a previously unknown fossil is tossed into the box labeled puzzle pieces for evolutionary processes.

Recognizing this gives us a more accurate view of the scientific landscape. It's a landscape where the majority of scientists are engaged in dedicated research with direct applications to health, technology, and understanding of the natural world. Many of these research areas are refining our understanding of the innate technological-like features found in nature and across the cosmos. These scientists are also diligently striving to replicate these natural mechanisms and systems. This effort reflects a recognition of the technological aspects woven into the fabric of the natural world. What contributions to science have figures like Dawkins made in the past fifty years, beyond their relentless attacks on religion?

Much of the progress in science comes from focused, detailed research that incrementally builds our understanding. This work is often less glamorous and less likely to be featured in popular media, but it is essential for scientific advancement—unlike engaging in gotcha questions about whether Jesus was born of a virgin or rose from the grave.[768] This focus on concrete scientific goals means that many researchers may not be engaged with or well-versed in the broader philosophical or speculative discussions that often captivate the public imagination. Topics such as the origins of life or the implications of macroevolutionary theory, while significant in some academic circles, rarely constitute the core of their day-to-day scientific work.

At the personal level, scientists, like any other individuals, grapple with their work's philosophical and existential implications. Discoveries that shake the very foundations of cosmic understanding, such as the nature of dark matter, the peculiarities of quantum mechanics, or the fine-tuning of universal constants, often strike at scientists' intellectual identity. When confronted with findings that defy the conventional wisdom of reality, a scientist may experience intellectual turmoil, perceiving it as an attack on their long-held 'correct' beliefs. This internal conflict is exemplary of the human aspect of scientific investigation, where objective analysis intersects with subjective interpretation and personal belief systems.

Thus, the cultural context in which science operates must be considered. The public often expects clear, definitive answers of what 'the research says.' However, in complex fields like cosmology and studies of origins, some questions may never be fully answered. Admitting to these unknowns is challenging for many but essential, even if it introduces conundrums that push the boundaries of one's understanding of reality. This level of humility and vulnerability requires a departure from the traditional public image of science as infallible and all-knowing.

The image of scientists as purely rational and emotionally detached often obscures the reality of these human vulnerabilities. This lack of recognition for the human element in science affects not only how scientists engage with their work and one another but also how the public perceives scientific authority.

Notes

Notes

1 Deuteronomy 4:9–10, King James Version.

2 William Bristow, "Enlightenment," *The Stanford Encyclopedia of Philosophy*, Spring 2025 ed., edited by Edward N. Zalta, accessed June 13, 2025, https://plato.stanford.edu/entries/enlightenment/.

3 Ibid.

4 Joachim Schaper, "The Question of a 'Biblical Theology' and the Growing Tension between 'Biblical Theology' and a 'History of the Religion of Israel': From Johann Philipp Gabler to Rudolf Smend, Sen.," in Hebrew Bible / Old Testament: The History of Its Interpretation, Volume III/1: From Modernism to Post-Modernism (The Nineteenth and Twentieth Centuries), ed. Magne Sæbø (Göttingen: Vandenhoeck & Ruprecht, 2013), https://www.academia.edu/10619421/_The_Question_of_a_Biblical_Theology_and_the_Growing_Tension_between_Biblical_Theology_and_a_History_of_the_Religion_of_Israel_from_Johann_Philipp_Gabler_to_Rudolf_Smend_Sen_?utm_source=chatgpt.com.

5 Michael G. Hasel, "Israel in the Merneptah Stela," *Bulletin of the American Schools of Oriental Research*, no. 296 (November 1994): 45–62.

6 Ibid., 13:00–44:00

7 "Proto-Sinaitic Inscriptions," net.lib.byu.edu, https://net.lib.byu.edu/imaging/negev/origins.html.

8 Shane M. Thompson, "Serabit El-Khadem: An Egyptian and Semitic Mining Community," *O. UBC Community and Partner Publications, Database of Religious History* (DRH), December 26, 2022, http://dx.doi.org/10.14288/1.0438242.

9 William H. Shea, "A Further Reading for the Hobab Inscription from Sinai," *Andrews University Seminary Studies* 27, no. 3 (Autumn 1989): 193–200.

10 Ibid.

11 Titus Kennedy, "The Land of the š3sw (Nomads) of yhw3 at Soleb," *Dotawo: A Journal of Nubian Studies* 6, no. 1 (2019): 175–192, https://doi.org/10.5070/D66146256.

12 Thomas E. Levy, Russell B. Adams, and Adolfo Muniz, *Archaeology and the Shasu Nomads: Recent Excavations in the Jabal Hamrat Fidan, Jordan*, in Archaeology, Anthropology and Cult: The Sanctuary at Gilat, Israel, ed. Thomas E. Levy (London: Equinox, 2018), chap. 6, accessed June 18, 2025, https://archive.org/details/ArchaeologyAndTheShasuNomadsRecentExcavationPages228.

13 Flavius Josephus, *Against Apion*, Book I, in *The Works of Flavius Josephus*, ed. H. St. J. Thackeray, vol. 1 (London: William Heinemann; New York: G.P. Putnam's Sons, 1926), accessed June 14, 2025, https://penelope.uchicago.edu/josephus/apion-1.html

14 Ibid.

15 Manfred Bietak and Gary A. Rendsburg, "Egypt and the Exodus," in *Ancient Israel: From Abraham to the Roman Destruction of the Temple*, rev. and expanded ed., ed. Hershel Shanks and John Merrill (Washington, D.C.: Biblical Archaeology Society, 2021), 17–58, 342–51.

16 Manfred Bietak, "Avaris/Tell el-Dab'a," in *The Encyclopedia of Ancient History*, ed. Roger S. Bagnall et al. (Chichester, UK: Wiley-Blackwell, 2022), 1–16, https://doi.org/10.1002/9781444338386.wbeah15052.pub2.

17 Henning Franzmeier, "The Foundation of Pi-Ramesse: Strengthening the Rule of the 19th Dynasty and Displaying Egypt to the Outside World," *The Journal of Egyptian Archaeology* 110, no. 1–2 (2024): 177–86, https://doi.org/10.1177/03075133241297651.

18 Kenneth A. Kitchen, "The Patriarchal Age: Myth or History? The Biblical Data Match Objective Facts from the Ancient World in an Almost Uncanny Way," *Biblical Archaeology Review* 21, no. 2 (March/April 1995): 48–57, 88–95.

19 The Exodus: Fact or Fiction? Evidence of Israel's Exodus from Egypt" Biblical Archaeology Society, April 10, 2025, https://www.biblicalarchaeology.org/daily/biblical-topics/exodus/exodus-fact-or-fiction/.

20 Ibid.

21 Daniel M. Keeran, Ancient Egyptian Ipuwer Papyrus (1250 B.C.) Describes the Biblical Plagues (Victoria, Canada: self-published, 2019), https://www.academia.edu/39655701/Ancient_Egyptian_Ipuwer_Papyrus_1250_B_C_Describes_the_Biblical_Plagues.

22 Christopher Pearson, Kostas Sbonias, Iris Tzachili, et al., "Olive Shrub Buried on Therasia Supports a Mid-16th Century BCE Date for the Thera Eruption," *Scientific Reports* 13 (2023): 6994, https://doi.org/10.1038/s41598-023-33696-w.

23 Intelligent design is a pseudoscientific argument for the existence of God, presented by its proponents as 'an evidence-based scientific theory about life's origins.'" *Wikipedia*, s.v. "Intelligent design," https://en.wikipedia.org/wiki/Intelligent_design.

24 James Tour, "Nanoscientist, Lee Cronin, says close to creating life in the lab! Origin of life and abiogenesis," YouTube video, 1:14, posted July 13, 2022, https://www.youtube.com/watch?v=yxm1CHyw8NU.

25 James Jeans, *Astronomy and Cosmogony*, 2nd ed. (Cambridge: Cambridge University Press, 2009; first published 1928), https://doi.org/10.1017/CBO9780511694363.

26 Barbara Ryden, Introduction to Cosmology, 2nd ed. (Cambridge: Cambridge University Press, 2017), 1.

27 Cosmogony," Wikipedia, last modified March 25, 2025, https://en.wikipedia.org/wiki/Cosmogony.

28 Ibid., Emphasis added.

29 Ibid.

30 George F. R. Ellis, "Cosmology," *Stanford Encyclopedia of Philosophy*, Fall 2020 Edition, edited by Edward N. Zalta, https://plato.stanford.edu/entries/cosmology/.

31 *American Dictionary of the English Language*, s.v. "cosmogony," Noah Webster, 1828, https://webstersdictionary1828.com/Dictionary/cosmogony.

32 Cosmogony," *Merriam-Webster.com Dictionary*, accessed May 17, 2025, https://www.merriam-webster.com/dictionary/cosmogony.

33 "Cosmogony," *Online Etymology Dictionary*, accessed May 17, 2025, https://www.etymonline.com/word/cosmogony.

34 James H. Jeans, The Problems of Cosmogony and Stellar Dynamics (Cambridge: Cambridge University Press, 1919), https://archive.org/details/problemsofcosmog00jeanrich/.

35 Georges Lemaître, *The Primeval Atom: An Essay on Cosmogony* (New York: D. Van Nostrand Company, 1950).

36 J. A. Wheeler and C. M. Patton, "Is Physics Legislated by Cosmogony?" in *The Encyclopedia of Ignorance*, ed. Ronald Duncan and Miranda Weston-Smith (Oxford: Pergamon, 1977), 44–45.

37 Ibid.

38 Ibid.

39 Ibid.

40 James Jeans, *The Mysterious Universe* (New York: Macmillan, 1930), https://archive.org/details/TheMysteriousUniverseSirJamesJeans.

41 John Archibald Wheeler, quoted in "John Archibald Wheeler Quotes," Today in Science History, accessed June 19, 2025, https://todayinsci.com/W/Wheeler_John/WheelerJohn-Quotations.htm.

42 Ibid.

43 "Cosmogony," *Merriam-Webster.com Dictionary*, archived comparison between April 25, 2009, and January 25, 2025, Internet Archive, https://web.archive.org/web/diff/20250125190332/20090425014943/https://www.merriam-webster.com/dictionary/cosmogony.

44 Ibid.

45 Ibid.

46 Stephen Hawking, *A Brief History of Time: From the Big Bang to Black Holes* (New York: Bantam Books, 1988).

47 Sean Carroll, The Big Picture: On the Origins of Life, Meaning, and the Universe Itself (New York: Dutton, 2016).

48 Barbara Ryden, Introduction to Cosmology. Ryden notes: "In a flat, radiation-only universe, as $t \to 0$, $\varepsilon r \to \infty$ (Equation 5.63). Thus, at the instant $t = 0$, the energy density of our own universe (well approximated as a flat, radiation-only model in its early stages) was infinite, according to this analysis; this infinite energy density was provided by an infinite number density of particles (Equation 5.66), each of infinite energy (Equation 5.65). Should we take these infinities seriously? Not really, since the assumptions of general relativity, on which the Friedmann equation is based, break down at $t \approx tP$."

49 Ibid., 203. Ryden notes: "Suppose the universe contains a scalar field whose value can vary as a function of position and time. Some early implementations of inflation associated the scalar field ϕ with the Higgs field, which mediates interactions between particles at energies higher than the GUT energy; however, to keep the discussion general, let's just call the field the inflaton field. 4 Generally speaking, a scalar field can have an associated potential energy $V(\phi)$. (As a simple illustrative example, suppose that the scalar field ϕ is the elevation above sea level at a given point on the Earth's surface. The

associated potential energy, in this case, is the gravitational potential $V = g\phi$, where $g = 9.8$ ms -2.)"

50 Barbara Ryden, "Inflation and the Very Early Universe," in *Introduction to Cosmology*, 2nd ed. (Cambridge: Cambridge University Press, 2017).

51 Ibid., Ryden lays out the inflationary scenario in explicitly staged terms: "suppose the exponential growth was switched on instantaneously at a time t_i, and lasted until some later time t_f, when the exponential growth was switched off instantaneously, and the universe reverted to its former state of radiation-dominated expansion." What follows is a sequence of ad hoc transitions: "after rolling off the plateau… the inflaton field oscillates," releasing photons that "reheat the universe after the precipitous drop in temperature caused by inflation." She adds that this process can be "thought of as the latent heat" from a phase transition. The model depends on a fictionalized timeline in which fields are toggled on and off, reheating occurs by analogy, and physics gives way to metaphor. This is not explanation—it's narrative structure.

52 Ibid., Ryden explains that a submicroscopic patch of space, approximately 4×10^{-29} meters, was inflated to macroscopic size—about 0.9 meters—in an extremely short period. While she doesn't convert this to centimeters or light-years, the scale of growth she describes is consistent with a jump from smaller than a proton to human-scale dimensions, within $\sim 10^{-34}$ seconds.

53 Ibid., Ryden calculates that if inflation involved 65 e-foldings, the visible universe today would have emerged from a region smaller than 6×10^{-28} meters—well below the threshold of direct observation. This supports that the model begins with a space far smaller than any known physical structure and assumes it expanded faster than causality allows under normal physics.

54 Alan H. Guth, "The Inflationary Universe: A Possible Solution to the Horizon and Flatness Problems," *Physical Review D* 23, no. 2 (1981): 347–356. https://doi.org/10.1103/PhysRevD.23.347

55 Barbara Ryden, "Inflation and the Very Early Universe," in *Introduction to Cosmology*. She writes: "If the inflaton field is coupled to any of the other fields in the universe… the energy of the inflaton field [is] carried away by photons or other relativistic particles. These photons reheat the universe after the precipitous drop in temperature caused by inflation. The energy lost by the inflaton field… can be thought of as the latent heat of that transition."

56 Ibid., Ryder explicitly describe reheating and particle formation following inflation, though still in generalized, theoretical terms—without specifying the precise mechanisms for these transitions.

57 Ibid.

58 Ibid., Ryder identifies the time of Big Bang nucleosynthesis as occurring when the universe was about 300 seconds (or 3–5 minutes) old, with temperatures around 6×10^8 K, during which protons and neutrons fused to form helium and trace amounts of other light elements. She also references Steven Weinberg's *The First Three Minutes* and goes into detail about the inefficiency of this nucleosynthesis process and the resulting helium fraction of the universe.

59 Ibid., Barbara Ryden affirms that the cosmic microwave background reflects conditions roughly 370,000 years after the Big Bang—not the origin itself, but the moment when the universe first became transparent to light.

60 Richard B. Larson and Volker Bromm, "The First Stars in the Universe," *Scientific American*, December 2004, 64–71. http://www.astro.yale.edu/larson/papers/SciAm04.pdf.

61 Ibid.

62 *"Star Formation,"* Center for Astrophysics | Harvard & Smithsonian, accessed June 20, 2025, https://www.cfa.harvard.edu/research/topic/star-formation.

63 "Graceful Exit Problem," *Wikipedia*, last modified April 2, 2025, https://en.wikipedia.org/wiki/Graceful_exit_problem.

64 Daniel Dennett, "Information, Evolution, and Intelligent Design," YouTube video, 1:07–1:55, Royal Institution, May 13, 2015, https://www.youtube.com/watch?v=AZX6awZq5Z0.

65 Jacob Berkowitz, "The Stardust Revolution: The New Story of Our Origin in the Stars" (Amherst, NY: Prometheus, 2012), ISBN 9781616145491.

66 Maria Kalambokidis and Michael Travisano, "The eco-evolutionary origins of life," *Evolution* 78, no. 1 (January 2024): 1–12, https://doi.org/10.1093/evolut/qpad195. Note: This article explores the concept of abiogenesis, focusing on the eco-evolutionary processes that might have led to the origin of life. The authors discuss the role of small energy increments in early prebiotic systems and the significance of environments like deep sea vents in providing suitable energy potentials and stable conditions for the emergence and evolution of life.

67 In the *Kitzmiller v. Dover* case, the court ruled that teaching intelligent design, including Behe's argument of irreducible complexity, was unconstitutional under the Establishment Clause of the First Amendment. Although Behe presented his argument as a scientific critique of evolutionary theory, the court dismissed it due to its implications, which were interpreted as religious—specifically the suggestion of a designer. As a result, the ruling effectively prohibits such arguments in public school science classes, not because of their form, but because of the religious implications drawn from them. However, the Earth is round, even if that somehow implies intelligence. See: https://law.justia.com/cases/federal/district-courts/FSupp2/400/707/2414073/

68 Richard Dawkins, *The God Delusion* (Boston: Houghton Mifflin Harcourt, 2006), 125.

69 Ibid., 126.

70 Ibid., 128.

71 "Expelled: No Intelligence Allowed (2008) - Trascript," IMDb, accessed March 3, 2024, https://www.imdb.com/title/tt1091617/characters/nm1468026.

72 Ibid.

73 *Encyclopædia Britannica*, "Oparin-Haldane Theory," accessed June 18, 2024, https://www.britannica.com/science/Oparin-Haldane-theory.

74 Tonći Kokić, "The Oparin Hypothesis is a Falling Star," *Athens Journal of Philosophy* 2, no. 1 (March 2023): 39-52, accessed March 5, 2024, https://www.researchgate.net/publication/368711576_The_Oparin_Hypothesis_is_a_Falling_Star

75 Ibid., 48.

76 Ibid.

77 Elizabeth O'Grady, Jason Cashmore, Marsha Hay, and Carol Wismer, *Principles of Biology: An Introduction to Biological Concepts*, adapted from Concepts of Biology by OpenStax (College of Lake County, 2021), 63, http://dept.clcillinois.edu/biodv/PrinciplesOfBiology.pdf.

78 Kevin Zahnle, Laura Schaefer, and Bruce Fegley, "Earth's Earliest Atmospheres," Cold Spring Harbor Perspectives in Biology 2, no. 10 (2010): a004895, 10.

Notes

79 Ibid.

80 Elizabeth O'Grady, Jason Cashmore, Marsha Hay, and Carol Wismer, *Principles of Biology: An Introduction to Biological Concepts.*

81 Ibid.

82 OpenStax, Microbiology, ISBN 978-1-947172-23-4, accessed June 18, 2024, https://openstax.org/books/microbiology/pages/7-introduction.

83 OpenStax, "Press," accessed June 18, 2024, https://openstax.org/press.

84 Creative Commons, "About," accessed June 18, 2024, https://creativecommons.org/about/.

85 OpenStax, "Is OpenStax Content High Quality?" accessed June 18, 2024, https://openstax.org/faq.

86 OpenStax, "How do OpenStax Books Stay Current?" accessed June 18, 2024, https://openstax.org/faq.

87 Ibid.

88 Khan Academy, "Origins of Life," August 1, 2016, 0:00-5:21, accessed June 18, 2024, https://www.khanacademy.org/science/ap-biology/natural-selection/origins-of-life-on-earth/v/origins-of-life.

89 Khan Academy, "Origins of Life," August 1, 2016, 0:00-5:21, video, accessed June 18, 2024, https://www.youtube.com/watch?v=rMuj2MGeIAc.

90 Ibid.

91 Ibid.

92 Ibid.

93 Ibid.

94 Ibid.

95 Ibid.

96 Carl Sagan, *Cosmos* (New York: Random House, 1980).

97 Charles Lyell, Principles of Geology: Being an Attempt to Explain the Former Changes of the Earth's Surface, by Reference to Causes Now in Operation (London: John Murray, 1830).

98 "Timeline of the Life of Charles Darwin," *Christ's College, University of Cambridge*, accessed February 16, 2025, https://www.christs.cam.ac.uk/timeline-life-charles-darwin.

99 Charles Darwin, Letter to W. D. Fox, January 15, 1839, Darwin Correspondence Project, accessed September 24, 2024, https://www.darwinproject.ac.uk/letter/?docId=letters/DCP-LETT-319.xml.

100 Ibid.

101 Charles Darwin, Letter to Leonard Horner, August 29, 1844, Darwin Correspondence Project, accessed September 24, 2024, https://www.darwinproject.ac.uk/letter/DCP-LETT-771.xml.

102 Charles Darwin, Letter to Charles Lyell, June 26, 1858, in The Darwin Correspondence Project, accessed September 15, 2024, https://www.darwinproject.ac.uk/letter/?docId=letters/DCP-LETT-2295.xml&query=letter.

103 *Charles Lyell, Life, Letters, and Journals of Sir Charles Lyell*, Bart., ed. Mrs. Lyell (London: John Murray, 1881), 1:17, accessed via Cornell University Library, Henry Williams Sage Endowment Fund, Ithaca, NY.

104 Ibid.

105 Ibid., 238.

106 "*Reflections in a Black Mirror: Analyzing Bloody Mary and Her Presence in 'The Wolf Among Us'*," Center for Writing and Public Policy, University of Missouri, April 14, 2016, https://cwp.missouri.edu/2016/reflections-in-a-black-mirror-analyzing-bloody-mary-and-her-presence-in-the-wolf-among-us/.

107 *Charles Lyell, Life, Letters, and Journals of Sir Charles Lyell*, Bart., ed. Mrs. Lyell., 238.

108 Ibid., 269.

109 "*Quarterly Review*," Wikipedia, last modified February 27, 2025, https://en.wikipedia.org/wiki/Quarterly_Review.

110 *Charles Lyell, Life, Letters, and Journals of Sir Charles Lyell*, Bart., ed. Mrs. Lyell. Emphasis added.

111 Ibid., 270.

112 Ibid.

113 Ibid., 271.

114 Ibid.

115 Ibid.

116 Ibid., 276.

117 Ibid.

118 Ibid., 252.

119 Ibid.

120 Ibid., 252-253

121 Ibid., 473.

122 Ibid., 276

123 Ibid.

124 Ibid., 271.

125 Ibid.

126 Ibid.

127 Charles Darwin to J. D. Hooker, *Letter*, 24–5 February 1863: "On Friday I had interview with Sir H. Holland, & found him going immense way with us (ie all Birds from one)—good, as showing how wind blows." *Darwin Correspondence Project*, Letter no. 4009, accessed October 13, 2024, https://www.darwinproject.ac.uk/letter/?docId=letters/DCP-LETT-4009.xml.

128 Charles Lyell, *Life, Letters, and Journals of Sir Charles Lyell, Bart.*, 468.

129 Note: Italics added for emphasis.

130 Charles Lyell, *Life, Letters, and Journals of Sir Charles Lyell, Bart.*, 468.

131 Italicized for emphasis.

132 Charles Lyell, *Principles of Geology* (New York: D. Appleton & Co., reprinted edition), 27-31. Accessed via Apple Books. https://books.apple.com/us/book/principles-of-geology/id497909056. (Emphasis added).

133 Ibid.

134 Ibid., (emphasis added).

135 Charles Lyell, *Life, Letters, and Journals of Sir Charles Lyell, Bart.*, 468.

136 Ibid.

137 "Presiding Deity," *Wisdom Library*, last modified February 16, 2025, https://www.wisdomlib.org/concept/presiding-deity.

138 "Presiding God," *Wisdom Library*, accessed September 23, 2024, https://www.wisdomlib.org/concept/presiding-god.

139 "Adhidaivata: 10 Definitions," *Wisdom Library*, last updated May 31, 2022, https://www.wisdomlib.org/definition/adhidaivata.

140 *Chandogya Upanishad (Madhva Commentary)*, *Wisdom Library*, last updated February 27, 2021, https://www.wisdomlib.org/hinduism/book/chandogya-upanishad-madhva-commentary/d/doc626557.html.

141 S. A. Cooper, *Natural Technology: The Theory of Everything.*, 233-234.

142 Erwin Schrödinger, *Mind and Matter* (Cambridge: Cambridge University Press, 1958), 129, http://strangebeautiful.com/other-texts/schrodinger-what-is-life-mind-matter-auto-sketches.pdf.

143 William Provine, "Scientists, Face It! Science And Religion Are Incompatible," *The Scientist*, September 1988, https://www.the-scientist.com/scientists-face-it-science-and-religion-are-incompatible-62695.

144 Charles Darwin, *The Life and Letters of Charles Darwin, Including an Autobiographical Chapter*, ed. Francis Darwin (London: John Murray, 1887), 3:105, https://darwin-online.org.uk/content/frameset?pageseq=154&itemID=F1452.3&viewtype=side.

145 Paul Harrison, *A History of Pantheism*, "Haeckel's Monism," Pantheism.net, December 16, 1996, https://www.pantheism.net/paul/history/haeckel.htm.

146 Nolan Heie, *Ernst Haeckel and the Redemption of Nature* (PhD diss., Queen's University, 2008), p. 39, https://central.bac-lac.gc.ca/.item?id=TC-OKQ-1016&op=pdf&app=Library&oclc_number=1032899443.

147 Ibid.

148 Ibid.

149 Charles Darwin, *The Autobiography of Charles Darwin 1809–1882*, edited by Nora Barlow (London: Collins, 1958), 85.

150 "The Death of Anne Elizabeth Darwin," in *Darwin Correspondence Project*, accessed November 2, 2024, https://www.darwinproject.ac.uk/people/about-darwin/family-life/death-anne-elizabeth-darwin.

151 Charles Darwin, *The Autobiography of Charles Darwin 1809–1882*, ed. Nora Barlow (London: Collins, 1958), 87.

152 Romans 3:9–20 (ESV): "[A]s it is written: 'None is righteous, no, not one; no one understands; no one seeks for God. All have turned aside; together they have become worthless; no one does good, not even one.'" Accessed May 23, 2025. https://www.biblegateway.com/passage/?search=Romans%203%3A9-20&version=ESV.

153 Charles Darwin, "Letter to Asa Gray," May 22, 1860, in *Darwin Correspondence Project*, accessed November 2, 2024, https://www.darwinproject.ac.uk/letter/DCP-LETT-2814.xml.

154 Charles Darwin to William Graham, 3 July 1881, *Darwin Correspondence Project*, Letter no. 13230, accessed November 15, 2024, https://www.darwinproject.ac.uk/letter/DCP-LETT-13230.xml.

155 Ibid.

156 Charles Darwin, "Letter to Charles Lyell," 25 August 1845, in *Darwin Correspondence Project*, "Letter no. 905," accessed October 13, 2024, https://www.darwinproject.ac.uk/letter/DCP-LETT-905.xml.

157 Charles Darwin, "Letter to G. R. Waterhouse," October 8, 1843, Darwin Online, accessed April 18, 2024, https://darwin-online.org.uk/converted/published/1939_CollingwoodLetter_F3408.html.

158 Keith Thomson, "Darwin's Enigmatic Health: After His World Travels, Darwin Became Ill—But the Cause Remains Unknown," American Scientist, accessed February 2025, https://www.americanscientist.org/article/darwins-enigmatic-health.

159 T.J. Barloon and R. Noyes, "Charles Darwin and Panic Disorder," *JAMA* 277, no. 2 (1997): 138–141, https://doi.org/10.1001/jama.1997.03540260052035.

160 Keith Thomson, "Darwin's Enigmatic Health: After His World Travels, Darwin Became Ill—But the Cause Remains Unknown."

161 Charles Darwin, "Letter to G. R. Waterhouse."

162 "Epizeuxis," LitCharts, accessed April 13, 2024, https://www.litcharts.com/literary-devices-and-terms/epizeuxis. Quoted in Ibid., "Some additional key details about epizeuxis: The immediate repetition of the same word or phrase in epizeuxis is blunt and powerful, but for that same reason should be used sparingly. In speeches, epizeuxis is usually forceful, vehement, and motivating, and can serve as a rallying cry.

163 "Holy, holy, holy is the Lord Almighty; the whole earth is full of his glory" (Isaiah 6:3); "Do not trust in these deceptive words: 'This is the temple of the Lord, the temple of the Lord, the temple of the Lord'" (Jeremiah 7:4); "Holy, holy, holy is the Lord God Almighty, who was, and is, and is to come" (Revelation 4:8); "My God, my God, why have you forsaken me?" (Matthew 27:46), Holy Bible, New International Version.

164 Ruth Barton, *The X Club: Power and Authority in Victorian Science* (Chicago: University of Chicago Press, 2018, eBook.), 171–72.

165 Ibid., Emphasis added.

166 Michael J. Behe, *Darwin's Black Box: The Biochemical Challenge to Evolution* (New York: Free Press, 1996).

167 Ibid.

168 Thomas Henry Huxley, *Evidence as to Man's Place in Nature* (London: Williams and Norgate, 1863), 127.

169 Thomas Henry Huxley, *Darwiniana: Essays* (New York: D. Appleton and Company, 1896), 77.

170 Charles Darwin, *On the Origin of Species*, 6th ed. (London: John Murray, 1872).

171 Ibid.

172 Manuela Fernández Pinto, "Methodological and Cognitive Biases in Science," *Perspectives on Science* 31, no. 5 (2023): 535-554, accessed April 13, 2024, https://direct.mit.edu/posc/article/31/5/535/115648/Methodological-and-Cognitive-Biases-in-Science.

173 "Six things Darwin never said," Darwin Correspondence Project, accessed April 26, 2024, https://www.darwinproject.ac.uk/people/about-darwin/six-things-darwin-never-said. Note: This page attempts to narrow the context of Darwin's admission regarding his speculations going beyond the bounds of 'true science' to a specific discussion about the geographic distribution of certain plant species. This interpretation minimizes the broader uncertainties that Darwin expressed about his evolutionary theories. For a contrasting view that reveals the integral role of Darwin's botanical studies in his broader scientific work, see "Getting to Know Darwin's Science: Orchids," Darwin Correspondence Project, https://www.darwinproject.ac.uk/learning/universities/getting-know-darwins-science/orchids. This discrepancy within the same website highlights the dogmatism of neo-Darwinian commentary, which often seeks to sanitize Darwin's uncertainties to portray a more unwavering figure in the face of complex scientific inquiry.

174 Ibid.

175 Ibid.

176 Bruce A. Thyer, "The X Club and the Secret Ring: Lessons on How Behavior Analysis Can Take Over Psychology," *The Behavior Analyst* 18, no. 1 (1995)

177 Ibid.

178 Ibid, 23-24.

179 Ibid.

180 Ibid.

181 Ibid.

182 Ibid., 25.

183 Ibid., 24.

184 Paul Lucier, "The Origins of Pure and Applied Science in Gilded Age America," *Isis* 103, no. 3 (September 2012): 527-536, https://doi.org/10.1086/667976.

185 "The Science of Biology: Basic and Applied Science," In *LibreTexts. General Biology (Boundless).* Accessed November 2, 2024. https://bio.libretexts.org/Bookshelves/Introductory_and_General_Biology/General_Biology_(Bou

ndless)/01%3A_The_Study_of_Life/1.04%3A__The_Science_of_Biology_-_Basic_and_Applied_Science.

186 Michael J. Behe, *Darwin's Black Box: The Biochemical Challenge to Evolution*.

187 Bruce A. Thyer, "The X Club and the Secret Ring."

188 Ibid, 25.

189 Ibid, 24.

190 Ibid, 23.

191 Ibid, 23.

192 Ibid, 23.

193 Barton, *The X Club: Power and Authority in Victorian Science*, Chapter 4, p. 267.

194 Ibid.

195 Ibid.

196 Ibid.

197 Ibid.

198 Bruce A. Thyer, "The X Club and the Secret Ring," 24.

199 N. R. Jenkins, An Institutional Capture Theory of Interest Group Influence (PhD diss., University of California, Riverside, 2022), https://escholarship.org/uc/item/08g7006p.

200 Barton, *The X Club: Power and Authority in Victorian Science* 289.

201 Ibid., 310.

202 Ibid.

203 Ibid., 311.

204 Ibid., 294.

205 Ibid., 309.

206 Ibid., 309-311.

207 Ibid., 363, 370.

208 Ibid., 16.

209 Lee, C.J., Sugimoto, C.R., Zhang, G., and Cronin, B. (2013). "Bias in Peer Review," *Journal of the American Society for Information Science and Technology* 64(1): 2-17. https://doi.org/10.1002/asi.22784, p. 9. Conservatism in peer review often leads to a bias against groundbreaking and innovative research, violating the impartiality of the process. This conservatism suggests a disparity in how evaluative criteria are interpreted and applied, posing a threat to scientific progress by stifling the development and articulation of alternative and revolutionary scientific theories.

210 Ibid., p. 2. "Confirmation bias is the tendency to gather, interpret, and remember evidence in ways that affirm rather than challenge one's already held beliefs. In peer review, this bias manifests as a tendency against manuscripts that present results inconsistent with the reviewer's theoretical perspective,

thereby challenging the impartiality of peer review and the ability of scientists to evaluate hypotheses independently of their personal and institutional preferences."

211 Ibid.

212 Ibid.

213 Ibid.

214 Kirsten Birkett, "Science & Religion: Must They Be in Conflict?," Henry Center, last modified December 2016, https://henrycenter.tiu.edu/2016/12/science-religion-must-they-be-in-conflict/.

215 Ibid.

216 Ibid.

217 Ibid.

218 "Aktion T4." *Wikipedia*. Last modified October 3, 2024. https://en.wikipedia.org/wiki/Aktion_T4.

219 Kirsten Birkett, "Science & Religion: Must They Be in Conflict?."

220 Neil deGrasse Tyson, interview by Jim Clash, Forbes, February 2, 2017, https://www.forbes.com/sites/jimclash/2017/02/02/neil-degrasse-tyson-the-next-time-youre-abducted-steal-something-off-the-spaceship/.

221 Reports of the National Center for Science Education, "Stanley Weinberg, NCSE Founder, Dies," Vol. 21, No. 3-4, May-August 2001, https://ncse.ngo/stanley-weinberg-ncse-founder-dies.

222 National Center for Science Education, "About," accessed December 23, 2024, https://ncse.ngo/about.

223 Ibid.

224 "Why is NCSE Now Concerned with Climate Change?" *National Center for Science Education*, January 13, 2012, https://ncse.ngo/why-ncse-now-concerned-climate-change.

225 Ibid.

226 Ibid.

227 Ibid., Emphasis added.

228 Ibid.

229 Ibid.

230 NASA, "Evidence," *Global Climate Change: Vital Signs of the Planet*, accessed January 9, 2025, https://science.nasa.gov/climate-change/evidence/.

231 Behe, Michael J. *Darwin's Black Box: The Biochemical Challenge to Evolution.*

232 Intergovernmental Panel on Climate Change (IPCC), *Climate Change 2007: The Physical Science Basis, Summary for Policymakers*, Contribution of Working Group I to the Fourth Assessment Report (Paris: IPCC, February 2007), 1–21, https://www.slvwd.com/sites/g/files/vyhlif1176/f/uploads/item_10b_4.pdf.

233 Discovery Institute, "Public Policy Think Tank Advancing a Culture of Purpose, Creativity, and Innovation," accessed September 14, 2024, https://www.discovery.org/.

234 Discovery Institute. "Darwin Dissenters Speak." Accessed May 6, 2024. https://www.discovery.org/v/darwin-dissenters-speak/.

235 A. Hallam, "Lyell's Views on Organic Progression, Evolution, and Extinction," *Special Publications of the Geological Society* 143, no. 1 (1998): 305–313, https://doi.org/10.1144/gsl.sp.1998.143.01.11.

236 P. J. Bowler, "That Huxley Was Darwin's Bulldog and Accepted All Aspects of His Theory," in *Darwin Mythology: Debunking Myths, Correcting Falsehoods*, ed. K. Kampourakis (Cambridge: Cambridge University Press, 2024), 137–147.

237 See the following quotes for additional relevant perspectives by Huxley:

"Those who take the trouble to read the first two essays, published in 1859 and 1860, will, I think, do me the justice to admit that my zeal to secure fair play for Mr. Darwin, did not drive me into the position of a mere advocate; and that, while doing justice to the greatness of the argument I did not fail to indicate its weak points. I have never seen any reason for departing from the position which I took up in these two essays; and the assertion which I sometimes meet with nowadays, that I have 'recanted' or changed my opinions about Mr. Darwin's views, is quite unintelligible to me....we still remain very much in the dark about the causes of variation..."

"If these questions can be answered in the affirmative, Mr. Darwin's view steps out of the rank of hypotheses into those of proved theories; but, so long as the evidence at present adduced falls short of enforcing that affirmation, so long, to our minds, must the new doctrine be content to remain among the former—an extremely valuable, and in the highest degree probable, doctrine, indeed the only extant hypothesis which is worth anything in a scientific point of view; but still a hypothesis, and not yet the theory of species."

"I do not quite see, myself, how, if the action of natural selection is certain, the occurrence of evolution is only probable; inasmuch as the development of a new species by natural selection is, so far as it goes, evolution. That the doctrine of natural selection presupposes evolution is quite true; but it is not true that evolution necessarily implies natural selection. In fact, evolution might conceivably have taken place without the development of groups possessing the characters of species."

"I adopt Mr. Darwin's hypothesis, therefore, subject to the production of proof that physiological species may be produced by selective breeding; just as a physical philosopher may accept the undulatory theory of light, subject to the proof of the existence of the hypothetical ether; or as the chemist adopts the atomic theory, subject to the proof of the existence of atoms; and for exactly the same reasons, namely, that it has an immense amount of prima facie probability: that it is the only means at present within reach of reducing the chaos of observed facts to order; and lastly, that it is the most powerful instrument of investigation which has been presented to naturalists since the invention of the natural system of classification, and the commencement of the systematic study of embryology."

238 Thomas Henry Huxley, *Life and Letters of Thomas Henry Huxley, Volume 2*, ed. Leonard Huxley (London: Macmillan and Co., Ltd., 1900), 279, https://ia601508.us.archive.org/22/items/in.ernet.dli.2015.97935/2015.97935.Life-And-Letters-Of-Thomas-Henry-Huxley--Vol-2_text.pdf. Emphasis added.

239 Thomas Henry Huxley, "Evolution in Biology," *Collected Essays II*, 1878, Clark University, http://aleph0.clarku.edu/huxley/CE2/EvBio.html.

240 Thomas Henry Huxley, *Darwiniana: Essays* (London: Macmillan and Co., 1893), 20. Emphasis added.

241 Jean-Baptiste Lamarck, *Philosophie Zoologique* (Paris: Dentu, 1809), translated and edited by Hugh Elliot, available at the Internet Archive, https://archive.org/details/philosophiezoolo00lama/page/n9/mode/2up.

242 Thomas Henry Huxley, *Lay Sermons, Addresses, and Reviews* (London: Macmillan, 1870), 298.

243 Michael J. Behe, John Lennox, and Stephen C. Meyer, interview by Peter Robinson, By Design: Behe, Lennox, and Meyer on the Evidence for a Creator, Hoover Institution, February 1, 2023, https://www.hoover.org/research/design-behe-lennox-and-meyer-evidence-creator.

244 Thomas Henry Huxley, *The Essays of Thomas Henry Huxley*, 75.

245 Union of Concerned Scientists, "*Defending Evolution in the Classroom: A Statement by the Union of Concerned Scientists*," National Center for Science Education, 2007, https://ncse.ngo/union-concerned-scientists-2007.

246 National Center for Science Education. "*Voices for Evolution.*" https://ncse.ngo/voices-evolution-0.

247 Union of Concerned Scientists, "*Defending Evolution in the Classroom: A Statement by the Union of Concerned Scientists*."

248 National Center for Science Education, "Understanding Evolution," February 5, 2004, https://ncse.ngo/understanding-evolution.

249 University of California Museum of Paleontology, "Understanding Evolution," accessed December 21, 2024, https://evolution.berkeley.edu/.

250 Robert Sanders, "Paleontology Museum Launches New Web Site on Evolution," Berkeley News, February 26, 2004, https://newsarchive.berkeley.edu/news/media/releases/2004/02/26_evolve.shtml.

251 National Center for Science Education, "Understanding Evolution."

252 Ibid.

253 University of California Museum of Paleontology. "Macroevolution." *Understanding Evolution*. Accessed December 21, 2024. https://evolution.berkeley.edu/wp-content/uploads/2022/02/Evo101_06_Macroevolution_UE.pdf.

254 Collins English Dictionary, s.v. "stasis," accessed January 9, 2025, https://www.collinsdictionary.com/us/dictionary/english/stasis.

255 Ibid.

256 University of California Museum of Paleontology. "Macroevolution."

257 Thomas H. Huxley, "Geological Contemporaneity and Persistent Types of Life," *Quarterly Journal of the Geological Society*, vol. 18 (1862): 249; reprinted in *Collected Essays VIII: Discourses Biological and Geological*, Project Gutenberg, https://www.gutenberg.org/cache/epub/10060/pg10060-images.html.

258 Ibid., Emphasis added.

259 University of California Museum of Paleontology, "Speciation," Understanding Evolution, PDF, accessed December 21, 2024, https://evolution.berkeley.edu/wp-content/uploads/2022/02/Evo101_05_Speciation_UE.pdf.

260 Rebecca J. Safran and Patrik Nosil, "Speciation: The Origin of New Species," *Nature Education* (2012), https://www.nature.com/scitable/knowledge/library/speciation-the-origin-of-new-species-26230527/.

261 Ibid.

262 Michael Behe, *Darwin's Black Box*, 12.

263 Thomas Henry Huxley, "Obituary," *Life and Letters of Thomas Henry Huxley — Volume 2*, ed. Leonard Huxley, Project Gutenberg, March 1, 2004, last updated December 28, 2020, https://www.gutenberg.org/files/6919/6919-h/6919-h.htm#c10.

264 Ibid.

265 Thomas Henry Huxley, "On Some of the Results of the Expedition of H.M.S. Challenger," *The Contemporary Review* (1875), *Collected Essays VIII*, Clark University, https://mathcs.clarku.edu/huxley/CE8/ExChal.html.

266 University of California Museum of Paleontology, "The Big Issues," Understanding Evolution, accessed December 21, 2024, https://evolution.berkeley.edu/wp-content/uploads/2022/02/Evo101_07_The_big_issues_UE.pdf.

267 Ibid.

268 Ibid.

269 D. J. Taylor, "Orwell: A (Brief) Life," *The Orwell Foundation*, accessed January 22, 2025, https://www.orwellfoundation.com/the-orwell-foundation/orwell/biography/.

270 *V for Vendetta*, directed by James McTeigue (2005; Burbank, CA: Warner Bros. Pictures), DVD.

271 James McTeigue, director, *V for Vendetta* (Warner Bros. Pictures, 2005).

272 M. Night Shyamalan, director, *The Village* (Touchstone Pictures, 2004).

273 George Orwell, *1984* (Harvill Secker, 1949).

274 Wikipedia contributors, "Newspeak," Wikipedia, last modified January 19, 2024, accessed February 11, 2024, https://en.wikipedia.org/wiki/Newspeak.

275 Wikipedia contributors, "Political geography of Nineteen Eighty-Four," *Wikipedia*, 22 December 2024, https://en.wikipedia.org/wiki/Political_geography_of_Nineteen_Eighty-Four.

276 University of California Museum of Paleontology, "Avoid Common Teaching Pitfalls," *Understanding Evolution*, accessed December 21, 2024, https://evolution.berkeley.edu/teach-evolution/teaching-guides/13-16-teaching-guides/avoid-common-teaching-pitfalls/.

277 Ibid.

278 Ibid.

279 Ibid.

280 Steven Hassan, *Combatting Cult Mind Control: The #1 Best-selling Guide to Protection, Rescue, and Recovery from Destructive Cults* (Rochester, VT: Park Street Press, 1990), 120, chap. 4, "Understanding Mind Control."

281 Ibid.

282 Ibid.

283 Antony Flew, "Theology and Falsification," in *New Essays in Philosophical Theology*, ed. Antony Flew and Alasdair MacIntyre (London: SCM Press, 1955), 96–99.

284 IDquest, "Antony Flew on God and Atheism," February 1, 2013, 0:11-18:17, YouTube video. In this video, Anthony Flew discusses scientific discoveries that led him to abandon atheism. https://www.youtube.com/watch?v=VHUtMEru4pQ.

285 "There is a God, leading atheist concludes," NBC News, December 8, 2004, https://www.nbcnews.com/id/wbna6688917.

286 Richard Dawkins, *The God Delusion* (Boston: Houghton Mifflin, 2006), 82. "Maybe Flew's alleged conversion will be rewarded with the Templeton Prize. A first step in that direction is his ignominious decision to accept, in 2006, the 'Phillip E. Johnson Award for Liberty and Truth'. The first holder of the Phillip E. Johnson Award was Phillip E. Johnson, the lawyer credited with founding the Intelligent Design 'wedge strategy'. Flew will be the second holder. The awarding university is BIOLA, the Bible Institute of Los Angeles. One can't help wondering whether Flew realizes that he is being used."

287 Victor Stenger, "Flew's Flawed Science," *Free Inquiry* 25 (2005): 18, accessed February 11, 2024, https://secularhumanism.org/wp-content/uploads/sites/26/2005/02/p18.pdf.

Quote: "Apparently, Flew is unaware that physicists and cosmologists are not as totally stumped by fine-tuning as he seems to be."

288 Lee et al., "Bias in Peer Review," *Journal of the American Society for Information Science and Technology* 64, no. 1 (2013): 10-11: "Conservatism. Peer review is often censured for its conservatism, that is, bias against groundbreaking and innovative research… Conservatism violates the impartiality of peer review by suggesting that reviewers do not interpret and apply evaluative criteria in identical ways since what count as the proper criteria of evaluation—and their relative weightings—are disputed."

289 "Trofim Lysenko," Wikipedia, last edited July 10, 2024, https://en.wikipedia.org/wiki/Trofim_Lysenko.

290 Richard P. Feynman, "What Is Science?" Feynman.com, accessed July 14, 2024, http://www.feynman.com/science/what-is-science/.

291 Richard Sternberg, "Smithsonian," accessed December 22, 2024, https://richardsternberg.com/biography/.

292 Richard Sternberg, "Biography," accessed December 22, 2024, https://richardsternberg.com/biography/.

293 Stephen C. Meyer, "The Origin of Biological Information and the Higher Taxonomic Categories," *Proceedings of the Biological Society of Washington* 117, no. 2 (2004): 213–239.

294 Richard Sternberg, "Smithsonian."

295 Ibid.

296 Ibid.

297 Ibid.

298 Richard Sternberg, "Statement of Facts / Response to Misinformation," Smithsonian Controversy, https://richardsternberg.com/smithsonian/statement/.

299 "NCSE Board Member Skip Evans Passes Away," Antievolution.org, accessed May 7, 2024, http://www.antievolution.org/cs/ncse_20120803.

300 Ibid.

301 NCSE. "Doubting Darwinism." https://ncse.ngo/doubting-darwinism-through-creative-license.

302 Ibid.

303 Ibid.

304 Pennock, Robert T. "Creationism and Intelligent Design." *Annual Review of Genomics and Human Genetics* 4 (2003): 143–63. https://doi.org/10.1146/annurev.genom.4.070802.110400.

305 Alan D. Attie et al., "Defending Science Education Against Intelligent Design: A Call to Action," *Journal of Clinical Investigation* 116, no. 5 (May 1, 2006): 1134–1138, https://www.jci.org/articles/view/28449. Emphasis added.

306 Ibid.

307 Ibid.

308 Ibid.

309 Ibid.

310 Ibid.

311 Ibid.

312 Ibid.

313 Ibid.

314 Ibid., 1136.

315 University of Oxford, "History of the University," accessed January 26, 2025, https://www.ox.ac.uk/about/organisation/history.

316 Ibid., 1136.

317 Ibid., 1135.

318 American Civil Liberties Union, "Frequently Asked Questions about Intelligent Design," last modified September 16, 2005, accessed February 11, 2024, https://www.aclu.org/documents/frequently-asked-questions-about-intelligent-design.

319 Ibid.

320 Eugenie C. Scott, *Evolution vs. Creationism: An Introduction*, 52.

321 "American Civil Liberties Union." Last modified August 26, 2023. https://www.aclu.org/.

322 American Civil Liberties Union," *Encyclopædia Britannica*, accessed February 6, 2024, https://www.britannica.com/topic/American-Civil-Liberties-Union.

Notes

323 American Civil Liberties Union. "Court Cases." Accessed February 8, 2024. https://www.aclu.org/court-cases.

324 American Civil Liberties Union, "Frequently Asked Questions about Intelligent Design."

325 Ibid.

326 Ibid.

327 Ibid.

328 Ibid.

329 Ibid., Italics added for emphasis.

330 "What the Experts Say About Intelligent Design," American Civil Liberties Union, November 23, 2005, accessed April 25, 2024, https://www.aclu.org/documents/what-experts-say-about-intelligent-design.

331 Miller, Kenneth R. "Science, Evolution, and Creationism." American Civil Liberties Union, 2006, https://www.aclu.org/files/evolution/statements/miller.pdf.

332 Ibid.

333 Ibid.

334 Pennock, Robert T. "Creationism and Intelligent Design." American Civil Liberties Union, 2006, https://www.aclu.org/files/evolution/statements/pennock.pdf.

335 Ibid.

336 Ibid.

337 Eugenie C. Scott, "Antievolutionism and Creationism in the United States," National Center for Science Education, accessed June 15, 2025, https://ncse.ngo/antievolutionism-and-creationism-united-states.

338 NOVA, "Board vs. Teachers," PBS, created October 2007, https://www.pbs.org/wgbh/nova/id/boardvsteachers.html.

339 Ibid., Note: The first stanza is sometimes omitted when this disclaimer is cited. Leaving out the first stanza can shape how it is perceived. Without the context provided by the first stanza, the disclaimer may appear more antagonistic toward evolution, making the board's actions seem more ideologically motivated. The first stanza is less emotionally or ideologically charged compared to the later portions. Critics may disregard it because it doesn't support their argument that the disclaimer is inherently biased or problematic.

340 Laurie Goodstein, "School Board Sued on Mandate for Alternative to Evolution," *The New York Times*, December 15, 2004, https://www.nytimes.com/2004/12/15/education/school-board-sued-on-mandate-for-alternative-to-evolution.html.

341 Pew Research Center, "Federal Court Strikes Down Intelligent Design Curriculum," December 20, 2005, https://www.pewresearch.org/religion/2005/12/20/federal-court-strikes-down-intelligent-design-curriculum/.

342 Tom Rosentiel, "The Darwin Debate: 20 Years after a Landmark Supreme Court Decision, Americans Are Still Fighting About Evolution," *Pew Research Center*, June 13, 2007, https://www.pewresearch.org/science/2007/06/13/the-darwin-debate/.

343 NOVA, "Board vs. Teachers."

344 National Center for Science Education, "Remembering *Kitzmiller v. Dover*," NCSE, https://ncse.ngo/remembering-kitzmiller-v-dover.

345 "Kenneth R. Miller," *Wikipedia*, https://en.wikipedia.org/wiki/Kenneth_R._Miller.

346 "Robert T. Pennock," *Wikipedia*, https://en.wikipedia.org/wiki/Robert_T._Pennock.

347 Robert T. Pennock, *Tower of Babel: The Evidence Against the New Creationism* (Cambridge, MA: MIT Press, 1999).

348 Chapman University, "Brian Alters," *Chapman University Faculty Directory*, accessed December 30, 2024, https://www.chapman.edu/our-faculty/brian-alters.

349 Brian J. Alters and Sandra M. Alters, *Defending Evolution: A Guide to the Evolution/Creation Controversy* (Sudbury, MA: Jones and Bartlett, 2001).

350 "Barbara Forrest," *Wikipedia*, last modified October 21, 2024, https://en.wikipedia.org/wiki/Barbara_Forrest.

351 Discovery Institute, "William A. Dembski," *Discovery Institute*, accessed December 30, 2024, https://www.discovery.org/p/dembski/.

352 Stephen C. Meyer Official Website, Stephen C. Meyer, accessed January 1, 2025, https://stephencmeyer.org/.

353 Stephen Meyer, "Intelligent Design and the Return of the God Hypothesis," *Hoover Institution*, accessed January 9, 2025, https://www.hoover.org/research/stephen-meyer-intelligent-design-and-return-god-hypothesis-1.

354 William A. Dembski, "Specified Complexity Made Simple: The Historical Backdrop," *Evolution News*, February 2024, https://evolutionnews.org/2024/02/specified-complexity-made-simple-the-historical-backdrop/.

355 Ibid.

356 Stephen C. Meyer, *Return of the God Hypothesis*.

357 Wikipedia, s.v. "Specified Complexity," last modified November 17, 2024, https://en.wikipedia.org/wiki/Specified_complexity.

358 William A. Dembski, *No Free Lunch: Why Specified Complexity Cannot Be Purchased Without Intelligence* (Lanham, MD: Rowman & Littlefield, 2002).

359 Thomas More Law Center, "Home," accessed December 30, 2024, https://www.thomasmore.org/.

360 Discovery Institute, "Setting the Record Straight about Discovery Institute's Role in the Dover School District Case," November 10, 2005, *Intelligent Design*, https://www.discovery.org/a/3003/.

361 Ibid.

362 Ibid.

363 Ibid.

364 Ibid.

365 Eugenie C. Scott. Interview by S. Joshua Swamidass and Nathan H. Lents. Peaceful Science. YouTube video, 1:03:20. April 6, 2022. https://www.youtube.com/watch?v=S4RVGtUxSUY&t=1170.

366 Eugenie Scott, "The Dover Trial: Evolution vs. Intelligent Design," interviewed by D.J. Grothe, *Point of Inquiry*, January 20, 2006, https://pointofinquiry.org/2006/01/eugenie_scott_the_dover_trial_evolution_vs_intelligent_design/.

367 Eugenie Scott, interview by S. Joshua Swamidass and Nathan H. Lents.

368 Ibid., 16:28-16:40.

369 Ibid., 15:59-16:35.

370 Eugenie Scott, "The Dover Trial: Evolution vs. Intelligent Design," interviewed by D.J. Grothe," 4:23-5:06.

371 Eugenie Scott, interview by S. Joshua Swamidass and Nathan H. Lents, 16:00-16:40.

372 Ibid.

373 Lauri Lebo, *The Devil in Dover: An Insider's Story of Dogma v. Darwin in Small-Town America* (New York: The New Press, 2008), 22, https://www.everand.com/book/418599642/The-Devil-in-Dover-An-Insider-s-Story-of-Dogma-v-Darwin-in-Small-Town-America.

374 Lauri Lebo, "Lauri Lebo," The New Press, https://thenewpress.com/authors/lauri-lebo.

375 Lauri Lebo, *The Devil in Dover: An Insider's Story of Dogma v. Darwin in Small-Town America*, 23.

376 RationalWiki. *RationalWiki: Kitzmiller v. Dover annotated transcript/P027*. Accessed January, 1, 2025, Retrieved from https://rationalwiki.org/wiki/RationalWiki:Kitzmiller_v._Dover_annotated_transcript/P027.

377 Ibid.

378 Ibid.

379 *The Ascent of Man*, accessed January 2, 2025, https://www.imdb.com/title/tt0069733/.

380 Lauri Lebo, "From Dover to DNA: How Science-Literate Communities Can Change the Narrative," *Pennsylvania Nonbelievers*, January 19, 2014, YouTube video, https://www.youtube.com/watch?v=uCwWaQwIC2M.

381 Ibid., 6:03-7:25.

382 Lauri Lebo, *The Devil in Dover: An Insider's Story of Dogma v. Darwin in Small-Town America*, 23.

383 Ibid., 24.

384 Stephen Jay Gould, *Wonderful Life: The Burgess Shale and the Nature of History* (New York: W. W. Norton & Company, 1989), 30, https://hiskingdom.us/wp-content/uploads/2019/02/Gould-WonderfulLife.pdf.

385 Eugenie C. Scott, *Evolution vs. Creationism: An Introductio, 43*.

386 RationalWiki. *RationalWiki: Kitzmiller v. Dover annotated transcript/P027*.

387 Ibid.

388 Ibid.

389 Lauri Lebo, *The Devil in Dover: An Insider's Story of Dogma v. Darwin in Small-Town America*, 33.

390 Ibid., 23-25.

391 Ibid., 26.

392 Ibid.

393 Ibid.

394 Ibid.

395 Ibid.

396 Ibid.

397 Eugenie Scott, interview by S. Joshua Swamidass and Nathan H. Lents, 32:14-32:46.

398 "Last Universal Common Ancestor," *Wikipedia*.

399 Michael J. Behe, *Darwin Devolves: The New Science About DNA That Challenges Evolution* (New York: HarperOne, 2019).

400 Cari Shane, "If Humans Evolved from Apes, Why Do Apes Still Exist?" *Discover Magazine*, February 16, 2022, https://www.discovermagazine.com/planet-earth/if-humans-evolved-from-apes-why-do-apes-still-exist.

401 Stephen Jay Gould, *Wonderful Life: The Burgess Shale and the Nature of History*, 30.

402 Ibid.

403 Ibid.

404 Eugenie Scott, interview by S. Joshua Swamidass and Nathan H. Lents.

405 Percival Davis and Dean H. Kenyon, *Of Pandas and People: The Central Question of Biological Origins*, 2nd ed. (Dallas: Haughton Publishing, 1993).

406 Eugenie Scott, interview by S. Joshua Swamidass and Nathan H. Lents," 17:26-17:56.

407 Ibid., 16:56-17:10.

408 Ibid., 17:35-18:10.

409 Stephen Jay Gould, *Wonderful Life: The Burgess Shale and the Nature of History*, 31.

410 Merriam-Webster, s.v. "captive audience," accessed January 9, 2025, https://www.merriam-webster.com/dictionary/captive%20audience.

411 *Edwards v. Aguillard*, 482 U.S. 578 (1987), https://supreme.justia.com/cases/federal/us/482/578/.

412 "Best High Schools: Dover Area High School," *U.S. News & World Report*, https://www.usnews.com/education/best-high-schools/pennsylvania/districts/dover-area-school-district/dover-area-high-school-16923.

413 Ibid., 17:26-17:56.

414 NOVA, "Board vs. Teachers," PBS.

415 Eugenie Scott, "The Dover Trial: Evolution vs. Intelligent Design," interviewed by D.J. Grothe," 4:23-5:06.

416 Eugenie Scott, interview by S. Joshua Swamidass and Nathan H. Lents, 18:00-1850.

417 Jeffrey Koperski, "Two Bad Ways to Attack Intelligent Design and Two Good Ones," *Zygon* 43, no. 2 (June 2008): 436.

418 Ibid., 439.

419 Ibid., 444.

420 *Kitzmiller v. Dover Area School District*, 400 F. Supp. 2d 707, 735 (M.D. Pa. 2005).

421 Jeffrey Koperski, "Two Bad Ways to Attack Intelligent Design and Two Good Ones.", 435.

422 Ibid., 440.

423 Eugenie Scott, interview by S. Joshua Swamidass and Nathan H. Lents, 47:30-47:50.

424 Eugenie Scott, "The Dover Trial: Evolution vs. Intelligent Design," interviewed by D.J. Grothe," 6:30-7:40.

425 Ibid.

426 *Kitzmiller v. Dover Area School District*, trial transcript, Day 6 (October 5), AM Session, Part 2, accessed January 2, 2025, https://www.talkorigins.org/faqs/dover/day6am2.html.

427 *Daubert v. Merrell Dow Pharmaceuticals, Inc.*, 509 U.S. 579 (1993), accessed January 9, 2025, https://supreme.justia.com/cases/federal/us/509/579/.

428 Barbara Forrest, testimony, *Kitzmiller v. Dover Area School District*, Day 6 (October 5), AM Session, Part 1, accessed January 2, 2025, https://www.talkorigins.org/faqs/dover/day6am.html.

429 Ibid.

430 Barbara Forrest, "Dr. Barbara Forrest on Dover/Kitzmiller 15 Years On," TheNMSR, YouTube video, 16:50, January 16, 2021, https://www.youtube.com/watch?v=abW7wWMJZ1Q&t=820s.

431 Ibid.

432 Ibid.

433 Ibid.

434 Isaac Newton, *The Mathematical Principles of Natural Philosophy*, trans. Andrew Motte (London: Benjamin Motte, 1729), General Scholium, quoted in Goodreads, "This Most Beautiful System of the

Sun, Planets, and Comets," accessed January 2, 2025, https://www.goodreads.com/quotes/232391-this-most-beautiful-system-of-the-sun-planets-and-comets.

435 D. L. Hartl, "Gregor Johann Mendel: From Peasant to Priest, Pedagogue, and Prelate," *Proceedings of the National Academy of Sciences of the United States of America* 119, no. 30 (July 26, 2022): e2121953119, https://doi.org/10.1073/pnas.2121953119.

436 M. Keynes, "Mendel—Both Ignored and Forgotten," *Journal of the Royal Society of Medicine* 95, no. 11 (November 2002): 576–77, https://doi.org/10.1177/014107680209501129.

437 Charles Darwin, The Variation of Animals and Plants Under Domestication (London: John Murray, 1868)

438 Charles Darwin to Alfred Russel Wallace, February 6, [1866], In The Darwin Correspondence Project, Letter no. 4989, accessed January 22, 2025, https://www.darwinproject.ac.uk/letter/?docId=letters/DCP-LETT-4989.xml.

439 Ibid.

440 Darwin, Charles. Letter to George John Romanes. June 11, [1877]. In The Darwin Correspondence Project. Letter no. 10996. Accessed January 22, 2025. https://www.darwinproject.ac.uk/letter/?docId=letters/DCP-LETT-10996.xml.

441 "2012 Richard Dawkins Award for Eugenie Scott," *YouTube video*, 0:20–2:50, posted by "Richard Dawkins Foundation for Reason & Science," September 2, 2012, https://www.youtube.com/watch?v=WgwaR7ExVdg.

442 "Creationism." *Wikipedia*. Last modified January 5, 2025. https://en.wikipedia.org/wiki/Creationism.

443 "Church of Antioch," *Wikipedia*, last modified January 5, 2025, https://en.wikipedia.org/wiki/Church_of_Antioch.

444 2 Peter 1:16 (King James Version).

445 Brandon D. Crowe, "Jesus Christ: The Last Adam," *The Gospel Coalition*, https://www.thegospelcoalition.org/essay/jesus-christ-last-adam/.

446 Galatians 1, *Holy Bible, New International Version*, https://web.mit.edu/jywang/www/cef/Bible/NIV/NIV_Bible/GAL+1.html.

447 "Creationism." *Wikipedia*.

448 Terry Mortenson, "Did Bible Authors Believe in a Literal Genesis?," *Answers in Genesis*, December 10, 2013, last featured November 26, 2021, https://answersingenesis.org/genesis/did-bible-authors-believe-in-a-literal-genesis/.

449 Ibid.

450 Ibid.

451 Eugenie Scott, "Here Come the Creationists…Again," *Center for Inquiry*, YouTube, March 27, 2024, 0:00–5:34, https://www.youtube.com/watch?v=UCKNUgPNBQ4.

452 Ibid.

453 Ibid.

454 Ibid.

455 Ibid.

456 Ibid.

457 Ibid.

458 Ibid.

459 Ibid.

460 Ibid.

461 Ibid.

462 Ibid.

463 Ibid.

464 Eugenie Scott, "Here Come the Creationists…Again."

465 Ibid.

466 Ibid.

467 Ibid.

468 National Center for Science Education, "Our Financials," accessed January 6, 2025, https://ncse.ngo/our-financials.

469 Ibid.

470 Eugenie Scott, "Here Come the Creationists…Again," 6:20-24:00.

471 *Kennedy v. Bremerton School District*, 597 U.S. ___ (2022), https://www.supremecourt.gov/opinions/21pdf/21-418_i425.pdf.

472 *Lemon v. Kurtzman*, 403 U.S. 602 (1971), https://supreme.justia.com/cases/federal/us/403/602/.

473 Ibid.

474 Ibid. 19:00-29:20

475 Ibid.

476 Ibid.

477 Ibid.

478 Ibid.

479 Ibid.

480 Ibid.

481 Ibid.

482 *Kitzmiller v. Dover Area School District*, 400 F. Supp. 2d 707 (M.D. Pa. 2005), accessed December 30, 2024, https://www.pamd.uscourts.gov/sites/pamd/files/opinions/04v2688a.pdf.

483 *Kitzmiller v. Dover Area School District*, 400 F. Supp. 2d 707, 745 (M.D. Pa. 2005).

484 Robert A. Linsenmeier and Lissa Padnick-Silver, "Metabolic Dependence of Photoreceptors on the Choroid in the Normal and Detached Retina," *Investigative Ophthalmology & Visual Science* 41, no. 10 (September 2000): 3117–3123, https://doi.org/10.1167/iovs.41-10-3117.

485 Ibid.

486 David C. Beebe, "Maintaining Transparency: A Review of the Developmental Physiology and Pathophysiology of Two Avascular Tissues," *Seminars in Cell & Developmental Biology* 19, no. 2 (April 2008): 125–133, https://doi.org/10.1016/j.semcdb.2007.08.014.

487 Ibid.

488 Ibid.

489 Jasmin Matuszak, Arata Tabuchi, and Wolfgang M. Kuebler, "Ventilation and Perfusion at the Alveolar Level: Insights From Lung Intravital Microscopy," *Frontiers in Physiology* 11 (2020), https://doi.org/10.3389/fphys.2020.00291.

490 Ali Saab et al., "Impact of Airways Geometry on Transport of Gases to Blood," *arXiv* (2021), https://arxiv.org/abs/2111.07627.

491 Jasmin Matuszak, Arata Tabuchi, and Wolfgang M. Kuebler, "Ventilation and Perfusion at the Alveolar Level: Insights From Lung Intravital Microscopy."

492 H. Kadry, B. Noorani, and L. Cucullo, "A Blood–Brain Barrier Overview on Structure, Function, Impairment, and Biomarkers of Integrity," *Fluids and Barriers of the CNS* 17, no. 69 (2020), https://doi.org/10.1186/s12987-020-00230-3.

493 Ibid.

494 Jeffrey J. Lochhead et al., "Structure, Function, and Regulation of the Blood-Brain Barrier Tight Junction in Central Nervous System Disorders," *Frontiers in Physiology* 11 (2020), https://doi.org/10.3389/fphys.2020.00914.

495 Ibid.

496 Ibid.

497 Einstein, Albert. *Relativity: The Special and General Theory*. Translated by Robert W. Lawson. London: Methuen & Co. Ltd., 1920. Accessed January 13, 2025, https://archive.org/details/einstein-1.

498 "Philipp Lenard," *Wikipedia*, last modified January 10, 2025, https://en.wikipedia.org/wiki/Philipp_Lenard.

499 Stephen Hawking, "A Brief History of Relativity: What Is It? How Does It Work? Why Does It Change Everything? An Easy Primer by the World's Most Famous Living Physicist," *Time*, December 31, 1999, https://content.time.com/time/magazine/article/0,9171,993017,00.html.

500 Ibid.

501 Richard Dawkins, "Put Your Money on Evolution," The New York Times Book Review, April 9, 1989.

502 National Center for Science Education, "Friend of Darwin Awards," *National Center for Science Education*, accessed December 30, 2024, https://ncse.ngo/friend-darwin-awards.

503 Ibid.

504 Ibid.

505 Ibid.

506 Ibid.

507 Richard E. Lenski, "Revisiting the Design of the Long-Term Evolution Experiment with *Escherichia coli*," *Journal of Molecular Evolution* 91, no. 3 (2023): 241–253, https://doi.org/10.1007/s00239-023-10095-3.

508 Edward Humes, *Monkey Girl: Evolution, Education, Religion, and the Battle for America's Soul* (New York: HarperCollins, 2009), https://www.everand.com/book/202689307/Monkey-Girl-Evolution-Education-Religion-and-the-Battle-for-America-s-Soul.

509 Kenneth R. Miller, *Only a Theory: Evolution and the Battle for America's Soul* (New York: Viking, 2008).

510 Monica Lam, "PROFILE / EUGENIE SCOTT / Berkeley Scientist Leads Fight to Stop Teaching of Creationism," *San Francisco Chronicle*, February 7, 2003, https://www.sfgate.com/bayarea/article/PROFILE-EUGENIE-SCOTT-Berkeley-scientist-2672260.php.

511 Edward Humes, *Monkey Girl: Evolution, Education, Religion, and the Battle for America's Soul* (New York: HarperCollins, 2009), 487.

512 Ibid., 9.

513 Ibid., 129.

514 Ibid., 161.

515 Lauri Lebo, *The Devil in Dover: An Insider's Story of Dogma v. Darwin in Small-Town America*, 79.

516 Ibid., 314.

517 Ibid., 315.

518 Lauri Lebo, *The Devil in Dover: An Insider's Story of Dogma v. Darwin in Small-Town America*, 79.

519 Ibid., 9.

520 Ibid., 9.

521 Ibid., 159.

522 Ibid.

523 Ibid.

524 Ibid., 153.

525 Ibid., 160.

526 Ibid., 287.

527 Eagle Scout, *Wikipedia*, last edited January 10, 2025, https://en.wikipedia.org/wiki/Eagle_Scout.

528 History of the Boy Scouts of America," *Wikipedia*, last edited December 22, 2024, https://en.wikipedia.org/wiki/History_of_the_Boy_Scouts_of_America.

529 "Scout Promise," *Wikipedia*, last edited July 21, 2024, https://en.wikipedia.org/wiki/Scout_Promise.

530 *Boy Scouts of America v. Dale*, 530 U.S. 640 (2000), https://supreme.justia.com/cases/federal/us/530/640/.

531 Edward Humes, Monkey Girl, 28.

532 Ibid.

533 Ibid.

534 Ibid., 29.

535 Ibid.

536 Robert Sanders, "Paleontology Museum Launches New Web Site on Evolution," Berkeley News, February 26, 2004, https://newsarchive.berkeley.edu/news/media/releases/2004/02/26_evolve.shtml.

537 Ibid., 271.

538 Ibid., 25.

539 "Teaching Evolution to Students of Faith," *Reports of the National Center for Science Education* 42, no. 2 (Spring 2022), https://ncse.ngo/sites/default/files/pdfs/REPORTS42_2links.pdf.

540 Edward Humes, Monkey Girl, 27.

541 Ibid., 74.

542 Ibid., 52.

543 Eugenie Scott, "The Dover Trial: Evolution vs. Intelligent Design," interviewed by D.J. Grothe.

544 Jerry A. Coyne, *Why Evolution Is True* (London: Viking Penguin, 2009), Kindle edition, https://www.amazon.com/Why-Evolution-True-Jerry-Coyne-ebook/dp/B001QEQRJW.

545 Ibid., 67.

546 Ibid.

547 Ibid.

548 Luca Poliseno, Leonardo Salmena, Jiang Zhang, et al., "A Coding-Independent Function of Gene and Pseudogene mRNAs Regulates Tumor Biology," *Nature* 465 (2010): 1033–1038, https://doi.org/10.1038/nature09144.

549 Ibid.

550 Ibid.

551 Xinling Hu, Liu Yang, and Yin-Yuan Mo, "Role of Pseudogenes in Tumorigenesis," *Cancers* 10, no. 8 (2018): 256, https://doi.org/10.3390/cancers10080256.

552 Ibid.

553 "ENCODE Data Annotations," *ENCODE Project*, accessed January 19, 2025, https://www.encodeproject.org/data/annotations/.

554 Jerry A. Coyne, *Why Evolution Is True*, 68.

555 Ibid., 80.

556 Daniel Albert, Prachi Thakur, and Varun Batura, "Embryology, Lanugo," in *StatPearls*, StatPearls Publishing, updated July 10, 2023, https://www.ncbi.nlm.nih.gov/books/NBK526092/.

557 Kenneth R. Miller, "Life's Grand Design," *Technology Review* 97, no. 2 (February/March 1994): 24–32, http://www.millerandlevine.com/km/evol/lgd/index.html.

558 Ibid.

559 Emphasis added.

560 "*Judgment Day: Intelligent Design on Trial*," produced by NOVA and Vulcan Productions, Inc., in association with The Big Table Film Company (2007; Boston: WGBH Educational Foundation and Vulcan Productions, Inc.), PBS, November 13, 2007, https://www.pbs.org/wgbh/nova/video/judgment-day-intelligent-design-on-trial/.

561 *Judgment Day: Intelligent Design on Trial*, transcript, NOVA, PBS, November 13, 2007, https://www.pbs.org/wgbh/nova/transcripts/3416_id.html.

562 Ibid.

563 Ibid.

564 Ibid.

565 Ibid.

566 Ibid.

567 Ibid.

568 "Madalyn Murray O'Hair," *Wikipedia*, last modified January 31, 2025, https://en.wikipedia.org/wiki/Madalyn_Murray_O%27Hair.

569 Ibid.

570 Ibid.

571 Ibid.

572 "*Judge Joe Brown*," IMDb, accessed January 31, 2025, https://www.imdb.com/title/tt0235927/.

573 "*Judgment Day: Intelligent Design on Trial*," transcript, NOVA, PBS.

574 Ibid.

575 Ibid.

576 "The Intelligent Design Trial: A Producer's Story," NOVA, October 1, 2007, https://www.pbs.org/wgbh/nova/article/intelligent-design-trial-producers-story/.

577 Anika Smith, "What NOVA Won't Tell You about Dover: The Truth about 'Judgment Day: Intelligent Design on Trial,'" Discovery Institute, November 13, 2007, https://www.discovery.org/a/4300/.

578 DiscoveryScienceChannel, Stephen Meyer Discusses the Big Bang, Einstein, Hawking, & More - Science Uprising Expert Interviews, YouTube video, 26:30–31:30, October 5, 2021, https://www.youtube.com/watch?v=m_AeA4fMHhI&t=166s.

579 Discovery Science, "Why Intelligent Design Was Not Over at Dover," YouTube video, 16:30–16:47, July 6, 2021, https://www.youtube.com/watch?v=_dSBf0k0o30.

580 Ibid., 13:32-14:05.

581 Ibid., 16:30-17:20.

582 Jovana Drinjakovic, "A Cell Holds 42 Million Protein Molecules, Scientists Reveal," *Temerty Faculty of Medicine, University of Toronto*, January 17, 2018, https://temertymedicine.utoronto.ca/news/cell-holds-42-million-protein-molecules-scientists-reveal.

583 Philip Ball, *Life's Matrix: A Biography of Water* (Berkeley: University of California Press, 2001)

584 Chaplin, Martin. "Water Hydrogen Bonding." *London South Bank University*, last modified 2023, https://water.lsbu.ac.uk/water/water_hydrogen_bonding.html.

585 Ed Miller, "Proteins," *Genomics Education Programme*, last modified 2023, https://www.genomicseducation.hee.nhs.uk/genotes/knowledge-hub/proteins/.

586 Elizabeth Brunk et al., "Recon3D Enables a Three-Dimensional View of Gene Variation in Human Metabolism," *Nature Biotechnology* 36, no. 3 (2018): 272–281, https://doi.org/10.1038/nbt.4072.

587 Victor Sojo, Barry Herschy, Alexandra Whicher, Eloi Camprubí, and Nick Lane, "The Origin of Life in Alkaline Hydrothermal Vents," *Astrobiology* 16, no. 3 (2016): 181–197, https://doi.org/10.1089/ast.2015.1406.

588 Clio Byrne-Gudding, "Q&A: How Many Stars Are There in the Universe?" *Yale Scientific Magazine*, March 23, 2016, https://www.yalescientific.org/2016/03/qa-how-many-stars-are-there-in-the-universe/.

589 "Hidden-Variable Theory," Wikipedia: The Free Encyclopedia, last modified January 31, 2024, https://en.wikipedia.org/wiki/Hidden-variable_theory.

590 "Boltzmann Brain," *Wikipedia: The Free Encyclopedia*, last modified January 31, 2024, https://en.wikipedia.org/wiki/Boltzmann_brain.

591 Discovery Science, "Why Intelligent Design Was Not Over at Dover," 40:20-40:35, (Emphasis added).

592 Ibid., 17:12-17:45.

593 Ibid.

594 "Richard Dawkins on the Truth of Evolution," BillMoyers.com, March 1, 2013, https://billmoyers.com/2013/03/01/moyers-moment-2004-richard-dawkins-on-the-truth-of-evolution/.

595 *Avengers: Age of Ultron*, directed by Joss Whedon (Marvel Studios, 2015), film.

596 Steven D. Greydanus, "The Theology and Philosophy of Avengers: Age of Ultron," Decent Films, accessed June 20, 2025, https://decentfilms.com/articles/theology-of-ultron.

597 Ibid.

598 TV Tropes, "Quotes/AvengersAgeOfUltron," accessed June 20, 2025, https://tvtropes.org/pmwiki/pmwiki.php/Quotes/AvengersAgeOfUltron.

599 George Orwell, *1984* (Mercy House, 2021), 98, accessed January 6, 2025, https://www.everand.com/book/511975326/1984.

600 Ibid., 279-330.

601 Ibid.

602 Ibid.

603 Ibid.

604 Ibid.

605 Ibid.

606 Ibid., 356.

607 Eugenie Scott, "The Dover Trial: Evolution vs. Intelligent Design," interviewed by D.J. Grothe," 18:36-18:50.

608 Council on Foreign Relations, "What Is the Enlightenment and How Did It Transform Politics?" last modified February 17, 2023, https://education.cfr.org/learn/reading/what-enlightenment-and-how-did-it-transform-politics.

609 Max Tegmark, Scientific American, January 2014, "Is the Universe Made of Math?"

610 "Max Tegmark." MIT Department of Physics. Accessed January 27, 2024. https://physics.mit.edu/faculty/max-tegmark/.

611 Max Tegmark, *Our Mathematical Universe: My Quest for the Ultimate Nature of Reality* (New York: Alfred A. Knopf, 2014), first edition.

612 Francis Sullivan, "Our Mathematical Universe: My Quest for the Ultimate Nature of Reality," *Physics Today* 67, no. 7 (1 July 2014): 51–52, https://doi.org/10.1063/PT.3.2453. "To be clear, he is not merely discussing the use of mathematics in modeling physical phenomena, nor is he speculating about the 'unreasonable effectiveness' of mathematics when applied to physical problems. Rather, he is arguing that the physical universe is itself an aspect of mathematics."

613 Max Tegmark, "Is Mathematics Eternal?," Closer To Truth, April 18, 2022, 0:00-9:03, accessed April 22, 2024, https://www.youtube.com/watch?v=4EObRQuhaPI.

614 Ibid.

615 Max Tegmark, *Our Mathematical Universe*.

616 Tegmark, "Max Tegmark - MIT".

617 Nagel, Thomas. *Mind and Cosmos: Why the Materialist Neo-Darwinian Conception of Nature Is Almost Certainly False*. Oxford: Oxford University Press, 2012. ISBN 978-0-19-991975-8.

618 Tegmark, Max. "The Mathematical Universe." *Foundations of Physics* 38, no. 2 (2008): 101-150. https://link.springer.com/article/10.1007/s10701-007-9186-9.

619 Max Tegmark, "Is Mathematics Eternal?," Closer To Truth.

620 Ibid.

621 Ibid.

622 Ibid.

623 Mark, Joshua J. "Ma'at." *World History Encyclopedia*. Published September 15, 2016. "Ma'at (pronounced may-et) is the ancient Egyptian goddess of truth, justice, harmony, and balance (a concept known as ma'at in Egyptian) who first appears during the period known as the Old Kingdom (c. 2613 - 2181 BCE) but no doubt existed in some form earlier." Accessed January 11, 2024. https://www.worldhistory.org/Ma'at/.

624 Adrian Currie, "Science & Speculation," *Erkenntnis* 88, no. 2 (2021): 597-619, doi:10.1007/s10670-020-00370-w, 612.

625 Hawking, *The Grand Design*.

626 Krauss, "What is 'Nothing'?," 4;00–4:07. Krauss states: "It sounds like the ultimate free lunch, and it potentially is. Now, these things are strange…"

627 Ellis and Silk. "Scientific method."

628 Max Tegmark, "What Exists?," video, 6:41-7:00, posted by "Closer To Truth," April 9, 2024, https://www.youtube.com/watch?v=FIsD70ZLUbo. "To falsify my conjecture here is to find some physical phenomena… yeah that cannot be described [mathematically]… if it ain't mathematical that doesn't exist."

629 Ibid.

630 Sabine Hossenfelder, "The Crisis in Physics Is Real: Science Is Failing," YouTube video, 7:27–8:17, November 4, 2024, https://www.youtube.com/watch?v=HQVF0Yu7X24&t=195s.

631 Weingart, Peter, and Guenther, Lars, "Science communication and the issue of trust," *JCOM* 15, no. 05 (2016): C01, https://doi.org/10.22323/2.15050301. In the article, the authors state: "…the economic pressure under which the mass media operate drives journalists to use well-known 'news values' such as sensationalizing, personalization, and use of emotion to 'sell' stories."

632 CNN, "Astrophysicist explains why dinosaurs died when crocodiles survived," YouTube video, 4:00, November 2023, https://www.youtube.com/watch?v=fW6bM5swNgo.

633 Ibid.

634 Fox News, "Scientists discover seven Earth-sized planets," YouTube video, 2:15, February 2017, https://www.youtube.com/watch?v=df85nCwhrmA.

635 Wikipedia, s.v. "Kristin Fisher," last modified July 3, 2024, https://en.wikipedia.org/wiki/Kristin_Fisher.

636 Ibid.

637 "Carl Zimmer, 'About: Bio,'" accessed February 17, 2024, https://carlzimmer.com/about/bio/.

638 Ibid.

Notes

639 Carl Zimmer, "Evolution and the Media," *Evolution: Education and Outreach* 3, no. 3 (2010): 236-240, https://doi.org/10.1007/s12052-010-0212-6.

640 Ibid., p.238

641 Ibid., p. 236.

642 Ibid., p. 238.

643 Ibid., p. 238.

644 National Geographic Society, "Who Was Ida?" *Education National Geographic*, accessed January 9, 2025, https://education.nationalgeographic.org/resource/who-was-ida/.

645 Ibid., p. 239.

646 Ibid.

647 "YouTube Channel: Professor Dave Explains," YouTube, accessed June 9, 2024, https://www.youtube.com/@ProfessorDaveExplains.

648 Professor Dave Explains. "Welcome to Professor Dave Explains!" YouTube video, 2:36. July 28, 2018. https://www.youtube.com/watch?v=pYVgB2lnztY.

649 Ibid.

650 Farina, David. *Is This Wi-Fi Organic? A Guide to Spotting Misleading Science Online*. New York: Mango Publishing, 2021. Accessed June 7, 2024. https://www.amazon.com/This-Wi-Fi-Organic-Spotting-Misleading/dp/1642504157.

651 Rice University, 'Faculty Profiles: James Tour,' https://profiles.rice.edu/faculty/james-tour.

652 Professor Dave Explains. "Elucidating the Agenda of James Tour: A Defense of Abiogenesis." YouTube video, 0:46. Posted by "Professor Dave Explains," August 28, 2020. https://www.youtube.com/watch?v=SixyZ7DkSjA&t=243s.

653 "Poisoning the well," Wikipedia, last modified April 27, 2024, https://en.wikipedia.org/wiki/Poisoning_the_well.

654 Ibid.

655 Dixon, Cantor, and Pumfrey, *Science and Religion*, 27.

656 "Anti-Christian Sentiment." Wikipedia, The Free Encyclopedia. Last modified June 1, 2024. https://en.wikipedia.org/wiki/Anti-Christian_sentiment.

657 "Elucidating the Agenda of James Tour: A Defense of Abiogenesis."

658 Ibid.

659 Philp Ball, How Life Works: A User's Guide to the New Biology (London: Pan Macmillan, 2023).

660 Xin Li et al., "Applications of Quantum Computing to Protein Folding Prediction," *Molecular Biotechnology* 65, no. 3 (2023): 227–244, accessed January 9, 2025, https://link.springer.com/article/10.1007/s12033-023-00765-4.

661 Arndt F. Török and colleagues, "Stochastic Gene Expression: Approaching Quantum Many-Body Problems in Biology," *arXiv*, accessed January 9, 2025, https://arxiv.org/abs/cond-mat/0301365.

662 Ball, Philip. "Science Must Move with the Times." *Nature*, November 5, 2019. https://www.nature.com/articles/d41586-019-03307-8.

663 Ben Stein. "Expelled: No Intelligence Allowed," IMDb.

664 "Elucidating the Agenda of James Tour: A Defense of Abiogenesis."

665 Hebrews 11:1: "Now faith is the assurance of things hoped for, the conviction of things not seen." GotQuestions.org further defines faith as "trusting in something you cannot explicitly prove." Accessed June 9, 2024, https://www.gotquestions.org/definition-of-faith.html.

666 Ball, Philip. "Science Must Move with the Times," 2.

667 Ibid., 4.

668 Ibid., 3.

669 Ibid., 4.

670 Ball, Philip. "Science Must Move with the Times."

671 Philip Ball, *Organisms as Agents of Evolution* (John Templeton Foundation, April 2023), 13, https://www.templeton.org/wp-content/uploads/2023/06/Biological-Agency_1_FINAL_2.pdf.

672 Henry D. Potter and Kevin J. Mitchell, "Naturalising Agent Causation," *Entropy* 24, no. 4 (March 2022): 472, https://doi.org/10.3390/e24040472, Excerpt: "We contend, however, that not all systems can be coherently decomposed into separable parts in this machine-like manner. As we have seen above, living organisms are dynamic, holistically integrated systems, whose parts constantly act in concert, influencing and constraining one another, in order to maintain the holistic pattern. Even the simplest organisms show substantial degrees of integration.... We see increasing degrees of holistic design as we scale up to more complex organisms with brains and nervous systems. Fuelled by recent technological advances... we are now learning that brain areas we once understood as single-mindedly carrying out their work in relative isolation are, in fact, highly sensitive to the activity in other brain areas.... To decompose this process into a set of functionally-independent (machine-like) 'parts' carrying out their work in isolation, and then combining to cause the system's next state, is to entirely miss the essentially dynamic and holistic nature of it. The evidence therefore suggests that biological systems are too holistic, too integrated and too relational to submit to a machine-like analysis.... If a system is so holistically integrated that to understand any given part, you must also understand the whole, then causal power will meaningfully inhere at the level of the whole. You cannot horizontally reduce such a system to identify a particular part (or set of parts) that is determining the system's next state, because the activity of that part is, itself, being determined by all the other parts in the whole. Therefore, we suggest that holistic integration is a necessary condition for agent causality."

673 "Elucidating the Agenda of James Tour: A Defense of Abiogenesis."

674 Preiner., et al. "The Future of Origin of Life Research."

675 "What Does 'The Internet is Forever' Really Mean?", *Reliable Tech*, accessed June 8, 2024, https://reliabletech.ca/what-does-the-internet-is-forever-really-mean/, quoting, "Anything posted online can be saved permanently, before you get the chance to delete it."

676 NASA, "NASA Invites Public to Share Excitement of Webb Space Telescope Launch," last modified December 7, 2021, https://www.nasa.gov/general/nasa-invites-public-to-share-excitement-of-webb-space-telescope-launch/.

677 "How Disorderly Young Galaxies Grow Up and Mature," Lund University, *Science Daily*, August 27, 2021, https://www.sciencedaily.com/releases/2021/08/210827121447.htm#google_vignette.

678 Nell Greenfieldboyce, "This New Space Telescope Should Show Us What the Universe Looked Like as a Baby," *NPR*, December 17, 2021, https://www.npr.org/2021/12/17/1064724045/this-new-space-telescope-should-reveal-what-the-universe-looked-like-as-a-baby.

679 Ibid.

680 Ibid.

681 Ibid.

682 Ibid.

683 Ibid.

684 Jonathan O'Callaghan, "Astronomers Grapple with JWST's Discovery of Early Galaxies," *Scientific American*, December 6, 2022, https://www.scientificamerican.com/article/astronomers-grapple-with-jwsts-discovery-of-early-galaxies1/.

685 B.W. Johnson and B.A. Wing, "Limited Archaean Continental Emergence Reflected in an Early Archaean ^{18}O-Enriched Ocean," *Nature Geoscience* 13 (2020): 243–248, https://doi.org/10.1038/s41561-020-0538-9.

686 John Eliot Allen, Marjorie Burns, and Scott Burns, *Cataclysms on the Columbia: The Great Missoula Floods* (Portland, OR: Ooligan Press, 2009).

687 Aaron Micallef, Giuseppe Barreca, Christian Hübscher, et al., "Land-to-Sea Indicators of the Zanclean Megaflood," *Communications Earth & Environment* 5, no. 794 (2024), https://doi.org/10.1038/s43247-024-01972-w.

688 Valentina Yanko-Hombach, Allan S. Gilbert, Nicolae Panin, and Pavel M. Dolukhanov, eds., The Black Sea Flood Question: Changes in Coastline, Climate and Human Settlement (Dordrecht: Springer, 2007).

689 Idaho State University, "Lake Bonneville Flood," *Digital Geology of Idaho*, https://www.isu.edu/digitalgeologyidaho/bonneville/.

690 Gusiakov, Viacheslav, Dallas Abbott, Edward A. Bryant, W. Bruce Masse and Dee Breger. "Mega Tsunami of the World Oceans: Chevron Dune Formation, Micro-Ejecta, and Rapid Climate Change as the Evidence of Recent Oceanic Bolide Impacts." (2009).

691 Jason Lisle, "The James Webb Space Telescope," *Biblical Science Institute*, January 21, 2022, https://biblicalscienceinstitute.com/astronomy/the-james-webb-space-telescope/.

692 Ibid.

693 Ibid.

694 NASA, "NASA's Webb Draws Back Curtain on Universe's Early Galaxies," *NASA*, accessed May 27, 2024, https://www.nasa.gov/universe/nasas-webb-draws-back-curtain-on-universes-early-galaxies/.

695 Jonathan O'Callaghan, "Astronomers Grapple with JWST's Discovery of Early Galaxies."

696 Ibid.

697 Robert Lea, "James Webb Space Telescope discovers some early universe galaxies grew up surprisingly fast," *Space.com*, April 26, 2024, https://www.space.com/james-webb-space-telescope-discovers-some-early-universe-galaxies-grew-up.

698 Ibid.

699 Ibid.

700 Ibid.

701 Dr. Jason Lisle, "Dr Jason Lisle JWST," *Denver Society of Creation*, May 4, 2024, YouTube video, 1:15:54, https://www.youtube.com/watch?v=EOx7tbSLGk0&t=1854s.

702 Ibid.

703 Gray AJ, "Worldviews," *Int Psychiatry* 8, no. 3 (2011): 58-60, "Everyone has a worldview. If you think you do not have a worldview then probably your view is the default one of your society, which in the UK's case is a form of agnostic, capitalist, scientific materialism. A worldview is a collection of attitudes, values, stories and expectations about the world around us, which inform our every thought and action. Worldview is expressed in ethics, religion, philosophy, scientific beliefs and so on ...When you encounter a situation and think'That's just wrong', your worldview is active. We have a natural tendency to think that what we believe is normal: his views are backward and superstitious; your views are a result of how you were brought up; my views are rational, balanced and true," PMID: 31508085; PMCID: PMC6735033.

704 Ibid.

705 "Cognitive Dissonance," *Psychology Today*, "Cognitive dissonance is a term for the state of discomfort felt when two or more modes of thought contradict each other.," accessed February 15, 2024, https://www.psychologytoday.com/us/basics/cognitive-dissonance.

706 Wikipedia, s.v. "Stephen C. Meyer," last edited July 10, 2024, https://en.wikipedia.org/wiki/Stephen_C._Meyer#Work.

707 Richard E. Lenski, "Evolution: Fact and Theory," National Center for Science Education, accessed June 15, 2025, https://ncse.ngo/evolution-fact-and-theory.

708 "Discovery Institute.'What is Intelligent Design?' Accessed December 20, 2023. https://www.discovery.org/v/what-is-intelligent-design/."

709 "Chock," The Free Dictionary, accessed April 23, 2024, https://www.thefreedictionary.com/chock. (Definition: "A block or wedge placed under something else, such as a wheel, to keep it from moving.")

710 May, Joshua, "Bias in Science: Natural and Social," *Synthese* 199 (1-2): 3345–3366, accessed November 4, 2023, https://philarchive.org/rec/MAYBIS.

711 Robert T. Blackburn and Molly D. Hakel, "An Examination of Sources of Peer Review Bias," *Psychological Science* 17, no. 5 (2006): 378–382. Quote: "In peer review, bias can occur when reviewers make judgments that deviate from objective criteria, potentially influenced by their own preferences, beliefs, or affiliations."

712 Carole J. Lee, Cassidy R. Sugimoto, Guo Zhang, and Blaise Cronin, "Bias in Peer Review," *Journal of the American Society for Information Science and Technology* 64, no. 1 (2013): 8.

713 Ibid., 9.

714 Ibid.

715 Ibid.

716 Ibid., 6.

717 Ibid., 7.

718 Ibid., 6.

719 Denis Noble interview, conducted by Ard Louis and David Malone, "Why Are We Here?", accessed July 13, 2024, https://www.whyarewehere.tv/people/denis-noble/. (Note, since I first viewed this video in July of 2024, it has been taken down, but the transcripts are still available.)

720 Ibid.

721 Ibid.

722 Ibid.

723 Ibid.

724 Ibid.

725 Ibid.

726 Denis Noble, Proselyte of Yah, "Atheist Denis Noble on Antitheistic Bias in Science," YouTube video, June 18, 2023, https://www.youtube.com/watch?v=IAM_mIFsLZo.

727 Ibid.

728 Ibid.

729 This quote was heard and recorded from a video. The original source has been misplaced and cannot be located. Efforts to find the reference were unsuccessful.

730 Valerie Tarico, "Two Liars for Jesus and an Aging Philosopher," AwayPoint, November 12, 2007, https://valerietarico.com/2007/11/12/two-liars-for-jesus-and-an-aging-philosopher/.

731 Michael Behe, "A (R)evolutionary Biologist."

732 Behe, Michael J. "Correspondence with Science Journals." Discovery Institute. Accessed December 21, 2023. https://www.discovery.org/a/450.

733 Michael Behe and 'Intelligent Design' on National Public Radio." National Center for Science Education. Accessed December 21, 2023. https://ncse.ngo/michael-behe-and-intelligent-design-national-public-radio.

734 Sabine Hossenfelder, "I Was Asked to Keep This Confidential," YouTube video, 0:00–3:51, February 15, 2025, https://www.youtube.com/watch?v=shFUDPqVmTg.

735 Ibid.

736 Ibid.

737 Ibid.

738 Sam Harris, *Letter to a Christian Nation* (New York: Alfred A. Knopf, 2006)

739 "What is the New Atheism?," GotQuestions.org, accessed April 27, 2024, https://www.gotquestions.org/new-atheism.html.

740 Paul Wallace, "Atheism's Bronze Age Goat Herder Conceit," HuffPost, January 9, 2013, updated December 6, 2017, https://www.huffpost.com/entry/atheisms-bronze-age-goat-herder-conceit_b_2398220.

741 Steven Soter and Neil deGrasse Tyson, eds., *Cosmic Horizons: Astronomy at the Cutting Edge* (New York: New Press, 2000), American Museum of Natural History, accessed November 5, 2024, https://www.amnh.org/learn-teach/curriculum-collections/cosmic-horizons-book/georges-lemaitre-big-bang.

742 Snobelen, S.D. "Newton's Theology." In *Encyclopedia of Early Modern Philosophy and the Sciences*, edited by Dana Jalobeanu and Charles T. Wolfe, Cham: Springer, 2020. https://doi.org/10.1007/978-3-319-20791-9_106-1.

743 Richard Dawkins, *The God Delusion*.

744 Newton, Isaac. *General Scholium*. Translated by Andrew Motte. In *Newton's Principia: The Mathematical Principles of Natural Philosophy*, 501. New York: Daniel Adee, 1825.

745 Wikipedia contributors. "Ministries in Nineteen Eighty-Four." Last modified January 22, 2024. In Wikipedia, The Free Encyclopedia. https://en.wikipedia.org/wiki/Ministries_in_Nineteen_Eighty-Four#Ministry_of_Truth, accessed February 18, 2024.

746 Declan Fahy, *New Celebrity Scientists: Out of the Lab and into the Limelight* (Lanham: Rowman & Littlefield, 2015), ISBN-10: 1442233427, ISBN-13: 9781442233423.

747 "Declan Fahy - School of Communications - Dublin City University." Dublin City University. Accessed December 2, 2023. https://www.dcu.ie/communications/people/declan-fahy.

748 Declan Fahy, *New Celebrity Scientists: Out of the Lab and into the Limelight*.

749 Ibid.

750 Shanks, Niall, and Richard Dawkins. *God, the Devil, and Darwin: A Critique of Intelligent Design Theory*. New York, 2004. Online edition, Oxford Academic, January 20, 2005. https://doi.org/10.1093/0195161998.001.0001.

751 Krauss, Lawrence M. "When Worldviews Collide: Science and Religion Face Off Again." *American Physical Society News*, April 2006. https://www.aps.org/publications/apsnews/200604/backpage.cfm.

752 Ibid.

753 Ibid.

754 Ibid.

755 Ibid.

756 Kari Edwards and Edward E. Smith, "A Disconfirmation Bias in the Evaluation of Arguments," *Journal of Personality and Social Psychology* 71, no. 1 (1996): 5-24, https://doi.org/10.1037/0022-3514.71.1.5.

757 Ibid., In this study, Edwards and Smith observed that "arguments incompatible with prior beliefs are scrutinized longer, subjected to more extensive refutational analyses, and consequently are judged to be weaker than arguments compatible with prior beliefs."

758 Ibid.

759 Krauss, "When Worldviews Collide."

760 Ibid.

761 Ibid.

762 Ibid.

763 Ibid.

764 Ibid.

765 Ibid.

766 "Cognitive Dissonance," *Psychology Today*, "Though a person may not always resolve cognitive dissonance, the response to it may range from ignoring the source of it to changing one's beliefs or behavior to eliminate the conflict," https://www.psychologytoday.com/us/basics/cognitive-dissonance.

767 Ibid.

768 Alex O'Connor, *Did It Really Happen? Jordan Peterson vs. Richard Dawkins*, November 1, 2024, YouTube video, 20:57, https://www.youtube.com/watch?v=wmz6Pi2RCCo. O'Connor, as moderator, interestingly frames Dawkins' questioning of Peterson on events like the virgin birth and resurrection of Jesus as an inquiry into "scientific truth." This framing is notable given that they treat these as scientific questions, while similar questions raised by figures like Michael Behe (on irreducible complexity) and Stephen Meyer (on the origin of specified functional information) are often dismissed as religious, rather than scientific, inquiries.

Illustration Credits

Within chapters: Figures are labeled with the chapter number followed by the figure number within that chapter. For example, "Figure 1.4" refers to the fourth figure in Chapter 1, and "Figure 4.3" refers to the third figure in Chapter 4.

> * The usage of these photographs, illustrations, or images does not suggest any endorsement by the copyright holders or creators. All images are used under appropriate licenses or permissions.

Figure 1.1 From *An American Dictionary of the English Language* by Noah Webster (1828). **Image source**: https://archive.org/details/americandictiona01websrich/page/480/mode/2up?q=cosmogony.

Figure 2.1 (Left) Introductory section of Chapter 7, "Microbial Biochemistry," Image source: https://openstax.org/books/microbiology/pages/7-introduction.

Figure 2.2 (Right) Introductory section of Chapter 3, "Biologically Important Molecules," from the College of Lake County's textbook, adapted from OpenStax. **Image source:** College of Lake County textbook, page 63, https://dept.clcillinois.edu/biodv/PrinciplesOfBiology.pdf

Figure 3.1 Charles Lyell, age 43, painted by Alexander Craig during the British Association meeting in Glasgow, 1840. **Image source:** Fæ, https://commons.wikimedia.org/wiki/File:Lyell_1840.jpg.

Figure 5.1 Thomas Henry Huxley. Known as "Darwin's Bulldog." **Image source:** Wikimedia Commons, https://commons.wikimedia.org/wiki/Category:Thomas_Henry_Huxley#/media/File:T.H.Huxley(Woodburytype).jpg.

Figure 8.1 The missing 'March of Progress' mural from Dover Area High's science class, featured in the PBS/NOVA documentary on the Dover trial, https://www.pbs.org/wgbh/nova/id/program.html.

Figure 8.3 Cari Shane, "If Humans Evolved from Apes, Why Do Apes Still Exist?" *Discover Magazine*, February 16, 2022, https://www.discovermagazine.com/planet-earth/if-humans-evolved-from-apes-why-do-apes-still-exist.

Figure 8.3 Image excerpted from *A Wonderful Life: The Burgess Shale and the Nature of History* by Stephen Jay Gould (W. W. Norton & Company, 1989).

Figure 9.1 The entrance to the Glendive Dinosaur and Fossil Museum in Montana. **Image source:** Wikimedia Commons, https://commons.wikimedia.org/wiki/File:Glendive_entrance.JPG.

Figure 9.2 A fossil of a Tyrannosaurus rex skull nicknamed "Stan," on display at the Glendive Dinosaur and Fossil Museum in Montana. **Image source:** Wikimedia Commons, https://en.wikipedia.org/wiki/Glendive_Dinosaur_and_Fossil_Museum#/media/File:Glendive_stan.JPG.

Figure 9.3 The Ark Encounter, a full-scale replica of Noah's Ark, located in Williamstown, Kentucky. **Image source:** https://commons.wikimedia.org/w/index.php?title=User:Cimerondagert&action=edit&redlink=1.

Figure 9.4 The exterior of the ICR Discovery Center for Science and Earth History in Dallas, Texas, a facility dedicated to promoting young-earth creationism and exploring scientific evidence through a Biblical lens. **Image source:** Wikimedia Commons, https://commons.wikimedia.org/wiki/File:ICR_Discovery_Center_-_Exterior.jpg.

Index

100 Authors Against Einstein, 168
1984, 211
   Ingsoc (English Socialism), 99
   Minister of Truth, Orwellian, 255
   Ministry of Love, 213
   Newspeak, 99, 101
   Room 101, 213
   the Party, 99, 103, 211, 212, 213, 215
   thoughtcrime, 84, 103, 104
   unpersoning, 104
   Winston Smith, 212, 213
abiogenesis, 225, 231, 234, 235
abstract and physical reality, separation between, 218
ACLU, 115
Adhidaivata, 54
Advancing Creation Truth, 158
   Glendive Dinosaur and Fossil Museum, 158
American Civil Liberties Union (ACLU), 114, 115
amino acids, 34
Answers in Genesis (AiG)
   Ark Encounter, the, 159
   Ham, Ken, 156
Answers in Genesis (AIG), 160
atheism and antitheism, 251
Attie, Alan D., 107
Avengers: Age of Ultron, 211
baby universe, 238
Baier, Bret, 224
Ball, Philip, 232, 233, 236, 237
Barton, Ruth, 77, 78, 79, 80

Behe, Michael J., 83, 91, 92, 95, 113, 121, 145, 258
Berceau, Terese, 107
Big Bang (cosmology), 239
Birkett, Kirsten, 83
Blackburn, Robert T., 247
blending inheritance, 151
Bloomberg, Michael, 227
Boltzmann Brain, 202
Boy Scouts of America v. Dale *(2000)*, 180
Bradač, Maruša, 238
Brown University, 121
Brown, Judge Joe, 194
Buckingham, Bill, 120
Buckland, William, 47
Cancers, 185
carbohydrates, 33
carbon dioxide, 34, 38
climate change, 84
College of Lake County, 32, 35
Combatting Cult Mind Control, 101
constants, 262
Copley Medal, 76
cosmogony, 45, 53
Cox, Beth, 107
Cox, Michael M., 107
Coyne, Jerry, 184, 185, 186
creation science, 116
Creationism, C-word, 84, 121, 149, 155
Creationism's Trojan Horse
   The Wedge of Intelligent Design, 149
Creationism's Trojan Horse: The Wedge of Intelligent Design, 121

Creative Commons (CC) license, 35, 37
Crick, Francis, 240, 250
Currie, Adrian, 220
Dance to the Tune of Life: Biological Relativity, 232
Darwin Day, 109, 113
Darwin, Charles, 42, 50, 51, 69, 251
    doubts of, 70, 73
    frustration, 51, 60
Darwinian evolution, 104
Darwinius masillae fossil, 227
Daubert v. Merrell Dow Pharmaceuticals, 148
Dawkins, Richard, 30, 256, 278
De, Jean-André, 47
deep time, 37, 57
Defending Evolution: A Guide to the Evolution/Creation Controversy, 121
deGrasse, Neil, 29
Dembski, William A., 123
Dennett, Daniel, 202
Descent of Man, The, 66
diluvian periods, Buckland and Luc's, 47
Discovery Institute, 81, 199
Doppler model, 243
Draper, John William, 82
Dunning-Kruger effect, 235
dystopian fiction, 98
    1984, 98
    The Village, 98
    V for Vendetta, 98
Edwards v. Aguillard (1987), 138, 156, 206
Edwards, Kari, 259
Einstein's calculations, 218
Elwick, James, 79
ENCODE project, 185
Establishment Clause, 121, 162, 166, 267
Evans, Skip, 105
evolution
    divergence, 95
    natural selection, 68, 69, 70, 72, 87, 94, 231
    speciation, 90, 93, 95
evolution education, 'one-stop shopping' for, 93
extraterrestrial life, 225, 226
Fahy, Declan, 257
Farina, Dave, 229, 230, 234
Feynman, Richard, 104
Fisher, Kristin, 224
Flew, Antony, 103, 252
Forrest, Barbara, 148
Forrest, Barbara C., 148, 149
fossils, 226, 227, 228, 262
Friend of Darwin award, 169
Friend of Darwin award, recipients, 169
Galileo, Galilei, 83
gemmules, 151
Genome Project, 236
geology, 44, 68
Glendive Dinosaur and Fossil Museum, 158
God Delusion, The (book), 30
Gould, Stephen Jay, 137
Graham, William, 64
Gray, Asa, 73
GULO pseudogene (ψGLO), 185
Haeckel, Ernst, 81
Hakel, Molly D., 247
Hassan, Steven, 101
Hebrew cosmogony, 44, 45
Herschel, Sir John, 52
Hindu, 54
History of the Conflict between Religion and Science (book), 82
Hooker, Joseph Dalton, 77, 78
Horner, Leonard, 41
Hossenfelder, Sabine, 253

How Life Works: A User's Guide to the New Biology, 237
Humes, Edward, 170
Hutton, James, 46
Huxley, Thomas Henry, 50, 74, 77, 78, 79, 80, 82, 87, 88, 89, 90, 91, 92, 112
    doubt of, 71
    doubts of, 70, 71, 89
Ida, 227, 228
Illingworth, Garth, 238
in-crowd, 179, 195
    Edward Humes, 171
    PBS/NOVA, 188
    The Discovery Institute, 197
inflaton, 25
Institute for Creation Research (ICR), 161
    Museum, 160
institutional capture, 78
Intelligent Design (ID), 87, 104, 105, 106, 109, 116, 117, 120, 122, 124, 136, 145, 257, 258, 260
    community, 258
    debate around, 113
    proponents of, 81
irreducible complexity, 30, 91, 92
    alveoli, 167
    blood clotting cascade, 166
    cblood-brain barrier (BBB), 168
    vascular arrangement of eye, 167
James Webb Space Telescope (JWST)
    observations, 238, 239, 241, 242, 243
Jones, John E., III, 143, 166
Judgement Day
    Intelligent Design on Trial
        DI, 197
Judgment Day
    Intelligent Design on Trial, PBS/NOVA, 170, 188, 189, 190, 194

Justice Gorsuch, Neil, 162
Kalambokidis, Maria, 267
Kennedy v. Bremerton School District, 162
Kenneth R. Miller
    Life's Grand Design, 187
Khan Academy, 37, 39
Kitzmiller v. Dover, 120
    Behe, Michael J., 122, 141, 144, 191
    Bonsell, Alan, 120, 190
    decision to sue, 126
    Dembski, William A., 123
    Devil in Dover, the, 124
    Dover High School, 121
    Kitzmiller, Tammy, 121, 174
    methodological naturalism, 144
    Miller and Levine, textbook of, 136
    Miller, Kenneth R., 121, 143
    Minnich, Scott, 122
    Rothschild, Eric, 191
    ruling, 110
    Scott, Eugenie C., 124
Kokić, Tonći, 32
Koperski, Jeffrey, 141, 142, 144
Krauss, Lawrence M., 29, 258
lanugo, embryonic hair, 186
Lebo, Lauri, 127, 128, 129
Lee, Carole, 248
Lemon Test, 206, 207
Lemon v. Kurtzman, 162
    Lemon Test, 162
Lemon v. Kurtzman (1971), 206
Lenard, Philipp, 168
Lents, Nathan H., 133, 164
life
    Alexander Oparin's hypothesis on the origin of, 32
    ignorance in origins of, 30
    origin of, 39, 230

primordial soup hypothesis, 32
lipids, 33
Lisle, Jason, 242, 243
lncRNA, 185
Louis, Ard, 249
Luskin, Casey, 199, 200, 203, 204, 205, 207, 209
Lyell, Charles, 42, 44, 46, 51, 52, 53, 73, 81, 87
Lyell's cosmogongy, 54
Lysenko, Trofim, 104
Ma'at, 219
Malone, David, 249, 250
March of Progress, 137
Materialism, 82, 103, 225
materialist problems, 243
  cognitive dissonance, 261
Mathematical Universe Hypothesis, 218
mathematics, as the intrinsic fabric of universe, 220
May, Joshua, 247
McLean v. Arkansas, 156
metaphysics, 218, 220, 222
methodological naturalism, 142, 215
Meyer, Stephen C., 91, 104, 123, 245, 258
Miller, Kenneth R., 116, 171, 191
Miller, Stanley, 33
Miller-Urey experiment, 33, 34, 37
Mitchell, Kevin J., 237, 295
monism, 54
Monkey Girl
  Evolution, Education, Religion, and the Battle for America's Soul, 170, 171, 174, 175
Mosaic narrative, 51
Mosaico-geological system, 47
Muise, Robert, 148
nanotechnology, 230
NASA, 224, 242

National Center for Science Education (NCSE), 84, 92, 105, 108, 121
  Understanding Evolution, 93, 97, 101
National Institutes of Health (NIH), 104
natural selection, 51, 87, 231
neo-Darwinism, 227
New Celebrity Scientists: Out of the Lab and Into the Limelight, The, 257
Newton, Isaac, 256
Noah's Ark, 159
Noble, Denis, 232, 249, 250, 251
NPR, 238
Numbers, Ronald L., 107
O'Callaghan, Jonathan, 242
O'Hair, Madalyn Murray, 192
Of Pandas and People, 119, 136, 148, 199, 200
Oluseyi, Hakeem, 223
online educational platform, 34, 35, 37
Only a Theory: Evolution and the Battle for America's, 171
Open Source Curriculum, 32
OpenStax textbook, 34, 35, 36, 37
Origin of Species, On the, 51, 63, 68
Orwell, George, 98
  Blair, Eric, 98
paleontology, 227
pangenesis, 151
pantheism, 54, 220
PBS/NOVA, 170
peer review bias, 247, 248
peer-review process, 247
Pennock, Robert, 121
Phillip, Abby, 223
Potter, Henry D., 237, 295
Presiding Mind, 52, 53
primates to humans, 29, 38, 39, 267
primordial soup (hypothesis), 32, 33

Principles of Geology: Being an Attempt to Explain the Former Changes of the Earth's Surface, by Reference to Causes Now in Operation, 53
Proceedings of the Biological Society of Washington, 104
Professor Dave, 230, 231, 232, 233, 234, 235, 236, 237, 245, 260
proteins, 33
   folding, 232
pseudogenes genes, 184
PTENP1, 184
quantum mechanics
   entanglement, 232
   wave-function collapse, 232
Rees, Martin J., 29
Reeser, Larry, 127, 128, 130, 131, 132
religion and science, conflict between, 81, 82, 250
Return of the God Hypothesis: Three Scientific Discoveries That Reveal the Mind Behind the Universe, 122
RNA World Hypothesis, 38
Rogan, Joe, 246
Rothschild, Eric, 190
Royal Society, the, 74, 76, 78
   X Club manipulating elections of Royal Society, 77
Ryden, Barbara, 19
SafeInsights, 35
Sagan, Carl, 29
Sapolsky, Robert, 202
science, 32, 47, 74, 82, 83, 227, 256, 260
   "pure" science, 75
   applied science, 75
   confirmation bias in, 73
   pure science, 75, 76
scientific discourse

   personal beliefs on, 259
Scientific Dissent from Darwinism, A declaration, 87
scientism, 30, 257, 258
Scott, Eugenie C., 84, 153, 155, 156, 166
   interview with DJ Grothe, 125, 139, 146
   interview with Swamidass and Lents, 133, 136
   surveillance of Christian cultural expressions, 154, 156, 159, 161, 162
Scrope, George Poulett, 45, 47, 48
sensational science
   mainstream media, 223, 226, 227
   CNN, 223
   Fox News, 224
   media bias, 222
sensationalized science
   social media, 228, 229
singularity, the initial, 239
skepticism about Darwinian evolution, 87, 259
Smith, Edward E., 259
Sober, Elliot, 107
social media science communications, 229
Special Creation, 155
specified complexity, 122
Spottiswoode, William, 77
star bars, 243
stardust, 29
Stein, Ben, 30
Stenger, Victor, 278
Sternberg, Richard, 104, 105
Stough, Stephen, 177
Swamidass, S. Joshua, 126, 136, 163
Technology Review, 187
Tegmark, Max, 219, 220
   Mathematical Universe Hypothesis, 218

Mathematical Universe Hypothesis (MUH), 220
pseudoscience, 219
The Ascent of Man, 128
The Devil in Dover
   An Insider's Story of Dogma v. Darwin in Small-Town America, 129
The Devil in Dover: An Insider's Story of Dogma v. Darwin in Small-Town America, 127
The Variation of Animals and Plants Under Domestication, 151
The Village
   M. Night Shyamalan, 98
   Those We Don't Speak Of, 98
The X Club and the Secret Ring: Lessons on How Behavior Analysis Can Take Over Psychology, 74
Theology and Falsification essay, 103
Thomas More Law Center (TMLC), 123
Thought Reform and the Psychology of Totalism
thought reform, 100
Thyer, Bruce A., 74, 77
Tour, James, 230, 231, 232
Tower of Babel: The Evidence Against the New Creationism, 121
Travisano, Michael, 267
Two Bad Ways to Attack Intelligent Design and Two Good Ones (Koperski), 141
Tyndall, John, 50, 78, 80
Tyson, Neil deGrasse, 260
University
   Brown, 116
   Durham, 243
   Florida State, 74
   Lund, 238
   Michigan State, 121
   of Alabama, Birmingham, 247
   of California, Davis, 238
   of California, Santa Cruz, 238
   of Chicago, 33
   of New South Wales, 83
   of Oxford, 249
   of Split, Croatia, 32
   Rice, 35, 230
University of
   Washington, 248
Urey, Harold, 33
vernix caseosa, 186
viewpoint discrimination, 207
Waters, David Roland, 193
Watson, James, 240
Webb, Beatrice, 80
wedge strategy, 81
Weinberg, Stanley L., 84
Wikipedia, bias, 245
Wizard of Oz, 195
X Club, 74, 77, 81
X Club: Power and Authority in Victorian Science, The, 70, 74, 75, 76, 256
Zimmer, Carl, 227

www.ingramcontent.com/pod-product-compliance
Lightning Source LLC
Chambersburg PA
CBHW071709180426
43192CB00053B/2219